RESOURCES FOR TEACHING

Approaching Literature in the 21st Century

Fiction • Poetry • Drama

Peter Schakel
Hope College

Jack Ridl
Hope College

D1456816

Bedford/St. Martins

Boston ◆ New York

For information, write: Bedford/St. Martin's, 75 Arlington Street, Boston,
MA 02116 (617-399-4000)

ISBN: 0-312-40757-2
EAN: 978-0-312-40757-5

Preface

Aims and Approaches

The heart of *Approaching Literature in the 21st Century,* and the central purpose of its authors, is to help students discover what lies within the world of literature, to build their confidence in ways of responding to literary works, to lead them to a variety of ways to interact with individual stories, poems, and plays, and to help them find the worthwhile pleasure that can come from reading and responding to works. The approach and explanations are intended to alert and inform students about the basic aspects of literature in a tone that is engaging, thoughtful, and inviting.

Entry Points

This manual does not provide a reading of each work in mini-essay form, as some manuals do. Our fear is that such little essays run the danger of becoming authoritative interpretations of a text and tempt instructors to turn classes into ways of getting such a reading across to the students, either by presenting it through lecture or by arriving at it through a set of guided questions. The reader-response approach used in this book runs against such predetermined conclusions about the work or the class. Instructors don't need authoritative readings: They too will want to arrive at their own positions, preferably through interaction with their students.

Of more value to instructors are "entry points," suggestions for ways to get at the key questions and issues a text raises and to introduce a work successfully in class. Often having a successful class turns on having a few good questions or topics for discussion. Other questions or topics can then flow out of those as the class proceeds. This manual gives for each work several such entry points, varied ideas that work in class. They are a healthy reminder, for instructors and students alike, that there are many ways of opening up a work, many ways of entering it besides the usual "What does it mean?" or "What is it about?"

Starters

Beginnings are difficult, whether in writing or in opening a class or discussion. In keeping with its focus on being basic and practical, this manual offers "starters" for each selection contained in the elements chapters. A starter may be a "watch for this as you read"-type assignment to give students the previous class or an activity to focus their attention as they arrive at class. Some starters will work better than others, of course, or will suit one instructor better than another, but all are ones that we have used. They are offered in part to stimulate your thinking and help you come up with better ideas yourself.

Provocative Pairings

For each selection in *Approaching Literature in the 21st Century,* at least one pairing — thematic or stylistic — with another work in the book is suggested. Pairings can be used for teaching — looking at similarities and differences between two works can be a helpful way of noticing important aspects of both — and can be used for exercises and paper topics. In almost every case, many more pairings could be suggested for each work, and often you will want to create your own instead of using ours. We've tried to foreground ones that we found provocative and illuminating but encourage you to pair works in your own interesting ways.

Sustained Themes

The multicultural emphasis in the choice of selections in the book leads naturally into several themes — borders, voices, and outsiders — that can be traced in a sustained way throughout a course. In organizing the book, borders was the particular focus in the section on fiction, voices in the section on poetry, and outsiders in the section on drama. But each theme is present in all three sections, and the three are closely interrelated.

BORDERS   The first sustained theme is *borders.* Political borders separate and divide one country and its people from another. The dividing line may be artificial, but the differences and alienation created can be very real. The border on a page, a piece of fabric, a carpet, or a section of property defines its space and creates a sense of inclusion and exclusion. Borders can also be used metaphorically for whatever beliefs, attitudes, or ideas define, divide, or alienate people (old and young, parents and children, one ethnic group from another, and so on). Many of the works selected for *Approaching Literature in the 21st Century* deal with literal borders: streets, walls, fences, or whatever physical barriers separate, restrict, or contain people. Others deal with metaphorical borders that divide or constrict.

The world in the twenty-first century must deal with the issue of borders, in part by recognizing that borders are not just lines of division and separation — they also provide points of meeting. A political border is where two countries abut and where their people can encounter and engage with each other. Most borders have crossing points where exchange and interaction can take place. The world in the twenty-first century, more than ever, needs to have borders crossed (if they can't be eliminated entirely). People need to use those crossing points and come to know each other, to get past stereotypes and superficial differences, and to find common ground in their shared humanity. In one sense, this book models such border crossings. It moves across (or wipes out) canonical boundaries and moves freely between ethnicities and nationalities, demonstrating the unity of the literary enterprise. And many of the works included in it explore such border crossings — literal or figurative — as part of their content and themes.

VOICES   A second sustained theme unifying *Approaching Literature in the 21st Century* involves *voices*. This book treats voice, in Chapter 11, as an important technical feature of writing. A writer needs to find her or his distinctive voice, and that voice can make her or his writing authentic and effective. Students need assistance in learning to listen for the voice in the poetry and prose they read. But literature is also the expression of a multitude of varied voices, expressing in their own ways that which is central to their existence.

We in the twenty-first century need to listen for and listen to all voices, those different from our own as well as those similar to our own. *Approaching Literature in the 21st Century* provides a model by offering a wide range of voices through the diversity of the authors and backgrounds represented in its selections. Reading and writing about literature give voice to thoughts and emotions that we may not be able to express adequately in any other way. We hope this book, through its rich variety of selections, will help students see how literature can express the hopes, dreams, and aspirations; the hatred, fear, and anguish; the courage, love, and compassion of many people and many voices.

OUTSIDERS   A third theme running through *Approaching Literature in the 21st Century* involves the fact or sense of being an outsider. The theme can relate to borders, both literal and figurative: Borders divide those who are inside, accepted, approved of, from those who are outside, excluded, not welcomed or accepted. This too is a major problem facing the twenty-first-century world: The gap between industrialized and nonindustrialized countries continues to grow, accentuating the sense of insiders with economic and political clout and outsiders who lack such power. And the increasing immigration of people between countries creates growing tensions. Minority ethnic groups and subcultures — adults and young people — often are treated as outsiders by the majority culture. The inclusive approach taken in *Approaching Literature in the 21st Century* is intended to avoid creating literary outsiders, and many of the selections deal with exclusion and the need for inclusion. The sense of being an outsider has further ramifications for the majority of the student population. Many from various backgrounds are treated as outsiders, even by their peers, for reasons of class, appearance, personality, or accent, to name a few. Many selections in this anthology concern people wrestling with feelings of exclusion and struggling to find a sense of self and acceptance.

Contents

PART **3** Approaching POETRY   53

9 Reading Poetry   53

10 Words and Images   55

11 Voice, Tone, and Sound   61

15 **Writing about Poetry**   **86**

A Collection of Poems   **88**

PART 4   Approaching DRAMA   199

16   Reading Drama   199

17   Character, Conflict, and Dramatic Action   200

18   Setting and Structure   202

19   Theaters and Their Influence   205

20   Dramatic Types and Their Effects   208

21   Writing about Drama   211

A Collection of Plays   212

Reading Literature   CHAPTER **1**

We consider this chapter to be of great importance. Many students come to a college literature course trained to focus on the text and convinced they need to dig out what is "in" there, perhaps hidden and inaccessible except to those initiated into its mysteries. We think it is important to set a different tone and approach from day one, emphasizing that the book and the course focus on process rather than on product, on active reading rather than on passive reception.

Taking a reader-oriented approach to literature incurs certain risks. Students may believe that focusing on the reader means that a work means whatever an individual reader says it means, or they may say that the only thing they are interested in is how they personally "respond" to a work. Emphasizing reading as a *transactional* activity counters such tendencies: The text is important, and close attention must be paid to it; the text (especially as interpreted by a community of readers, such as a class or group of students) does serve as a check on individual readings. These tendencies are also countered by focusing on ways students are actively involved in the *process* of reading (not just by "responding" to what the text says): selecting from their banks of memories to fill words with meaning and images with sensory qualities, anticipating what will come, revising those expectations, filling in gaps left by the text, and reacting intellectually and emotionally.

Sherman Alexie

Superman and Me   (p. 4)

STARTER   Assign students in advance (or have the assignment posted as they come in, to complete as they wait for class to begin) to select a sentence in "Superman and Me" they like especially well either for its style or for its content.

1

ENTRY POINTS   This is a straightforward piece of writing, and Chapter 1 discusses its most powerful idea, "I was [reading] to save my life" (p. 5). For this point in the semester, it seems best to concentrate on some basic writing techniques, such as the importance in good writing of using specific, concrete details, which Alexie does well. Point out (if students don't) his effective use of lists.

An underlying theme in the essay, which can be rewarding to explore, is the search for personal identity by someone who felt like an outsider.

Perhaps the best use of the essay is to ask students to compare Alexie's background in reading with their own. Were their parents readers? Are they readers? If so, what do they like to read? If not, why don't they read? Does Alexie convince them reading is important?

This essay relates well to the multigenre casebook on Alexie in Chapter 24 (p. 1319). Encourage students to watch Alexie's enjoyable film *Smoke Signals* (1998) and to ask themselves to what extent the character Thomas Builds-the-Fire seems similar to Alexie.

PAIR IT WITH   Julia Alvarez, "Daughter of Invention" (p. 10); Judith Ortiz Cofer, "Not for Sale" (p. 134).

Julia Alvarez

Daughter of Invention   (p. 10)

STARTER   Ask students to bring to class a list of as many mangled maxims in the story as they can find — give a mock prize to the student with the most examples.

ENTRY POINTS   Much of the wit in "Daughter of Invention" derives from the mother's mangling of proverbial sayings, with which students may or may not be familiar. Missing most of them only loses some humor, but missing the one behind the title loses significant meaning. Going quickly in class through the lists students compiled brings out the humor in the story and provides a way to check if they catch the point of the title maxim. If no one has it on a list, bring it up and ask students to come up with several ways "Necessity is the mother of invention" fits the story (including the seventeenth-century rhetorical meaning of *invention*).

This story works well as a first-day reading. Students relate well with its parent-child tensions and issues of identity and assimilation. It's a witty and enjoyable narrative, with some good narrative tension along the way.

Like Alexie's "Superman and Me," it describes the importance of reading and writing for a young person trying to fit in, trying to find a place and a self. You might ask students (as the fifth "Approaching the Reading" prompt on page 19 suggests) to what extent the narrator is writing to save her life, and what that means. Follow these questions by asking students what they have done to "save their lives."

After publishing "Daughter of Invention" as a first-person account in *Unholy Alliances: New Fiction by Women* in 1988, Alvarez changed the point of view to third person when she incorporated the story into her book *How the Garcia Girls Lost Their Accents* (1991). Comparing the effects of the two versions can be a good exercise or paper topic for Chapter 5 on point of view.

PAIR IT WITH   Judith Ortiz Cofer, "Not for Sale" (p. 134).

CHAPTER 2 Responding to Literature

This is a long, detailed chapter. It is not meant to be read straight through, nor will students want to. It's a chapter that deals not just with writing but also with the many ways of responding to writing. We think it wise to introduce it early, long before the first paper is due. Doing so gives students another way to think about writing in terms of what they discover works well for them as a way of responding.

The chapter affirms individual differences in abilities and sensibilities. Too often students are given only one way to articulate their responses. Students whose strengths mesh with that particular way do well. Others may conclude they are weak at response instead of realizing they are better at some ways of responding than at others.

We suggest assigning the section on "Writing in the Margins" (p. 22) in the first week, perhaps paired with Chapter 1, as a helpful way to reinforce the idea of active reading. The sections on "Discussing Literature" (p. 26) and "Thinking Critically" (p. 28) could be combined with "Writing in the Margins" or assigned for the following class.

Whether you use the section on "Journal Writing" (p. 24) depends, of course, on whether journals are required for the course. If so, you might include this section with the first assignment of a journal entry. If not, you still might assign the section (perhaps for the class following the first section) and talk about the value of journaling in preparation for class and more broadly as a way of recording and tracking their reading and thinking. If you think journaling is a valuable way for students to prepare for class, it is usually a good idea to incorporate journals in the class itself so that the students do in fact experience the worth of their work. Journals lend themselves to small-group work where the students can exchange what they've written. Students who are reticent to talk in class can "let their journals talk for them."

The section on "Writing Essay Examination Answers" (p. 29) should wait until the first exam. If your course does not include essay exams, you might call students' attention to the section as worth their attention in courses that use such exams.

When the first course paper is assigned, the section on "Writing Short Papers" (p. 32) could be paired with Chapter 8, 15, or 21 on writing about a specific genre. The section focuses on the whole writing process, from thinking of ideas and framing a topic to proofreading and formatting. It is important that students read the section before they start looking for a topic rather than just before they sit down to begin composing the paper. Note that Chapter 2 does not include a sample paper — models of short papers appear in Chapters 8, 15, and 21, and a sample research paper is included in Chapter 26.

Whether you use the section on "Responding Through Other Art Forms" (p. 46) depends on the course and your preferences. If you want to encourage the option of "nonpaper" assignments, point out or assign this section early because it will set a tone for your course and interest students who respond strongly to alternative response possibilities. We encourage this as at least an occasional option to writing a traditional paper. But students whose confidence in their abilities to use such an approach is low should not be required to do a "nonpaper." If you decide to allow nonpaper alternatives, it is important that such projects not be evaluated by standards applied to other arts. One can assess the quality of insight and understanding rather than the successful implementation of the formal elements of an art form.

In a course that must focus on writing, you can point students to "Responding Through Other Art Forms" and indicate that nonwritten responses are valid and important, even though you won't be able to accept them as work for credit in your course.

Alice Walker

The Flowers   (p. 20)

STARTER   Ask students to look closely at the opening paragraph. Have them bring to class a list of examples of particularly effective writing — places where Walker's style, expression, or insight impresses them.

ENTRY POINTS   This short short story is a fine example of an initiation story, handled with subtlety and grace. It exemplifies effective employment of basic storytelling techniques in a very small space: point of view, plot construction, depiction of character, use of images, handling of rhythm and style.

The student writings about "The Flowers" in Chapter 2 discuss most of the key points about the work. You could ask students to read the student writings and use them as a means of focusing on raising questions: For example, ask students to identify (perhaps write down) the questions that each piece of writing raises or responds to.

You might also point out the value of connecting a work such as this to information about its author and to other works by the author. Walker's mother was a gardener, and Walker seems to have acquired a love of flowers, and nature generally, from her. Other works by Walker, including *The Color Purple*, rely heavily on nature imagery, including flowers specifically.

PAIR IT WITH   Sandra Cisneros, "The House on Mango Street" (p. 91); Elizabeth Bishop, "In the Waiting Room" (p. 506).

Reading Fiction

CHAPTER 3

Students sometimes ask what the "point" or "message" of a story is. In discussing literature, we try to avoid words like *point* or *message,* because they make it seem like stories are written just to get an idea or moral lesson across. It seems to us stories are written to depict *an experience* or capture *a character,* not mainly to convey an idea (essays and lectures do that). If so, a more helpful place to start is to ask what is striking, what stands out, about the experience or the character described in the story? Usually students can talk or write helpfully about a story by looking at a central character or experience and identifying what seems interesting or unusual or problematical about it.

The "Approaching the Reading" suggestions provide good starting points for discussion topics: paying attention to a story's title, looking closely at the first sentence and first paragraph of a story, and considering the ending, especially the final sentence, of a story. It's also important to encourage students from the start of the course to look up words, facts, places, or other details that they don't recognize. Looking things up is an important part of active reading and critical thinking. It is the first and most basic kind of research and fosters an attitude of inquiry that leads to broader kinds of research.

CHAPTER 4 Plot and Characters

Dagoberto Gilb

Love in L.A. (p. 55)

STARTER On page 57 the narrator says Jake feels "both proud and sad about his performance." Ask students to write a few sentences describing Jake's character in which they answer the questions, Why *proud?* Why *sad?* Why *performance?*

ENTRY POINTS Chapter 3 shows how plot and character can be used as ways to enter and explore this brief and well-crafted short story. Alicia Abood's student paper (p. 213) illustrates some other ways to approach the story: through its language (especially its use of sounds, similes, and verbs) and through the different meanings given to *love* in the story.

Another approach is to experiment with how much one can tell about Jake by looking closely at just the first and last sentences of the story.

PAIR IT WITH John Updike, "A & P" (p. 386).

Louise Erdrich

The Red Convertible (p. 67)

STARTER Ask students to make a list of gaps in the story and to identify different kinds of gaps: inconsequential ones (How did the brothers pay for gas to drive to Alaska?) and crucial ones (What did Henry experience as a soldier and as a prisoner of war?).

ENTRY POINTS   This is a very teachable story, one that students like to discuss. Although point of view isn't covered until the next chapter, this story can be used to anticipate that topic by having students pay attention to the importance of who tells the story and to consider how different the story would be if told from Henry's perspective. Also, although the term *naïve narrator* isn't introduced until Chapter 5, the concept can be brought up here by asking students what Lyman doesn't know: The things he hasn't experienced and doesn't know make the story powerful because they force us to be active readers and to fill in what he leaves out and doesn't understand.

Lyman mentions the draft and not needing to think about what his number was. You may need to explain to students how the draft was used to fill vacancies in the military forces from 1948 through 1973, when the United States converted to an all-volunteer military; and about the lottery of 1969, in which the days of the year were arranged from 1 to 366, and young men whose birthdays fell at the top were likely to be called up for military service, while those whose birthdays were near the bottom could feel confident they would not be called up.

This is a good story to illustrate active reading: The reader is forced to participate in sorting out the story and completing its meaning. Ask students about gaps they needed to fill as they read, and how they needed to engage with the story by grasping ironies and supplying understanding the characters lack. Ask students to describe ways the effect of the opening paragraph is different when it is reread after finishing the story.

One way into the story is to ask students to discuss its plot, the way it is constructed (organized, arranged). What do the episodes about their travels — the place under the willows where they rested, and their taking Suzy home to Alaska — add to the story? What would be lost if they were not there?

You could also ask students to identify borders in the story — literal ones, like the boundaries of the reservation, and figurative ones, like that which was crossed when Henry moved from the Native American culture to the culture of the U.S. Marine Corps.

Another way into the story is to ask students to describe the character of the speaker and the character of Henry, to consider what ways they are similar and different. How does analyzing character help to understand why Henry walked into the river? What had happened to him? In what ways did he change, and what caused him to change? Did he intend to die, or was his death accidental? Why did Lyman roll the car into the river?

PAIR IT WITH   James Baldwin, "Sonny's Blues" (p. 138).

Joyce Carol Oates

Where Are You Going, Where Have You Been?   (p. 75)

STARTER   Ask students to write a short paragraph in which Connie's mother describes Connie — not the way Connie thinks her mother sees her, but what the mother herself might say about Connie.

ENTRY POINTS   One way of entering the story is by looking at its plot. Ask students to pick out steps in the story's development — perhaps outline the plot on the board. Then have them reflect on why the story includes sections that don't seem directly connected to the Arnold Friend section (such as the paragraphs about June, the trips to the mall, the evenings with Eddie and other friends). The plot divides and changes direction with the innocuous phrase, "One Sunday Connie got up at eleven" (p. 78), which leads to the encounter with Arnold Friend. Ask why the first part is needed; how would the second part be different without the first? Work through the second part to show how its organization helps the plot build in intensity and suspense.

Another way into the story is character. Students will be most interested in two characters, Connie and Arnold Friend. This is a good story to show how plot and character often relate to and depend on each other. The earlier part of the story is largely concerned with developing Connie's character: her adolescent self-centeredness, her romantic sense of life, her preoccupation with "boys" (who are not important to her as individuals but as an idea), her worshiping of the icons of youth culture. The title can tie in here as well: Students might consider what it suggests in the first few pages of the story and what it suggests at the end.

Oates says the story, and the character of Arnold, grew out of reading an account of an actual serial rapist and murderer in Arizona — probably in a *Life* magazine article entitled "The Pied Piper of Tucson" by Don Moser (4 Mar. 1955). Details about Arnold (such as his height and him stuffing his boots to make himself look taller) come out of that account. Some critics allegorize the story and treat Arnold as a fiend or devil figure. It seems to us that such an interpretation isn't needed and isn't advisable for first- or second-year college students. The story works well on its literal level as a psychological horror story, as we watch (from within her consciousness) what a young girl goes through as she is coerced to go out to her death. This already gives students a lot to deal with, emotionally and technically, without complicating the process by suggesting that there is another, "deeper" level to the story.

One of the things students may want to discuss is why Connie goes out to Arnold. It's a point students should be able to discuss well: Let them express opinions, but ask for evidence in the text to support their reasoning. Connie is alone; she is being physically threatened (Arnold says he won't break through the screen door as long as she does what he tells her, but there are clear implications if she crosses him); she is so panicky she can't use the telephone.

Beyond all this, Arnold says that if she doesn't come out to him, he will harm others in her family — that might be his decisive ploy. She seems almost brainwashed, completely unable to resist what he tells her.

Another way into the story is music. Connie lives in a world filled with music, presumably the sentimental, romantic pop music of the mid-1960s. Ask students to pick out as many references to music as they can, and to explain their effect on the story, especially on our sense of Connie's character. Notice especially how music and movies have shaped her vision of boys and love and life. The story is dedicated to Bob Dylan, whose music reacted against the kind of music Connie likes. Dedicating a story to someone does not necessarily mean the story should be interpreted in light of that person's work or ideas, and there may be no need to bring Dylan into a discussion of the story. But the story does seem to have connections with the titles and lyrics of some Dylan songs, such as the line "in the jingle jangle morning I'll come followin' you" from "Mr. Tambourine Man" (1964) and the title "It's All Over Now, Baby Blue" (1965) with such lines in it as "You must leave now . . . something calls for you." (Lyrics for both pieces can be found on the Internet.) The connection, of course, may be no more than an ironic verbal allusion to works of pop culture current at the time the story appeared.

PAIR IT WITH   Mishima Yukio, "Swaddling Clothes" (p. 438).

CHAPTER 5 Point of View and Theme

Sandra Cisneros

The House on Mango Street (p. 91)

STARTER Invite students to draw a sketch of the house on Mango Street or of the building the family lived in earlier on Loomis Street. Ask some students to show their drawings in class and explain what in the text shaped the visual images they produced.

ENTRY POINTS The discussion of the story in Chapter 5 focuses on point of view. "The House on Mango Street" illustrates well the use of a naïve narrator. Cisneros uses that perspective to illustrate how the American dream looks through the eyes of a child, epitomized in the specific detail of home ownership. The dream fades and reality sets in as the child realizes the house is far from what they have talked about and planned for. It's still not one the narrator can point to with pride.

Another way into the story is to focus on the handling of details. Cisneros does not generalize: She renders everything through the specific details that would define renting or owning for a child — the landlord banging on the ceiling, pipes that work or don't work, having to warn people when you're going to take a bath. The narrator doesn't complain about her family's economic deprivation: She describes her life simply and objectively, and readers draw their own conclusions.

A further way into "The House on Mango Street" is to notice what is implied about the narrator's family. Students may not notice, because of the narrator's naïve, understated style, that the story says a good deal about the family. They have moved frequently, but the parents seem to provide a solid sense of stability in their children's lives. The mother's bedtime stories and the protective bars the father nails across the windows are little things that demonstrate the care and love that later stories in *The House on Mango Street* develop further.

PAIR IT WITH   Patricia Grace, "Butterflies" (p. 420).

Alice Walker

Everyday Use   (p. 101)

STARTER   Ask one group of students to compare and contrast Dee and her mother, another group Dee and Maggie, and still another Maggie and her mother, either to hand in as a written assignment or to report on in class.

ENTRY POINTS   This is an accessible, powerful story that students respond to well. Although its author and characters are African American, its situation and themes are universal. It perhaps relates especially to college students, many of whom, like Dee, have left home and are pursuing opportunities for higher education that their parents did not or could not pursue.

One way to get into the story is through contrasts. Ask students to describe the three main characters by listing similarities and differences — for example, the mother is big-boned and stout, uneducated, and shy around white people, and Maggie is much like her (except for being thin), while Dee is attractive, educated, self-confident, and bold. Have students supply specific phrases and sentences to back up what they say in order to give attention to the careful, precise phrasing Walker gives to the narrator.

Another contrast is between Dee's former and current lifestyle — thus, between her current life and the lives of the narrator and Maggie. Get students to spell out how Dee has changed since she went off to college, especially the changes the mother has been unaware of (her African-type clothing, Afro hairstyle, and new name). This can lead into Dee and her mother's contrasting attitudes about heritage. Ask students to describe Dee's view of heritage and the views of the mother and Maggie: the way Dee reaches past her immediate, family heritage to Africa (selecting an African name, even though several generations of her family have been named "Dicie"); the way she takes (without asking) artifacts for their aesthetic qualities, though she cannot remember who made them and doesn't care about their continued practical value to her mother and sister. In contrast to Dee's separation from her immediate heritage, her mother and sister remain intimately connected to it: They live in the family house, eat the food their ancestors did, practice the traditional crafts (learned directly from their relatives, whom they remember clearly and remain connected with), and put to everyday use the objects Dee values only for their quaintness.

Don't let students miss the humor in the story. The mother has a wry way of expressing herself, as character and as narrator, that adds significantly to the effectiveness of the story.

Susan Farrell's essay "Fight vs. Flight: A Re-evaluation of Dee in Alice Walker's 'Everyday Use'" in Chapter 25 (p. 1366) provides quite a different way into the story, not defending Dee totally, but reminding us that we view Dee only through her mother's eyes. Farrell argues that looking at Dee from a different perspective might modify our conclusions about her and bring out similarities between Dee and her mother.

PAIR IT WITH   Lan Samantha Chang, "The Eve of the Spirit Festival" (p. 228).

William Faulkner

A Rose for Emily   (p. 108)

STARTER   Ask students to write an obituary notice for Miss Emily Grierson. Have them read some obituaries in a newspaper if they need a model.

ENTRY POINTS   This is an eminently teachable story. Students engage readily with its carefully crafted buildup and surprising, gruesome ending. One way into the story is to focus on Faulkner's skillful plotting by asking students to point out as many examples of foreshadowing as they can. It should become increasingly clear to them that the conclusion is not a trick ending — it is fully anticipated. Also have students pay attention to the way Faulkner diverts readers' attention from the foreshadowings so that we don't notice this effect until later.

Another way into the story is through Miss Emily's character. Many of the details that would go into an obituary (her birth into an upper-crust family, her genteel education, her lifetime spent in Jefferson, the deaths of her parents that leave her alone) help explain why she does the things she does. But understanding her fully also requires attention to things an obituary omits — the way her father dominated her life, her emotional emptiness, her difficulty in accepting reality.

A further way into the story is its unusual use of first-person plural point of view. Have students try substituting *I* for *we* and observing the difference. What is the advantage of having the narrator be not just a townsperson but a spokesperson for the community?

Students are likely to ask about the story's title. No roses appear in the story: The closest are the rose-colored curtains and light shades in the upstairs bedroom. A rose is a traditional symbol of love. Is it significant that no rose for Emily appears in the story? Is the story itself, its tribute to her, the rose she is being given?

Theme is probably not the first place one should enter a story; theme can be a good way to pull a story together as one leaves it. Ask students to consider what the story as a whole adds up to. One approach has been to take the story as exploring the way southern culture has held onto the past, resisting change even when that past is dead and change is essential. Another way of framing the issue would be in terms of borders and of insiders vs. outsiders (not racial or ethnic, but of class and status).

PAIR IT WITH   James Joyce, "Eveline" (p. 280).

CHAPTER 6 Setting and Symbol

Ernest Hemingway

Hills Like White Elephants (p. 120)

STARTER Ask students to diagram the setting (the station and what surrounds it) or to do a sketch of the way they visualize it. If there are differences in the way various students depict the setting, ask them to point out passages in the text that shape their imaginings.

ENTRY POINTS Several issues involving the importance of setting and symbols in the story are explored in the chapter. You might ask the members of your class what kind of operation the American is urging on Jig (is it an abortion, as we suggested?), and have them point to specific details in the relevant passages that back up what they think.

You might raise questions about the story's point of view. In what ways is the use of an objective point of view effective? How would the story be different if told from the perspective of one of the characters?

Jig's lines, "Yes. . . . Everything tastes of licorice. Especially all the things you've waited so long for, like absinthe" (p. 121), seem pivotal in the story. Before these lines, she and the American converse quite pleasantly; after them, she becomes more cutting and bitter. What is it in the lines that changes things or brings out tensions that had been below the surface?

The eight-line exchange beginning "I said we could have everything" (p. 122) may need discussing. What does Jig's line, "It [the world?] isn't ours any more" mean? And what does she mean by, "And once they take it away, you never get it back"? (Who is "they"? Why or how do they take it away?)

Ask the class to discuss the ending (perhaps using "Approaching the Reading" question 5 on p. 124). Are the students uneasy with the ambiguity of the ending since we aren't told what Jig decides? Ask what decision they think she reaches. If the story went on further, how would the relationship between the American and Jig have progressed? Does ending where it does suggest that the process of reaching the decision is more important than what the decision is? What's the point of Jig's final lines? Does she reach a decision with which she is at ease? (If so, is she won over by the American's arguments, or does she decide not to follow his wishes?) Or is she hiding what she really feels?

PAIR IT WITH   Raymond Carver, "Cathedral" (p. 217).

Judith Ortiz Cofer
Not for Sale   (p. 134)

STARTER   Ask students to bring to class two lists: the first identifying similarities and differences between "Not for Sale" and "Daughter of Invention" (p. 10), and the second identifying one or two connections between "Not for Sale" and "Superman and Me" (p. 4).

The lists should provide some talking points in class (feeling like an outsider; tensions between father and daughter, especially over the daughter wanting to be more American; supportive mothers; search for identity; the importance of reading and imagination). If no student brings it up, ask the class about affinities between Ortiz Cofer's line "Books kept me from going mad" (p. 134) and Alexie's line "I was [reading] to save my life" (p. 5).

ENTRY POINTS   The topics and questions raised in the third "Approaching the Reading" question (p. 138) deserve attention in class. The bedspread, of course, is central to the story. The daughter identifies with Scheherazade, through her love of stories (like Scheherazade, the speaker becomes a storyteller), her love of romantic adventures, and her sense of being a prisoner. The speaker sits Indian-style, much as Scheherazade sits in each panel of the bedspread. The bedspread brings beauty, mystery, and romance into the speaker's life. The mother understands her daughter's love of story and need for a vision beyond the apartment walls that enclose her, and thus buys the bedspread, despite its cost. The speaker loves the stories until she finds that El Árabe intends that his son should become the prince who rescues her from her prison. She had objected to the happily-ever-after endings of the Scheherazade tales; now she has to deal with a real story, with a real ending.

The father's reaction when he returns home opens up at least two strands — the clash of (or lack of mutual understanding between) cultural traditions, and the father-daughter relationship. The speaker thought her father's denials meant he didn't care for her; his impassioned rejection of El Árabe's offer shows her she was wrong.

The final paragraph is worth close attention for what it says about story, voice, and dreams.

Note: The reference to Papillon in paragraph 2 alludes to the book *Papillon* (1969) by Henri Charrière (1906–1973), the true story of a man incarcerated for a crime he didn't commit and his numerous escapes.

PAIR IT WITH   Julia Alvarez, "Daughter of Invention" (p. 10).

James Baldwin

Sonny's Blues (p. 138)

STARTER Assign half the class to write a paragraph arguing that Sonny is the most important character in the story, and the other half to write a paragraph arguing that the brother is the most important character.

Both groups should be able to come up with good arguments, for both brothers are important, in the end probably equally important. At the heart of "Sonny's Blues" is the conflict between Sonny and his brother, who narrates the story. The brothers are separated by more than just the seven years' difference in their ages. They have different values and attitudes and have never communicated effectively with each other. The story tells how the narrator learns to understand himself and Sonny better, which, without totally resolving the conflict or solving Sonny's problems, leads to at least a partial reconciliation between them. A criss-cross movement emerges as the older brother becomes the "younger" and the younger becomes the "older," and the narrator (the teacher) finally, in the last section, begins to listen to and learn from his younger but wiser brother.

ENTRY POINTS One way of getting into "Sonny's Blues" is through its structure. You might ask students to outline the story as a way of making sure they are following the plot and grasping its structural principles. One way to look at its structure is to divide it into seven sections, the first two and last two bracketing a flashback in the middle three:

1. Pages 138–42: This section recounts how the narrator reads in a newspaper about Sonny's arrest and talks to a former friend of Sonny who feels he may have encouraged Sonny to experiment with heroin.
2. Pages 142–45: After ignoring Sonny for a long time, the narrator writes to him and then brings him home after his release.
3. Pages 145–49: Flashback to the narrator's memories of their father, their home, and his last talk with their mother, when she tells him about the death of their father's brother.
4. Pages 149–52: After their mother's funeral, the narrator tries to talk to Sonny but can't understand Sonny's love of jazz.
5. Pages 152–54: Sonny's troubles: his piano playing at Isabel's house, his problems with her family, his enlistment in the navy, and his estrangement from the narrator following his return after the end of the war. The narrator's troubles: the death of little Grace.
6. Pages 154–59: The narrator and Sonny talk at length on a Saturday afternoon and the narrator tries to listen.
7. Pages 159–63: The narrator goes to listen to Sonny play in a nightclub and finally comes to understand him.

The structure of the story emphasizes the distance between the narrator and Sonny, with the flashback in sections 3–5 separating the arrest and the reconciliation. At the very center of the story (section 4) is Sonny's attempt to convey to his brother the place of music in his life; the failure of the narrator to understand becomes the biggest separation between them.

The story is unified partly through its narrative structures. There is the movement in time — from past, briefly to present, then to more distant past, and finally again to present. There is the balance supplied by the three times the narrator tries to talk to Sonny, in sections 2, 4, and 6 (the narrator is unable to talk at all, then unable to listen and try to understand, and then finally he makes himself listen and try to empathize). And there is the parallelism between the father and uncle (who loves music and was killed) with the narrator and Sonny (who loves music and is in danger of self-destruction).

Another way into the story is its setting. If your students aren't already acquainted with where and what Harlem is, suggest that they do some Internet searching to learn more about its location, history, and atmosphere. Then ask them to think further about the setting and its associations for Sonny, what he feels about it. Among the responses should be a sense of entrapment. That is, Sonny, after their mother dies, feels trapped in Harlem, desperately wants to leave, and eventually escapes to the navy; subsequently he is confined in an institution to cure his drug habit. The narrator thinks that he, in contrast to Sonny, has escaped the confinement of Harlem and racial stereotypes by becoming an algebra teacher and picking up the values of white society: He blocks out Sonny's problems and old friends (has no room for them inside himself) and listens to classical music rather than to jazz. Sonny's return forces the narrator to realize that he hasn't escaped — after all, he lives in a small apartment in a housing development. He realizes that everyone in the projects is "encircled by disaster. Some escaped the trap, most didn't. Those who got out always left something of themselves behind" (p. 144).

Another way into the story is through symbols. Ask students to pick out symbols. Among the answers should be darkness, which in this story is both literal and symbolic — in a recurrent pattern. It works well to have students contribute to a list of examples. Another symbol might be music: In addition to what music is in and of itself, it is also a means of escape, of attaining freedom. Music (especially the blues) relates also to suffering. When Sonny hears the Sister singing at the sidewalk revival meeting, he is struck by "how much suffering she must have had to go through — to sing like that" (p. 157). Music, Sonny says, is an attempt to escape suffering (and darkness and meaninglessness). Ultimately we cannot escape — "there's no way not to suffer," the narrator says (p. 157). But, Sonny replies, "you try all kinds of ways to keep from drowning in it" (p. 157).

The "cup of trembling" in the story's last line might also be a symbol. It is a biblical allusion (Baldwin was a preacher in his teen years and knew the Bible well). The phrase occurs twice in Isaiah 51. In verse 17, the phrase seems an injunction against the citizens of Jerusalem: The city has drunk deeply from God's cup of wrath, his cup of trembling, and has collapsed from exhaustion. In verse 22, God lifts up and restores Jerusalem: "Behold, I have taken out of thine hand the cup of trembling" and given it to Jerusalem's enemies and oppressors; "thou shalt no more drink it again."

PAIR IT WITH   Langston Hughes, "The Weary Blues" (p. 1266).

CHAPTER 7 Style, Tone, and Irony

Kate Chopin

The Story of an Hour (p. 167)

STARTER Ask students to bring to class a brief written description of what they think the Mallards' marriage was like.

ENTRY POINTS Chopin's brief story works well with students, partly because of the surprises in it: They're caught off guard by the unexpected ending, of course, but are surprised also by Mrs. Mallard's reaction to her husband's death. The discussion of the story in Chapter 7 discusses these effects through the story's use of style, tone, and irony, which are effective ways to enter the story.

Another way to get into the story is through the character of Mrs. Mallard. Ask students what she is like and whether they find her a sympathetic character. If you are fortunate, your students may divide, some accusing her of being self-centered and unfeeling, others defending her. Have students point out specific passages that indicate one interpretation or the other: ones showing that she does grieve, ones showing why she experiences a sense of freedom and relief. Relate this to the starter, to the way students view the Mallards' marriage.

Another way to examine the story is through plot. Ask students to pick out examples of foreshadowing (this can be helpful if students complain of a trick ending). Look also at the way the story builds, at its use of contrasts and juxtapositions, at its compression and economy.

PAIR IT WITH Henrik Ibsen, *A Doll House* (p. 926).

Toni Cade Bambara

The Lesson   (p. 183)

STARTER   Ask students to bring to class a brief written description of the character of Sylvia, the narrator in "The Lesson," based solely on their first impressions from the first paragraph of the story. (They should write the description when they finish reading that paragraph, before they go on to the rest of the story.)

ENTRY POINTS   Two striking features of this story are voice and style. The diction, syntax, and rhythms in the opening paragraph are so lively and audacious that it's hard not to read on. Ask students to comment on how they respond to that style (are they surprised, amused, offended, intrigued, whatever) and what effect they feel it contributes to the story.

The style relates directly to the character of Sylvia. Ask students to describe her character. She conveys a brash, know-it-all attitude. Ask students about their first impressions: Did they like Sylvia in the opening paragraph? Did they find her a sympathetic character initially? If not, did that impression change as the story went on? If that is the case, ask them to point out specific places where they began to feel differently about Sylvia. And ask why the author would choose to start that way.

Ask students to comment on the title. What is the lesson Miss Moore wants to teach? Do the children learn the lesson? (Is Sugar's statement of what she has learned in character, or has she learned the lesson too well to be convincing?) What does Sylvia learn? She starts out intending not to let Miss Moore get through to her. Have students pick out places where Sylvia is affected. A particularly important one is signaled by a shift in perspective as, for a moment, Sylvia gets outside herself and notices her own reaction: "'Unbelievable,' I hear myself say" (p. 186). Her intention is to be unflappable, but from that point on, she talks to Miss Moore, hesitates about entering the store, feels anger and irritation. Try to get students to explain what's going on inside Sylvia. Ask them to discuss the final paragraph, especially the last sentence.

This is a story in which borders — both literal and figurative — seem prominent and significant. Ask students to pick out and discuss examples.

Does the story succeed in conveying a theme without seeming to teach a heavy-handed lesson to its readers? If so, by what means does it do so?

PAIR IT WITH   Sandra Cisneros, "The House on Mango Street" (p. 91); John Updike, "A & P" (p. 386).

Amy Tan

Two Kinds (p. 189)

STARTER Suggest that students look closely at the list of "You could's" in the opening paragraph and be ready to comment on which seem to be realistic dreams that one could work toward and possibly attain, and which don't.

ENTRY POINTS "The Lesson" (p. 183) and "Two Kinds" are a natural pairing. You might ask students to list similarities between the narrators in the two stories, if both are being assigned (both stories are in the first person; both narrators have "attitude"; both narrators have lessons to learn about relationships and personal growth).

Tan's story foregrounds mother-daughter tensions and conflicts. Ask students to describe the mother's character and her goals for her daughter, and then to think about whether the goals are understandable for the mother and whether she pursues them in a prudent manner. Next, have students describe the daughter and her goals for herself. What brings the two characters into conflict? How is the conflict resolved or at least halted? Ask students whom they sympathize with in the story. The point of view makes the daughter's outlook more sympathetic (look for places where that seems particularly clear). Ask if anyone sympathizes with the mother, and why. If no one does, ask students to try to see the incidents from the mother's perspective and create a case for seeing her sympathetically.

The last section provides another way into the story. Mother and daughter seem to have put the conflict behind them. What is the point of the final section? Consider the last two paragraphs. Does the pairing of the two piano pieces provide a meaningful resolution to the story, or is it too easy and facile to be convincing and satisfying?

PAIR IT WITH Lan Samantha Chang, "The Eve of the Spirit Festival" (p. 228).

Writing about Fiction

It is important to have students read this chapter because — though the title says "Writing about Fiction" — the chapter, perhaps inevitably, deals with reading and thinking as well as writing. Chapters 3–7 approach reading by focusing on the elements of fiction. This chapter broadens the focus by showing a range of approaches to reading. Attention to the elements can be of value for reading analytically or contextually, both finding connections between a work and other literature and relating a work to the culture that informs or is influenced by it. These approaches tie in closely with ways of thinking critically and imaginatively about literature.

These reading and thinking skills are given practical application in the chapter's discussion of writing. Our aim is to have this chapter apply to writing generally, by emphasizing techniques used in all argumentative writing and focusing especially on the widely useful methods of analysis and of comparison and contrast. It might be helpful for you as instructor to reinforce with the students that one reason to read this chapter carefully is that it will help improve their skills in all areas of writing and not just help them in writing papers about literature.

It's also important for students to read this chapter because later chapters on writing refer back to it. The framework established in this chapter — "Looking Inside the Story," "Looking at What Surrounds the Story," and "Looking Beyond the Story" — is used again in Chapters 15, 21, and 26. Rather than go through these topics in detail each time, we remind students in the later chapters of what already has been explained here.

We have tried to make our advice about writing very practical. Chapter 8 lays out the kind of structural features expected in writing paragraphs (topic sentence, expansion of its idea, development, and support) and papers (introduction, thesis, development, conclusion). But the chapter also clarifies, as does Chapter 2, what is needed beyond good structures to produce an effective paper and get a good grade: that it takes thorough and accurate knowledge of the material and sound and fresh thinking about it. It requires going beyond summarization and easy conclusions to having a point to make, a point that readers will find informative and interesting.

In many cases, an example of effective writing is the most valuable part of a chapter about writing. The student paper included in this chapter does a good job of illustrating the structural features expected of a short paper on literature and the kind of sound and fresh thinking students should strive for. Encourage students to read the sample paper carefully and to use it as a model. Because this is the first sample paper in the book, it is prefaced by an extended "A Student Writer at Work" section, which we think students will find helpful and enjoyable to read.

A Collection of Stories

Raymond Carver

Cathedral (p. 217)

WORKS WELL FOR Character; epiphany; symbol.

ENTRY POINTS This is a very teachable story that students are drawn into and like. It shows how factors other than race or ethnicity sometimes lead to prejudice and misunderstanding. In this case, a blind man is treated as Other, thought of as an outsider, by someone who has never met a blind person before.

The story focuses on the narrator, initially a narrow, prejudiced person, who has an unexpected encounter that opens him to new experiences. One way to initiate discussion is to ask students to describe the narrator's character: for example, the way he labels people (his first words are "this blind man"), his tendency to stereotype, his lack of openness to anything new (he calls drinking "one of our pastimes" — p. 221). Students probably will need little priming — striking examples are abundant.

Then ask how and why he changes — what evidences of change are there, and what leads to the change? Perhaps it helps, initially, that a blind man can keep up with the narrator at drinking, smoking, and eating. But the narrator is still uneasy and doesn't "want to be left alone with a blind man" (p. 223). The TV program on cathedrals (a documentary relying on visual images, rather than dialogue that Robert could follow) leads the narrator to describe what is on the screen. Even that attentiveness to someone else may be a slight breakthrough, as is the thought that Robert might not even understand what cathedrals are, and his attempt to inform him. And that leads to what seems to be a crucial exchange, when Robert asks if the narrator is religious. The narrator replies, "I guess I don't believe in it. In anything. Sometimes it's hard" (p. 226), which perhaps relates to the emptiness in his life that the examination of his character reveals.

25

The last pages may be the most difficult for students to grasp: Ask them to try. Is it significant that what the narrator and Robert draw is a cathedral, rather than some other impressive building? What is suggested by the way they go about it? Surely it is important that they are doing something together, and that the narrator is doing something new: "Never thought anything like this could happen in your lifetime, did you, bub?" (p. 227). Part of the newness is the narrator's experimenting with blindness: He keeps his eyes shut, explaining this by saying, "I thought it was something I ought to do" (p. 228). A cathedral, with the spiritual associations that go with it, must be at least part of what gives the experience something of a mystical quality: "I didn't feel like I was inside anything" (p. 228).

Other areas of interest in the story are its use of imagery dealing with sight, often with ironic overtone; its use of irony generally; and Carver's typical minimalist approach and style. Students also might want to discuss the relationship between the narrator and his wife (and the implied contrast of her relationship to Robert, with whom she might be better matched than with the narrator).

PAIR IT WITH   Galway Kinnell, "Saint Francis and the Sow" (p. 540).

Lan Samantha Chang

The Eve of the Spirit Festival   (p. 228)

WORKS WELL FOR   Point of view (first-person limited); symbolism.

ENTRY POINTS   One way into the story is through its tensions and conflicts: most importantly, the generational tensions between Emily and her father; but also the cultural tensions between the father and American society, epitomized by the chemistry department, and the religious tensions between the father and Buddhist tradition, as well as between Emily and those traditions. There is also tension between Claudia and Emily (try a comparison and contrast of the two). Ask students to list and explain the reasons for the various tensions and conflict, and their importance to the story.

A different way to get at some of the same issues is to describe the characters of the father, Emily, and Claudia, and discuss comparisons and contrasts among them.

This story relates well to the themes of outsiders and figurative borders. And it is a good story for symbolism and cultural values: Ask students to watch for details relating to the cultural and symbolic significance of hair and to be ready to discuss their role in the story. Or, ask students to consider the cultural/religious significance of the Eve of the Spirit Festival and to discuss its importance in the story.

PAIR IT WITH   Judith Ortiz Cofer, "Silent Dancing" (p. 1295).

Ralph Ellison

Battle Royal   (p. 237)

WORKS WELL FOR   Plot; social conflict; symbolism.

ENTRY POINTS   The opening paragraph of the story, as the narrator looks back on his life, is abstract and may be difficult for students to grasp on first reading. Suggest that they return to it after finishing the story. Discussing it after the class has examined the rest of the story can be helpful, too.

One sentence in the opening paragraph is very clear, however: "I was naïve." Asking students for evidences of his naïvete throughout the story can be a good way into the story. In what ways was he naïve, idealist, out of touch with reality? The story provides lots of examples: his belief that humility is the key to advancement for blacks; his confidence that the men wanted to hear his speech and would respect his abilities; his admiration for the important and influential citizens of his city.

Another way to get at key aspects of the story is to ask about the smoker: What dynamic is at work in selecting the entertainment? What is the underlying purpose of bringing the young black men there? Talking about what goes on there will probably bring out that it's a degrading type of entertainment: the stripper, like the black youths, is used, reduced to an object, rendered invisible. Beyond this, it will probably be evident also that the blacks are being shown their place: the allurements (sex, money) are being dangled before them only to make it clear that they are unattainable. The establishment whites have all the power and privilege, the blacks have none, and the evening's experience makes sure they will never forget it. Aggression must be used only against other blacks, in blind, chaotic flailing, never against whites (the narrator's effort to topple Mr. Colcord onto the electrified pad is met with vicious retribution). And the narrator's slip of the tongue — "social equality" (p. 246) — silences the room instantly and requires retraction.

This provides the context for rereading the opening paragraph and his grandfather's advice: pretend to accept what you are told about staying in your place, but don't believe a word of it. "Overcome 'em with yeses, undermine 'em with grins" (p. 237), but subvert them by maintaining your self-respect and integrity. The narrator's dream at the end of the story should be clear in this context. Ask students to explain it and comment on it.

PAIR IT WITH   Langston Hughes, "Freedom's Plow" (p. 1258).

Diane Glancy

Aunt Parnetta's Electric Blisters (p. 248)

WORKS WELL FOR Point of view (third-person omniscient); humor; style.

ENTRY POINTS Like Leslie Marmon Silko's "The Man to Send Rain Clouds" (p. 377), this story deals with cultural differences — the impingement of white values on Native Americans. Unlike Silko's story, Glancy's is filled with humor. One way into the story is to pay attention to the variety of comic devices (from the slapstick comedy of shooting the refrigerator to the verbal humor of the use of dialect, the fanciful comparisons, and the witty expressions) and to the role humor fills in the story.

The story takes a more serious turn in section 3, as Parnetta begins to identify with the refrigerator and through it to come to a deeper self-understanding. One way of entering this section is to focus on the details that link her to the refrigerator, and then on details that move from the refrigerator (and white culture) to a deeper connection with aspects of Parnetta's native culture.

PAIR IT WITH Leslie Marmon Silko, "The Man to Send Rain Clouds" (p. 377).

Nathaniel Hawthorne

Young Goodman Brown (p. 252)

WORKS WELL FOR Allegory; archetypes; psychological/spiritual conflict.

ENTRY POINTS This story illustrates well what allegory is and how it works. Students are inclined to read allegorically where it is not appropriate, to ask of a story "what is it *really* about?" and try to fashion a double layer of meaning. You might try to get them to figure out what signals this story sends to indicate that seeing multiple layers of meaning in this story is appropriate, though that might not be the best way of reading other stories.

The choice of names in the story provides an obvious place to start. Having the wife named "Faith" can suggest that while she is a person in the story, she can also be seen as embodying the concept of religious faith. The name thus sets up a line such as "My Faith is gone!" (p. 258), which begs to be read in multiple ways. The name of the title character suggests he is a typical or universal figure, an "everyman," rather than a unique and unusual individual. He is "young," or "Brown, Junior," to distinguish him from his father, Old Goodman Brown. But "young" also suggests that he is inexperienced and innocent, that he has not yet encountered evil in the world and learned how to deal with it. "Goodman" is a common seventeenth-century title, an equivalent to "Mister"; but it also suggests what the character is at the beginning of the story — a good, decent man — and it becomes ironic later in the story when he becomes convinced there is no good in any man or woman. "Brown" is an ordinary, commonplace name — nothing special about it or him. It is also a middle-course name, avoiding the absolute associations that the names "White" and "Black" carry.

The story opens with two contrasting archetypes that help signal that the story deals with universal issues rather than with just one specific, individual event. On the one hand is the village, with its archetypal associations of home, safety, community and accompanying imagery of light, order, and goodness. Goodman Brown undertakes a journey, a universal image for moving through life and acquiring experience; his journey is taken at night, with all the archetypal associations of danger and evil that traditionally have been ascribed to darkness. It is a journey into a forest, a contrasting image to the village: Forests carry archetypal associations of the untamed regions surrounding a home or community, places of danger, disorder, and confusion where one can easily become confused or lost.

Goodman Brown travels into the forest to meet the devil (or, he encounters the evil that exists in the world, from which until now he seems to have been sheltered). No reason is given for his undertaking the journey, but perhaps the day itself is not time specific — the journey may occur whenever a person faces that step in life (unless it is the case that Goodman Brown is deliberately seeking out an encounter with evil, instead of facing it when it naturally occurs). He meets a supernatural figure, able to travel from Boston to Salem in fifteen minutes. Other details (his snakelike staff, his sitting under a tree) indicate this is the devil, the tempter who undermined the goodness of Adam and Eve in Genesis 3. The story does not require readers to take this as a literal encounter with the devil; alternative explanations (the wriggling of the staff might be only an "ocular deception" — p. 254) create ambiguity.

What does seem clear, however, is that Goodman Brown is confronted with the reality of evil. Whatever he experiences during his night in the forest — whether it be a literal initiation into witchcraft or a dream — he comes away from it convinced that he is no longer good, and that no one else is either. He loses his faith in God's goodness (defined as God's grace). The emphasis at the end of the story is on the way awareness of evil poisons Goodman Brown's likeness — turns him into "a stern, a sad, a darkly meditative, a distrustful, if not a desperate man" (p. 262). The story seems to be Hawthorne's imaginative account of how some people in his community turned into what has become the (unfair) stereotype of the dark, dour, distrustful Puritan, unable to accept and take joy in God's salvation because she or he believes that "evil is the nature of mankind" (p. 261). Those, however, are the words of the devil, not of God. By walking away from Faith, Goodman Brown cuts himself off from what for Hawthorne was the way to salvation for human beings who are mixtures of good and bad in need of God's grace.

PAIR IT WITH   Naguib Mahfouz, "Half a Day" (p. 435).

Zora Neale Hurston

Sweat (p. 263)

WORKS WELL FOR Point of view (third-person omniscient); character; setting.

ENTRY POINTS One way into the story is to focus on the character of Delia and that of Sykes. Hurston uses the full range of characterization techniques: telling, showing, what they say, what others say about them. Listing traits of both brings into juxtaposition a good, loyal, hardworking woman and an abusive, cruel, self-centered, and manipulative man. The story explores the conflict between Delia and Sykes. Describe also what their marriage is like and connect it to character. Related to characterization is the title; consider its relevance.

Another avenue into the story is settings — the house and the town. Consider what the house means to Delia, and what it means and conveys to Sykes (and how it relates to his intentions). Consider also its location and how its isolation, on the edge of town, relates to what happens (to her vulnerability, to Sykes' demise). Consider the effect of having the story occur in a small town (probably similar to Hurston's hometown of Eatonville, Florida), not a large city. And consider the use of dialect. Note that the narration is in standard English and the dialogue in rural black dialect, which can be difficult for students to read (suggest that they read it aloud, so they *hear* it). Does the use of dialectic seem a good idea? What does it add to the story? What would be lost if the dialogue was written in standard English?

Another way to get at the heart of the story is the ending. Delia is not legally responsible for Sykes' death: She does nothing to *cause* him to die. And there probably is nothing she can do to prevent him from dying. But the question of moral culpability remains: Should she make an effort to help or save him? Ask students to assess the ending (do they find the story itself satisfying?) and to assess Delia's attitude and her decision to take no action (do they accept and defend her, or find her actions disturbing?). Is the ending clear-cut and decisive, or ambiguous? In either case, is that the best way to end the story?

PAIR IT WITH Bessie Head, "The Collector of Treasures" (p. 421).

Gish Jen

Who's Irish? (p. 272)

WORKS WELL FOR Point of view (first-person unreliable narrator); humor.

ENTRY POINTS   A key issue in the story is the handling of the narrator. Ask students to describe her strengths (for example, her independence, determination, fierceness, ability to succeed in difficult circumstances) and weaknesses (her tendency to stereotype, her prejudices, her difficulty in accepting change, and so on). As they talk about the narrator and the things that happen to her, ask to what extent the narrator is reliable and to what extent she understands herself and her situation. See if they pick up places where the narrator shades or covers the truth (hiding things from her daughter parallels hiding things from us — her account of her attempts to get Sophie to come out of the foxhole is a particularly striking example: from Sophie's bruises, the narrator's poking with the stick must have been more aggressive than she indicates).

The handling of narration relates also to where our sympathies lie: Hearing the story from the narrator's perspective may incline us to sympathize with her and not her daughter. Should we yield to that inclination, or resist it and look at things from other perspectives as well?

Students should be able to identify and illustrate a series of conflicts that give the story structure: between ethnic groups, between mother and daughter, between old and new ways of doing things, between Chinese and American practices and values.

An issue that may come up is the mother's Chinese American dialect: Does use of it contribute to realism? Does it help to convey her character? Or does it interfere with the story's effectiveness? (It contributes to the humor of what is often a very funny story. Is it an effective comic technique?)

Discuss the story's ending. Has anything changed? Has the narrator gained in self-understanding or grown through her experiences? Has she found a home or just a place to live? How close and compatible are the two women?

PAIR IT WITH   Amy Tan, "Two Kinds" (p. 189).

James Joyce

Eveline   (p. 280)

WORKS WELL FOR   Point of view (third-person limited: center of consciousness); character; epiphany.

ENTRY POINTS   The question students will want to discuss is why Eveline didn't go with Frank. Start by having them give reasons why she should go — for example, her need to *escape* (from her father's self-centeredness; from the ways her father takes her for granted, threatens her, and treats her as a child; and from her boring job and the general emptiness of her life in Dublin) and the fact that a good man loves and appreciates her and wants to give her a better life.

Then ask students to give reasons why she holds back and eventually decides not to go with Frank — for example, her memories; her promise to her mother to keep the house together; the times her father is nice, especially the day she was sick. Point students to the line "Everything changes" (p. 280). We may think change is good or inevitable, but Eveline seems to regret change: She would prefer that things stay the same. And now she's thinking of contributing to that sense of change. A key line is, "she prayed to God to direct her, to show her what was her duty" (p. 283). If she prays to be shown her duty, she will inevitably stay — to leave would be indulgent and satisfying herself. By staying she would be faithful to what is expected of her.

It's interesting to consider the story in the context of Joyce's life — the fact that he, unlike Eveline, did leave, and the love/hate relation he had toward Dublin (leaving it, but then writing about it).

PAIR IT WITH   William Faulkner, "A Rose for Emily" (p. 108).

Jamaica Kincaid

Girl   (p. 283)

WORKS WELL FOR   Voice; style and rhythm; humor.

ENTRY POINTS   Students respond well to this short work of poetic prose. Ask your students how many of them can identify with the title character receiving more parental advice than she or he could ever want. A good way into the piece is listening to the voice. Urge students to read the selection aloud and listen for the voice, and for the rhythms and sounds. You might also ask a student or two to read it aloud in class so students will hear the voice as others read it.

The voice heard most in the work is that of a mother giving her daughter practical advice on running a household, being a lady, and dealing with other situations a woman might face. A second voice, presumably that of the "girl" of the title, responds twice, indicated by italics. Another way into the work is asking students to list various types of advice the mother gives, and to identify the kinds of concerns she has about her daughter.

Still another way into the piece is to ask students to describe the effect of the stream of directives. What aspects suggest that it is an actual dialogue between mother and daughter? If so, are the italicized lines spoken aloud, or are they thoughts the daughter would like to express but doesn't? Are there aspects that suggest the work might be a summary of advice the mother gave over many years instead of a single speech? Are there aspects that suggest it is a memory piece, showing how the daughter, thinking back, remembers the kind of advice her mother passed out continually? What way of looking at it best accounts for the story's wonderful humor?

Yet another way in is to consider the title. Why is it entitled "Girl" when the girl speaks only two lines? What is indicated by the fact that it is not entitled "Mother"? What is suggested by the fact that it is entitled "Girl" rather than "Woman"?

PAIR IT WITH   Clarence Major, "Young Woman" (p. 687).

Jhumpa Lahiri

Interpreter of Maladies   (p. 285)

WORKS WELL FOR   Character; setting.

ENTRY POINTS   The story as a whole involves a series of misunderstandings. An important one is cultural misunderstanding. Mr. and Mrs. Das were born and grew up in the United States, and are visiting India as tourists. Note examples of the cultural gaps between them and Mr. Kapasi, despite their common ancestry (Mr. Kapasi, for example, is shocked by the Western clothes Mrs. Das, who is clearly of Indian ancestry, is wearing, and the Das children are more unruly than Mr. Kapasi would expect Indian children to be).

The misunderstandings are highlighted also by the title of the story. It relates to Mr. Kapasi's job, translating patients' descriptions of their ailments so the doctor can understand how to treat them. As Mr. Kapasi, in his other job as a driver, takes the Das family around, Mrs. Das shows interest in his uninteresting job and awakens an excitement in his unexciting life: Mr. Kapasi interprets her Western clothes, her conversation, and her giving her address to him as sexual interest, and he spends the day fantasizing about her.

She, however, is reaching toward him out of her deep need, the pain she lives with from a brief affair eight years before and the fact that her husband does not know that his friend, not he, is the father of her younger son. She expects Mr. Kapasai, who works for a doctor and helps alleviate pain, to provide a remedy. Instead, he is struck by the contrast between what pain means to her, in her secure, wealthy, privileged Western life, and what pain means for the poor, desperate people for whom he interprets in the doctor's office. When he offers Mrs. Das an interpretation — that it is guilt, not pain, she feels and needs to deal with — she is angered and cuts him off. His fantasy ends and he — like she — is brought back to the drab, disillusioned reality that stretches out before him.

PAIR IT WITH   Julia de Burgos, "Returning" (p. 773).

Toni Morrison

Recitatif (p. 300)

WORKS WELL FOR Point of view (first-person limited); plot; social and psychological conflict.

ENTRY POINTS Kristina Martinez's student paper in Chapter 26 (p. 1408) deals with several of the questions students raise about "Recitatif" (Morrison's only published short story): Which of the two girls is black and which is white, and why is it left ambiguous? What happens to Maggie? Why do the conflicting stories about Maggie arise?

It seems impossible to discuss this story without getting into the race of the two main characters. Ask students to say which girl is white and which is black and give supporting evidence and explanations. In many cases, the explanations will involve stereotypes, which in this case could be reversed; that seems to be one of the central points of the story. In the end, we think it's impossible to determine the race of either girl definitively.

Contrasts are a key technique in exploring the theme of identity and acceptance (self-acceptance and acceptance by others). Invite students to pick out and discuss comparisons and contrasts between Twyla and Roberta and between them and Maggie. The story provides an excellent example of how people are turned into outsiders and thus become Other, separated by literal walls and figurative borders and fences.

Someone is likely to ask about the title. Students should have looked up the word if they weren't already familiar with it — that's part of active reading. Recitatif is the style of musical declamation, a mix of speaking and singing, used for dialogue and narrative parts in opera and oratorio. It goes back to the same root as *recite*, to repeat something from memory. Thus the title directs our attention to the importance of memories — Twyla is reciting memories, in a five-section formal structure akin to an opera or oratorio (though the story shows that reciting is not reliable; memories can be distorted, and parts can be forgotten).

PAIR IT WITH Countee Cullen, "Incident" (p. 519); Emily Dickinson, "I'm Nobody! Who are you?" (p. 578).

Bharati Mukherjee

Orbiting (p. 315)

WORKS WELL FOR Character; epiphany; tone.

ENTRY POINTS The heart of the story is the encounter of cultures, set up in a most interesting (and humorous) way as an Indian American author creates an Irish American narrator in love with an illegal immigrant from Afghanistan, hosting her family for the quintessential American holiday, Thanksgiving. The story foregrounds ethnic/cultural differences, as lists of such details can clarify.

The title refers to the way Ro circled from one international airport to another until he found a country that would take him in. Invite students to find other applications for the title: If orbiting is "to revolve around (a center of attraction)," what other centers exist in the story, and what revolves around them?

Look closely at Ro's story about Afghanistan and the oppression he has suffered, and explore how and why it leads Rindy's family to see him in a different way and leads Rindy to see Ro — and her own family — in ways she hasn't before. Ask students to discuss and evaluate Rindy's sentence, "Ro's my chance to heal the world" (p. 327).

PAIR IT WITH   David Mura, "Grandfather-in-Law" (p. 535).

Tim O'Brien

The Things They Carried   (p. 327)

WORKS WELL FOR   Style; imagery (detail; lists).

ENTRY POINTS   The best way into the story is considering the implications of its foregrounding of "things." Instead of focusing on people, O'Brien describes in close detail the things that are important to them, and why they are important. As we come to understand the importance of possessions and equipment, we also come to understand the men and their situation in Vietnam. The indirect method may be more powerful than a direct depiction of character might be.

Another way into the story is to focus on a key technique, it's the story's use of lists. In a way, the entire story is a list, of things soldiers carry into war (external, physical things and inner emotions, attitudes, and beliefs). Students can be asked to list the characters in the story and to list the things each carries and what those things reveal about the character.

A further way in is to trace the references to Ted Lavender. References to the fact that he dies are sprinkled through the story as an unusually explicit type of foreshadowing. You might ask students to consider the effect of spreading the climactic event through the story, so that it doesn't seem a climax.

Although the story's omniscient, objective narrator moves from one character to another, the principal focus is on Jimmy Cross, the platoon leader. Another entry to the story would be Martha's photographs and letters. Consider why Cross burns them.

PAIR IT WITH   Yosef Komunyakaa, "Facing It" (p. 505).

Flannery O'Connor

A Good Man Is Hard to Find   (p. 341)

WORKS WELL FOR   Plot; setting; spiritual conflict; epiphany.

ENTRY POINTS   This story works well for analysis of plot. It is a carefully structured, mostly chronological work that uses accessible plot devices. Looking at it one way, it divides in half: before the accident/after the accident. First half: the grandmother as misfit in her family; conflict between her and the rest of the family. The first half climaxes in the accident. Second half: grandmother vs. the Misfit; conflict between her and him, her and the rest of the family, and within herself. The second half climaxes either when she touches the Misfit or when she dies.

Looked at another way, the plot shows a satisfying symmetry and balance:

Misfit — referred to (p. 341)

Accident — referred to (p. 342)

Plantation — referred to (p. 343)

———

Misfit — talked about (p. 345)

———

Plantation — going to it (pp. 345–46)

Accident — happens (p. 346)

Misfit — appears (p. 347)

Foreshadowings are woven throughout the plot: the references to the Misfit in the first paragraph (and throughout the first half of the story); reference to the grandmother taking the cat Pitty Sing along secretly (p. 342); reference to an accident ("In case of an accident" — p. 342); many references to death (starting with "anyone seeing her dead on the highway" — p. 342); and so on.

Students find the ending shocking and difficult to sort out. O'Connor herself provides a helpful discussion of the story in comments she made at a public reading of the story in 1963 (published as "The Element of Surprise in 'A Good Man Is Hard to Find'" in "On Her Own Work," *Mystery and Manners: Occasional Prose*, ed. Sally and Robert Fitzgerald; reprinted in many literature anthologies). O'Connor addresses several issues that students are likely to ask about or wonder about and that provide good ways to get into the story.

One is the character of the grandmother. Ask students to describe her. O'Connor says that some readers think of the grandmother as evil, some even taking her as a witch, with a cat. O'Connor resists that: To her the grandmother is the kind of woman she encountered frequently in the South, a self-centered, hypocritical elderly person lacking comprehension but having a good heart.

Another entry to the story is its title. Ask students how they understand it. Some may catch the allusion to the story of the rich young ruler in Matthew 19:16–22 (also Mark 10:17–31 and Luke 18:18–30), who says to Jesus "Good master, what good thing shall I do, that I may have eternal life?" And Jesus replies "Why callest thou me good? There is none good but one, that is, God." The grandmother thinks of herself, and of people who are like her in values, as good — the episode at Red Sammy's place brings that out with delicious irony. To that extent, she is not in tune with the Christian emphasis on grace.

Another is the exchange between the grandmother and the Misfit. Ask students to comment on it or to raise questions about confusing parts (such as, "his face was as familiar to her as if she had known him all her life" — p. 348, possibly suggesting that he seems to her an ordinary person, one of mixed good and evil like everyone she has ever met). O'Connor points out that the grandmother is facing death and is not prepared for it. She does everything she can to save herself, especially appealing to the Misfit as a "good man," not a bit "common." The Misfit (like Jesus) denies it: "Nome, I ain't a good man" (p. 349). He talks about his life (students may not pick up that the head-doctor who tells him he had killed his father is using terms from Freudian psychoanalysis).

O'Connor makes clear that the interaction between the grandmother and the Misfit relies heavily on Christian theology, growing out of her strong Catholic faith. The Misfit raises profound theological issues: "Jesus thrown everything off balance" (p. 351); "If He did what He said, then it's nothing for you to do but throw away everything and follow Him" (p. 352) (echoing Matthew 19:21). The Misfit in his genuine wrestling with spiritual matter may, despite his crimes and lack of faith, be closer to God than the grandmother with her pious God-talk.

O'Connor in introducing the story said that if the following sentence were omitted, there would be no story — what would be left would not be worth our attention: "She saw the man's face twisted close to her own as if he were going to cry and she murmured, 'Why you're one of my babies. You're one of my own children!' She reached out and touched him on the shoulder" (p. 352). Ask students why that line is so important: What is going on in this part of the story? (They may be confused by the line, asking if the Misfit is actually her child.) See if anyone connects the moment with James Joyce's concept of epiphany. O'Connor would call it a moment of grace. For the first time in the story she thinks of someone else instead of just herself and reaches out to touch someone. As is usual in O'Connor stories, a person in need of grace, of salvation, finds it in the most unlikely place, conveyed by the most unlikely person.

Students may question the violence in the story (especially her being shot — three times — immediately after her life is transformed). O'Connor says that violence has a way of turning characters to reality and preparing them to receive grace. The violence in her stories is not an end in itself: A person encountering a violent situation displays her or his basic, core qualities. As the Misfit puts it, "'She would of been a good woman . . . if it had been somebody there to shoot her every minute of her life'" (p. 352).

PAIR IT WITH Nathaniel Hawthorne, "Young Goodman Brown" (p. 252).

Tillie Olsen

I Stand Here Ironing (p. 353)

WORKS WELL FOR Point of view (interior monologue).

ENTRY POINTS This moving, haunting story of a single parent's regrets that she had not been a better mother for her oldest daughter takes the form of a dramatic monologue (if, in paragraph 2, a school social worker has stopped by the house and is speaking to the mother), or of interior monologue, if — as seems more likely — the second paragraph contains the words of a note the social worker sent home, or a message left on her answering machine (if such machines had been available in the early 1960s, though the story probably should not be limited in that way to a specific time). In the latter case, the words spin through the mother's mind as she does her ironing, and the rest of the story contains the thoughts she would like to express to the social worker: She goes over in her mind the speech she would like to give to the social worker, whether she ever gives it or not.

The story relates the difficult circumstances under which Emily grew up. The mother clearly feels guilty about them and about not giving Emily the kind of care she needed. The mitigating circumstances are quite starkly summed up in the next-to-last paragraph (p. 358). Ask students whether the paragraph is needed, and what the effect would be of having it earlier in the story, perhaps as an introductory summary before the more detailed account. Ask students if they think the mother is right to say, "Let her be." Should the daughter not receive all the help she can? (But of how much value was the help they were given in the past?) Are there evidences in the story as it is being told of genuine love and attention on the mother's part, however inadequate she now feels it was? Students might be asked to describe the character of the mother. Who does the story seem to be more about, the daughter or the mother?

PAIR IT WITH Gwendolyn Brooks, "the mother" (p. 615).

Edgar Allan Poe

The Cask of Amontillado   (p. 359)

WORKS WELL FOR   Point of view (first-person unreliable narrator); plot; tone.

ENTRY POINTS   Poe theorized that "unity of effect or impression is a point of the greatest importance in fiction," a result attainable only in short fiction, works that can be read "at one sitting." Ask students to describe the single effect or impression of this story, and how the various techniques contribute toward achieving it.

This is a good story to illustrate the importance of reader involvement. The horror felt by the reader, as the implications of what the narrator is doing become ever clearer, is the crucial effect. Because of the point of view, we cannot enter the mind of Fortunato and share what he feels. Active reading leads us to project our own feeling of horror onto him. The story's reliance on irony also requires active participation by the reader — both dramatic irony (as, for example, "The cough is a mere nothing; it will not kill me. I shall not die of a cough" — p. 361) and verbal irony ("My dear Fortunato, you are luckily met — p. 359).

Students may want to focus on the narrator's line, "My heart grew sick — on account of the dampness of the catacombs" (p. 364). Is his explanation accurate (or honest)? Or is this an inadvertent admission that the narrator is not as unmoved by what he is doing as he tries to act?

We are not distracted from the horror by evaluating the narrator's motive: The direct address in sentence 2 implies that we already know what the "thousand injuries" and the "insult" are — and we know that the narrator is not someone to mess with. The first paragraph lays out the requirements for adequate revenge.

The point of view focuses our attention on the narrator. We see into the mind of a murderer carrying out a premeditated, carefully planned killing. It raises the question of the narrator's reliability. Does the narrator exaggerate the seriousness of the offense against him? Was the narrator sane when he carried out these acts? Is he sane when he tells us about them?

PAIR IT WITH   Robert Morgan, "Mountain Bride" (p. 695).

Katherine Anne Porter

The Jilting of Granny Weatherall   (p. 364)

WORKS WELL FOR   Plot; character; point of view (center of consciousness and some stream of consciousness).

ENTRY POINTS   Students often have difficulty getting oriented at the beginning of the story. Going over half a page with them can be helpful, as the approach shifts abruptly from sentence to sentence: Sentence 1 is an objective statement by the narrator; sentences 2 and 3 are Granny's thoughts; sentences 4 and 5 are dialogue, spoken aloud. Paragraphs 3–7 are dialogue, Granny apparently speaking aloud to Doctor Harry in paragraphs 3, 5, and 7 because the doctor replies to her in paragraphs 4 and 6. But the last part of paragraph 7 could be spoken in her mind rather than aloud, as with much of what Granny seems to say thereafter, except where another character replies directly to what she says.

Clarifying the shifting point of view can be helpful to students in following the story. The point of view alternates between third-person objective, third-person center of consciousness, and a mild version of stream of consciousness. You might look at some specific passages to show how these shifts occur and invite discussion of the value of such alternations in achieving multiple effects. Stream of consciousness — used in some parts of the story where Granny's mind wanders — may be the most confusing and difficult for them. They should not, however, say the whole story is stream of consciousness. The story uses stream of consciousness, but only as one among several approaches.

Students often need help in figuring out what happens in the story because events are not related chronologically and sometimes need to be determined from Granny's confused memories. For example, he who has jilted her on their wedding day ("he had not come" — p. 367) is George. The memory of him and of that day she has suppressed until now, when it resurrects on her dying day. The person whose hand had caught her and who cursed like a sailor's parrot is John, whom she marries instead of George and with whom she has four children (Cornelia, Lydia, Jimmy, and Hapsy) and a good life before he died young and she had to carry on as a single parent.

The details about Hapsy cause the most confusion: There are references to the birth of Hapsy ("Yes, John, get the Doctor now" — p. 369), and Hapsy seems to have been her favorite child. There are also references to "Hapsy standing with a baby on her arm" (p. 368), after which Hapsy and the baby fade to shadows and Hapsy says, "I thought you'd never come." Apparently Hapsy died in childbirth some time ago.

It's usually helpful to have students discuss Granny's character. Some, in most classes, find her unsympathetic (except for being jilted) and attach such labels as proud, exacting, unforgiving. Other students may bring out more positive attributes, such as hard-working, tough, independent, organized, efficient, smart, practical, loving, and caring. In either case, be sure they base what they say on specific references in the text.

Details in the last couple of pages, as she approaches death and then dies, also cause difficulty for many students. Granny steps into a cart (which might remind students of Emily Dickinson's "Because I could not stop for Death" — p. 635), driven by a man whose face she doesn't see but whom she knows "by his hands." It seems to us the identity of the driver is left deliberately ambiguous — her husband or Death or Jesus seem the most likely possibilities, each of which could be meaningful. Students may not recognize that when Father Connolly "tickled her feet," he was administering the last rites of the church. The references to "looking down the road" and making "a long journey outward" are conventional archetypes. The attempt to describe the moment of death itself, in the last two paragraphs, is remarkable.

The final paragraph generally raises many questions. "For the second time" there is no sign (of God's presence?). When was the first time? (When she was in the "hell" of depression after being jilted?) "Again no bridegroom" — why again? (This would seem to be a reference to Jesus, who referred to himself as a bridegroom when he asked, "Can the children of the bridegroom mourn, as long as the bridegroom is with them?" — Matthew 9:15; Mark 2:19; Luke 5:34). And again a "priest in the house" — a priest is present now as one was sixty years ago when she was jilted. Granny seems to sense that she is being jilted again, that Christ is jilting her because she does not sense his presence at her deathbed. "There's nothing more cruel than this — I'll never forgive it," and blowing out the light, can be taken as despair, as her dying without grace. But the ending can also be read in the larger context of the last two pages: for a Catholic, God is present through a priest and through the sacraments, both of which are there even though Granny does not seem very aware of them. In her feisty independence, and the deep pain uncovered by the release of hurtful memories, she may feel abandoned by God, but God is there nonetheless — perhaps driving the cart in which she rides between rows of trees that lean over and bow to each other, and in which "a thousand birds were singing a Mass."

PAIR IT WITH Helena María Viramontes, "The Moths" (p. 391).

Nahid Rachlin

Departures (p. 371)

WORKS WELL FOR Plot; character.

ENTRY POINTS The departure of her son to join the army turns into a point of reassessment and reflection for Farogh. Students might be asked why that occasion would provide such a spark (perhaps concern over the wellbeing of what appears to be her only son and youngest child; the "empty nest" that will follow his departure, she and her husband alone in the house each evening; the fact that she is getting older and a stage in her life is passing, which often leads a person to consider what has been and what remains).

It may be the situation more than Ahmad's photograph that reminds her of Karim. Ask students why, after all these years, she would remember him and want to see him again. (He was, after all, the only man in whom she ever had a romantic interest, not counting her arranged marriage to Hassan. Also, she thinks Ahmad's eyes remind her of Karim, but later she admits she cannot remember what Karim looked like — perhaps she is nostalgic as much for what she herself was when she was fifteen as for what Karim was. And a dissatisfaction with what the future seems to hold for her may stir a dissatisfaction with the past and a wondering about what might have been.)

That she sent a letter to Karim would seem, in her society, a rather daring action. Ask students if doing so seems consistent with her character, as the story reveals it. Ask them to describe her. She seems to have been something of an outsider: wanting an education, raising philosophical questions, longing for her old job with its opportunities to talk to others about subjects like world affairs. Sending the letter may be an act of near desperation. Her husband is considerably older than she and spends a great deal of time at his shop and apparently very little with her; his reaction to his own emotions as Ahmad departs, looking away and "shutting her out" (p. 374), probably defines their relationship generally. Thus it is that she reflects "I need someone."

The story culminates in Farogh's meeting with Karim at his mother's house. Ask students to comment on what Farogh hoped for and what she found. She is disappointed — he has changed greatly, influenced especially by becoming American. But the disappointment must go deeper than that. A key sentence seems to be, "She looked at him, still hoping to reach the person he had been and to then see a reflection of herself, the way she was at fifteen, but none of it came" (p. 377). That sentence should lead back to the earlier time with Karim, when she remembers "feeling very carefree. The other person, the person I was then, was so much more real than the one I am now. Hassan's creation, she thought" (p. 374). Perhaps one can say she has, throughout, been looking for her self, feeling that she has lost that self in the years since Karim departed from her life. And the story ends with concerns about how much Ahmad will change now that he has departed from home, and how that will diminish her life still further. Thus she holds onto the street, the reality in front of her, "as if it [like the good things earlier in her life] were a mirage that might slip away from her at any moment" (p. 377).

PAIR IT WITH   Henrik Ibsen, *A Doll House* (p. 926).

Leslie Marmon Silko

The Man to Send Rain Clouds   (p. 377)

WORKS WELL FOR   Setting; cultural conflict.

ENTRY POINTS   One way to enter this story is through what is implied but not said or is not spelled out (that is, through its gaps), starting with "him" in line 1. Consider the effect of Silko's spare style and approach and how it relates to and depends on telling the story mostly from Leon's perspective (two paragraphs are from Father Paul's perspective). Consider how different the story would look from the priest's perspective.

Another way into the story is paying attention to the two sets of lifestyles, cultural values, and religious beliefs that exist side by side and are even intertwined. Students can be asked to make three lists — examples of native culture, western Catholic culture, and ways the two have intertwined (for example, that Louise wants holy water sprinkled on Teofilo's body, but for a reason that seems different from the priest's).

A crucial question is why the priest hesitates to accede to Leon's request, and why he finally decides to do what Leon asks. One might compare and contrast the priest to the teacher in Chinua Achebe's "Dead Men's Path."

PAIR IT WITH   Chinua Achebe, "Dead Men's Path" (p. 405).

Virgil Suárez

A Perfect Hotspot   (p. 381)

WORKS WELL FOR   Character; setting.

ENTRY POINTS   One way into the story is to focus on the generational conflict: the father vs. the son, the way the father thinks about customers vs. the way the son does (for example, "make the kill fast" — p. 384), what the father sees as best for the son vs. what the son wants to pursue for himself. That conflict may result in part from the contrast between the way the son relates to his father and the way he remembers his recently deceased mother. How do the father and son seem different? The contrast between working in the ice cream truck and what Tonio dreams of (spending time on the beach and swimming laps) relates closely to the generational conflict.

Another entry point is the story about his childhood that the father tells the narrator. It seems to come out of nowhere, and no explicit connections are made to the rest of the story. Consider its relevance. Does it anticipate and account for the father's change of heart at the end? Consider the final sentence: *Does* Tonio's father begin throwing things around? If so, why does the story stop there?

Students are likely to (or should) raise a question about the title. Some possible implications are that the ice cream truck sells the most products on a hot day. Tonio's father feels on a hotspot because of increasing competition and decreasing sales. And Tonio's father puts Tonio on a hotspot by pressuring him to follow in his footsteps and taking over the ice cream truck.

PAIR IT WITH   Charles Bukowski, "my old man" (p. 488).

John Updike

A & P   (p. 386)

WORKS WELL FOR   Style; character; epiphany; irony.

ENTRY POINTS   One way to enter the story is through its breezy colloquial style and what it reveals about the narrator — see the discussions of the
opening paragraph in Chapter 7 (p. 166). Asking what one can tell from just
the first sentence can be an effective way to start. The colloquial approach was
probably more startling as a way to write a story in 1962 than it seems now.
Students find Sammy's use of detail interesting. They should notice also his
use of figures of speech and what they indicate about his character (for example, "like a bee in a glass jar" — p. 387; "like a dented sheet of metal tilted
in the light" — p. 387; "buzzed to the other two" — p. 387; "sheep . . . traffic
. . . houseslaves" — p. 387; "chalked up on his fuselage already" — p. 388;
"sizing up their joints" — p. 388; "haggling with a truck full of cabbages" — p.
389; "scuttle into that door" — p. 389; "the two smoothest scoops of vanilla" —
p. 390; and so on).

The part of the story that is most fruitful to talk about — and that gives
students the most difficulty — is Sammy's decision to quit. Students often
take it as a mistake, or an empty gesture, or a failed attempt at heroism. And
any of these may be at least partly correct. It can also be seen in a more positive way. Sammy seems quite young and immature for a nineteen-year-old—
his parents got him his job; he's still living at home, and his mother irons his
shirts (and presumably washes his clothes, cooks his meals, etc.); he shows
very little independence for someone who's almost twenty. He's stuck in a
small-town rut, conforming to its ways, in a dead-end low-paying job, taking
orders from his boss and being careful not to upset his parents. Into his life
walk three girls who don't conform, who seem (to his small-town, late-ado-
lescent mind) to be independent, going against the grain, and Lengel steps up
to set them straight — make them conform to the store rules and small-town
mores.

Perhaps as a result of all that, Sammy has a sort of epiphany (a moment
of illumination) — this minor episode makes him see himself and the life he's
stuck in with new insight. He realizes how unlike those girls he feels. So,
maybe for the first time in his life, he makes a gesture, breaks with conformity, decides to be independent and do what he thinks is right, not just what
is safe and prudent. He hopes the girls will know what he does and admire
him for it — but that may not be why he does it; and it's more than a gesture.
The last line of the story is surely overdramatic, but there may be a grain of
truth in it too: Life is going to be harder for him if he continues to think for
himself and go against conformity rather than if he stays in a safe groove and
just does what others expect of him and tell him to do.

PAIR IT WITH   Dagoberto Gilb, "Love in L.A." (p. 55).

Helena María Viramontes

The Moths   (p. 391)

WORKS WELL FOR   Symbolism; magic realism; character.

ENTRY POINTS   One way into the story is the mixing of realistic and fantastic details in "magic realism," a method Viramontes carried over from her teacher Gabriel García Márquez (p. 415). Much of the story is realistic, as it relates the narrator's conflicts with her mother and sisters and the narrator's care for her grandmother, who is approaching death. Juxtaposed with realistic detail are magical images: of the narrator's hands becoming huge when she doubts the value of potato slices in reducing fever, of moths coming out of the grandmother's soul and flying out of her mouth as she dies. Neither image is explained: We are left to make of them what we can. (The latter seems an unusual way of imaging spirituality; ask students how they interpret the line, "I wanted to go to where the moths were" — p. 395.)

Another way into the story is the narrator herself. Ask students to list central traits of her character: the importance of memories to her, her appearance, the way she is treated by her family, and the way she is treated by Abuelita. Her grandmother's house seems to be the narrator's only escape to a place of normal life and positive acceptance. Only there can she let out her tender emotions, as, holding her grandmother's body in her arms as she washes it in the bathtub, she is able to cry, expressing her grief and loss.

A further way to get into the story is by paying attention to hands — the narrator's and other people's.

PAIR IT WITH   Judith Ortiz Cofer, "Cold as Heaven" (p. 558).

Richard Wright

The Man Who Was Almost a Man   (p. 395)

WORKS WELL FOR   Point of view (third-person, center of consciousness); irony.

ENTRY POINTS   One of the first things students will notice is the use of dialect. Some may find it hard to follow (reading the dialect passages aloud may help clarify them). Notice in the opening paragraph how objective statements of the narrator (in grammatical, academically correct style) alternate with thoughts going through Dave's mind (in dialect). It's worth asking students if Wright's use of dialect increases the realism of the work or interferes with the story's effectiveness.

Students should be able to pick out as a key issue Dave's desire for respect, to be treated like a man, not like a mule. And not like a *boy*. They might be asked if that desire in itself is something they respect and admire, and then if they respect and admire the way he seeks to attain it. Is owning and being able to use a gun a positive way to establish and demonstrate one's manhood? If not, why not? What alternatives, if any, were available for Dave? What do students think he should have done? What does the ending suggest? Will he find the respect he is searching for?

PAIR IT WITH   Alice Childress, *Florence* (p. 795).

STORIES FROM AROUND THE WORLD

Chinua Achebe

Dead Men's Path   (p. 405)

WORKS WELL FOR   Irony; cultural conflict.

ENTRY POINTS   This is a story of a clash of cultures — in this case of modern rationalist ideas against traditional nonrational beliefs. It is a story involving borders and barriers — literal as well as figurative — and outsiders trying to move into a community.

One way into the story is to ask students whom they identify with. Do they agree that the teacher is right to oppose what he considers old-fashioned and superstitious notions, and to teach children to laugh at them? Or are the old priest and the villagers right to follow the practices of their ancestors? In what ways could concepts of borders and outsiders help to understand and deal with the situation?

PAIR IT WITH   Leslie Marmon Silko, "The Man to Send Rain Clouds" (p. 377).

Isabel Allende

And of Clay Are We Created   (p. 407)

WORKS WELL FOR   Style (figures and images); character.

ENTRY POINTS   One way into the story is the contrast between the technical media (ask students to pick out examples of the emphasis on equipment) and the written word. Discuss the difference between the way television communicated the tragedy and the way the narrator's words in this story describe it. What can written words do that television images cannot? What does Allende's style (including her use of irony) contribute that visual media can't match?

Another way into the story is the effect Azucena has on Rolf. Ask students to focus on why Rolf is so deeply affected by Azucena (perhaps her inner strength and heroism?), and why the experience has the effect of slipping past the defenses he has built up over the years and enables him to confront a past he has repressed since his youth.

Look at the title as a way of encountering the story. Consider that Azucena is sinking into clay. Consider also the reversal of normal wording: "Are We," rather than "We Are."

PAIR IT WITH   Raymond Carver, "Cathedral" (p. 217).

Gabriel García Márquez

A Very Old Man with Enormous Wings   (p. 415)

WORKS WELL FOR   Magic realism; tone; humor.

ENTRY POINTS   Getting into this story should start with genre. García Márquez writes magic realism — stories that seem perfectly realistic in approach and detail, except for fantastic elements that are treated as realistically as the commonplace details, giving the sense that they are equally commonplace. In this case, the old man is recognized as unusual, but the townspeople are not in the least surprised at the arrival of an old man with enormous wings, any more than they are at the disobedient woman who has turned into a huge tarantula.

Getting into the story also requires attention to tone. It is a very funny story, with a variety of humorous techniques, from the verbal wit and irony of Pelayo and Elisenda's "magnanimity" in deciding to put the old man on a raft with three days' provisions out of gratitude for their child returning to health, to the hilarious "consolation miracles" the creature performs. Such humor is mixed with the awful cruelty of people toward him — throwing stones at him and burning him with a branding iron — and their sheer neglect and inattention to his needs.

Eventually one must face the question of what the very old man is, or represents. Students will probably raise the question, or it can be raised for them. Some critics read the story allegorically. We don't regard that as necessary, or as necessarily the best way to approach it for students in introductory literature courses. Our preference is to let images be themselves and explore their literal effect. Perhaps the very old man is simply a very old man with wings. Because he is different (no need to ask how or why he came to be different), he is treated as an outsider, as Other — with prejudice, rejection, and torment — and eventually he is rendered invisible — people no longer see him at all. If the townspeople are correct, that the old man is actually an angel, the same point comes through: The supernatural also is treated as Other — rejected and eventually ignored. The angel illustrates the old saying that a god appearing in our world would be rejected because the god would not match our expectations and therefore would not be recognized.

PAIR IT WITH Helena María Viramontes, "The Moths" (p. 391).

Patricia Grace

Butterflies (p. 420)

WORKS WELL FOR Irony; style.

ENTRY POINTS Like "The Eve of the Spirit Festival" (p. 228), "The Man to Send Rain Clouds" (p. 377), and "Dead Men's Path" (p. 405), "Butterflies" is about cultural differences. But in this case the differences stressed are more those of economic and class separation than the ethnic and cultural distinctions of the other stories. The contrast is between what moths mean to farmers and what they mean to nonfarmers.

One avenue into this brief story is considering the effect of its objective point of view and its spare, understated style. Students can be asked to point out the key ironies in the story and to discuss the way much is done through suggestion and implication.

PAIR IT WITH Chinua Achebe, "Dead Men's Path" (p. 405).

Bessie Head

The Collector of Treasures (p. 421)

WORKS WELL FOR Plot; character.

ENTRY POINTS One way into the story is to focus on the character of Dikeledi. The story begins by introducing her as a murderess, thus setting up a negative initial impression. Ask students to watch how their impressions of her build on that. Ask them to summarize what she is like and their (perhaps changing) reactions to her.

The story also deals in depth with relationships between men and women. Ask students to discuss the simple (perhaps oversimplified?) contrast between two kinds of men, and between Garesego and Paul. In what ways does living next to Paul and Kenalepe change Dikeledi's life?

Another way into the story is noticing and considering the attention paid to Dikeledi's hands in the story.

Several references to treasures occur in the story. Watch for these and use them as a way of having students discuss the suitability and meaningfulness of the title. In a way, calling someone whose life has been as hard and deprived as Dikeledi's a "collector of treasures" seems ironic. In what ways does the story overcome that and convey her life as one filled also with good things?

The final line does more than wrap up the plot. Consider ways it is crucially important to the Dikeledi we met at the beginning of the story.

PAIR IT WITH   Zora Neale Hurston, "Sweat" (p. 263); Susan Glaspell, *Trifles* (p. 822).

Naguib Mahfouz

Half a Day   (p. 435)

WORKS WELL FOR   Plot; allegory.

ENTRY POINTS   Mahfouz's works often deal with time, showing how time brings about change and how change can often cause pain. In this story, a lifetime is telescoped into what seems a day: the walk to school in the morning, a student's first day, and the return home in the evening. Ask students at what point in their first reading they began to realize the story was about more than a day. In a second reading, what details did they begin to read differently, as carrying additional meaning? Explore the way the story uses a double layer of meaning, at least on second reading: "Rivalries could bring about pain and hatred or give rise to fighting" (p. 436), for example, applies both to the schoolyard in an individual's life and to human life generally. (This involves allegorical techniques, though it does not employ the one-to-one parallels of formal allegory.)

The most difficult part of the story for students may be the final paragraph, with its abundance of realistic detail in a nightmarish scene. Ask students what they make of it. Why is the focus on noise, confusion, and disaster? To what extent is it a comment on change and the modern world?

PAIR IT WITH   Benjamin Alire Sáenz, "Elegy Written on a Blue Gravestone (To You, the Archaeologist)" (p. 716).

Mishima Yukio

Swaddling Clothes   (p. 438)

WORKS WELL FOR   Symbolism; psychological conflict.

ENTRY POINTS   One way into the story is its negative detail dealing with modern life in Japan. Toshiko dislikes the feel of her house with its "Western-style furniture," for example (p. 438). Her husband wears an American-style suit and lacks the decorum Toshiko expects of him (he shouldn't have told about "the incident" to strangers). Opposition to modernism was a central aspect of the author's life and thought. Thus the story may have an allegorical sense in which the new Japan (the nurse's baby) is destined, under American influence, to kill the traditional Japan (Toshiko's child).

Another way into the story is examining newspapers as a symbol (the story's original title was "Newsprint"; "Swaddling Clothes" is the title given to the translation). The child is wrapped in newspapers, not swaddled properly in flannel. Toshiko is preoccupied with these newspapers — she returns to them frequently in the story, focusing especially on the degradation she feels will attach to the child from them: "Those soiled newspaper swaddling clothes will be the symbol of his entire life" (p. 440). Consider whether the line says more about her or about the child and his situation. She is drawn by newspapers to the homeless man sleeping in the park, identifying him with the baby. (Why newspapers? Do they connect to the first point, associating the baby with the modern world?)

Another way into the story is Toshiko's character. She is shy, delicate, and sensitive. The baby's birth, and the newspapers, have laden her with guilt — partly from the contrast between her wealthy, comfortable life, and the poverty and desperation of the new mother and baby, and partly from observing the baby's shame. That shame leads her to conclude that the baby, when grown, will take revenge for its early embarrassment, and thus prepares her to go off (to her death?) with the homeless stranger in the park.

PAIR IT WITH   Anna Akhmatova, "The Song of the Last Meeting" (p. 770).

Salman Rushdie

The Prophet's Hair   (p. 442)

WORKS WELL FOR   Plot; tone; irony.

ENTRY POINTS   This story typifies Rushdie's fiction in its sense of irreverence and its use of magic realism. (For other examples of magic realism, see Gabriel García Márquez, "A Very Old Man with Enormous Wings," p. 415, and Helena María Viramontes, "The Moths," p. 391.) The story starts *in me-dias res* with a young man and his sister attempting to find a thief. Only later do we learn why, in a series of comical inversions: They are trying to find a thief who will steal from their father a precious relic that had earlier been stolen from a mosque and that he found floating in the water. The father wants the relic, not for its religious value but because he is a collector of rare and valuable objects. This one is the rarest of them all. It turns out that the relic has mysterious powers: No one is able to keep possession of the relic (whoever has it loses it), and it changes the lives of those near to it. Under its influence the father suddenly adopts the strictest form of Muslim practice. Miracles occur when the relic is around, whether they are desired or not. Eventually the presence of the relic destroys the entire family, as well as the lives of many others who come into its sphere of influence.

Students might be asked to consider the form and style of this carefully crafted work. If they have read other magic realism stories, they could explain what makes this story an example of the type and pick out characteristics of the form in the story. If they have not read other such stories, its characteristics can be pointed out (see the preceding discussions on Viramontes and García Márquez, on pp. 45 and 47). They may want also to talk about its comedy. This tragic tale is full of irony and comic scenes and details. In many cases, the most gruesome scenes have at least a humorous edge, which students may find disconcerting.

Students may also find the irreverence of the story unsettling. It speaks of the most sacred things in a rather flippant manner. True believers within the story are depicted unsympathetically. Fantastic, magical things happen in the presence of the relic. It appears to cause destruction on the one hand and miraculous cures on the other. The story raises the questions of whether the relic does have true spiritual powers, what such powers would mean if they are present, and what the story implies about commitment to religious faith.

PAIR IT WITH   David Henry Hwang, *As the Crow Flies* (p. 903).

Reading Poetry

We find the poetry unit in a Writing and Literature or Introduction to Literature course challenging and satisfying. Students usually are more comfortable with stories and enjoy the fiction unit. But many approach the poetry unit with apprehension. Often they have had less experience with poetry than with fiction and feel less sure of themselves. Even the form of poetry — its lines and rhythms, its compactness and reliance on figurative language — seems foreign. In some cases a grade school or high school teacher, perhaps by insisting or implying that a poem has a correct interpretation, has made poetry seem mysterious and inaccessible, something only teachers or other professionals know how to unlock and appreciate.

Convincing students that poetry can be pleasurable, readable, and understandable isn't always easy, or always successful, but it is exhilarating (it takes so little to brighten the life of a teacher) to see a student who had been looking puzzled and unhappy suddenly light up as she or he "gets" a poem, or to have a student come up after class and say, "Before this course I didn't care much for poetry, but now I'm starting to like it and think I'll read more." This chapter is intended to lay the groundwork for helping students reach that point.

We've tried in this introductory chapter to meet students where they are, by reminding them that poetry doesn't exist just in literature books. Many people write poetry, especially in response to major or emotional events in their lives — 9/11, the birth of a baby, a death in the family, the need to express one's love or concern. The students we are teaching may write poems (just for themselves, of course). Many people write poetry even though they don't like to read poetry. We hope that by giving students a sense of what poetry does and why people read it, it will begin to seem less remote or peculiar.

The most important part of the chapter might be the list of suggestions for reading poetry. If you agree, you might encourage students to read the list more than once, or you might encourage students to return to it a few days or a week later and be reminded of what it suggests. Of the suggestions in the list, the one we think might be most important is that which encourages them to read for what the words say rather than what the poem means. "Meaning" can be elusive and mysterious, perhaps even (as students may think initially) arbitrary. Instead of emphasizing the meaning of a poem, we try to focus on things that are going on in the poem (sounds, images, rhythms, and so forth), and we encourage students to realize that they can enjoy parts and aspects of a poem even when they don't understand fully what it "means."

Perhaps the other vitally important point in this chapter is the necessity of rereading poetry. Students usually find it helpful and comforting to be told that even teachers don't grasp most poems on first reading — that we too need to read a poem repeatedly, and live with it, before we feel we are beginning to "know" it well, and in some cases we don't "really know" it until years later. In saying this we're not trying to lower expectations, but to raise them by being honest about our own experience with poetry and by instilling confidence as students realize that poems can be appreciated for a variety of qualities, and that their appreciation will grow if they open themselves to poetry and give it a chance to become an important part of their lives.

Words and Images   CHAPTER 10

Robert Hayden

Those Winter Sundays   (p. 462)

STARTER   Ask students to look up *austere* and *offices* and be able to explain how different denotations apply in the poem.

ENTRY POINTS   The analysis of the poem in the chapter deals with the poem's choices of words — how the poem builds on precise, skillful handling of denotative meanings. "Approaching the Reading" questions 1 and 3 (p. 463) can be good ways to initiate class discussion.

"Approaching the Reading" question 2 (p. 463) provides another way to approach the poem: Ask students to describe the father-son relationship, and the family situation, from whatever indicators the poem offers. Several factors can be considered. This is a memory poem, looking back some forty years: Many of the details are ones the older poet realizes now, but the boy wouldn't have noticed or cared about them. Why do the details included stand out in the poet's memory? The memories are mixed — love with fear, warmth with cold. What is conveyed about what the boy felt then and what the poet feels now?

The multiple meanings of *austere* and *offices* in the final line make them particularly important. These are words students should look up, even if they aren't asked to. *Austere*, with definitions including "strict; self-disciplined; abstinent (thus, sacrificial); without excess; sober; solemn; lacking softness," has a range of implications regarding the father's personality and relationship toward his son. *Offices* is rich in applicable meanings: "A position of duty, trust, or authority; the duty or function of a particular person; responsibility; the prescribed order or form for a religious service." Ask students to discuss what each contributes to the meaning of the poem.

PAIR IT WITH   Theodore Roethke, "My Papa's Waltz" (p. 492).

Gwendolyn Brooks
The Bean Eaters   (p. 464)

STARTER   Ask students to stop at the end of line 1 and write a response to the words "this old yellow pair" — what ideas and feelings did those words evoke on first reading?

ENTRY POINTS   The analysis in the chapter focuses on the connotations of words. Because some students have difficulty grasping the concept of connotation, it could be worthwhile to spend some time contrasting denotations and connotations in the poem, to clarify the difference.

This is not a memory poem, but it deals with the importance of memories, especially for elderly people. Ask students to focus on the final stanza and pick out techniques that make it effective, that make it tender, respectful, and deeply human. You might have them consider questions such as, Why repeat *remembering*? Why the word choice *twinklings* and *twinges*, connected and emphasized by their sounds? Why the use of the unexpectedly long, prose-like final line, and why the particular details chosen for it?

PAIR IT WITH   Rita Dove, "The Satisfaction Coal Company" (p. 641).

Maxine Kumin
The Sound of Night   (p. 466)

STARTER   Ask students to look up and bring to class definitions of *huggermugger, vesper, prink, knickers, thrum,* and any other words new to them.

ENTRY POINTS   The chapter asks students to focus on the images in the poem, especially images of sound created by verbs. Following up on this can be a good way to initiate discussion in class.

This is a poem students like and respond to enthusiastically. It is accessible and deals with a situation familiar to many of them. Students enjoy pointing out words and phrases they find particularly apt, striking, or memorable.

The poem creates a contrast of dark and night with light and day. Ask students to pick out examples of that contrast and ways it is explored and developed (ways and reasons "day creatures" enjoy sounds of night but also defend themselves from dark).

PAIR IT WITH   Garrett Kaoru Hongo, "Yellow Light" (p. 473).

William Carlos Williams

The Red Wheelbarrow   (p. 468)

STARTER   "Approaching the Reading" question 2 (p. 468) asking students to sketch the scene described in the poem can be a good start.

ENTRY POINTS   It's such a slight, simple poem, and so beautiful in the mental images it creates, that readers have always felt there must be more to it than meets the mind's eye. Perhaps depths of abstract meaning can be found through and behind the images; if so, we don't believe that finding them — or searching for them — is essential. This issue in itself might provoke a valuable class discussion. Is there more to this poem than the picture it creates through its choices and combinations of words? Can a poem be profound without being abstract, without having a "theme"? Might it be better to approach this poem the way we approach a still-life painting than the way we usually approach poetry? What does this suggest about the variety of ways literature can be approached?

PAIR IT WITH   Angelina Weld Grimké, "A Winter Twilight" (p. 550).

Allison Joseph

On Being Told I Don't Speak Like a Black Person   (p. 470)

STARTER   The subject of this poem begs for it to be read aloud. Read it aloud to the class yourself or ask one or two good readers in the class to be ready to read it aloud.

ENTRY POINTS   This poem contrasts to "The Red Wheelbarrow" (p. 468) in that it foregrounds an abstract idea, a theme (even a thesis). Ask students to summarize the point it is making. Then ask them to explain in what ways it might be more effective to make the point in a poem instead of in an essay (for example, a poem is more succinct; the case doesn't need the detailed analysis and illustration that prose is good at but instead needs illustrating, which poetry can do well; the case is about the way words *sound*, which falls more within the area of poetry than that of prose).

The poem is pretty straightforward in meaning and implication. Students should be able to recognize the way it examines the stereotypes people fall into readily. And they may notice that it relates to the motifs of labeling people as outsiders, and to the emphasis on a variety of voices, that run through the book.

PAIR IT WITH   Caleen Sinnette Jennings, *Classyass* (p. 812).

Garrett Kaoru Hongo

Yellow Light   (p. 473)

STARTER   Ask students to hand in, or have ready to contribute in class, lists of images of sights, sounds, smells, tastes, and touch/feel.

ENTRY POINTS   This poem does a marvelous job of capturing in words the intimacy, energy, and diversity of a neighborhood and contrasting it with the vastness and impersonal nature of the city surrounding it.

Students might discuss how and why a group of particular, individual images can combine to create the cumulative effect this poem conveys. Consider why the poem isolates a specific woman for attention — is she important for herself or mainly as a focal point? Ask them to point out images and phrases they think are particularly striking or effective as a way of getting the class to look closely at specific images.

Does this poem, like "The Red Wheelbarrow" (p. 468), mainly give us images to experience (in this case, ones of the sort a video camera might record), rather than a theme to reflect on?

PAIR IT WITH   Dennis Brutus, "Nightsong: City" (p. 548).

Robert Frost

After Apple-Picking   (p. 475)

STARTER   Ask students to pay attention to the "dream poem" section in lines 17–26, and to be ready to comment on how it and the images of looking through a pane of ice set up the way of visioning in the poem (things in the poem look wavy and distorted, not clear and sharp).

ENTRY POINTS   This is a good poem for discussing symbolism. It's the kind of poem that may lead a student to ask, "But what's it *really* about?" Our response is that it's *really* about the end of the apple-picking season. There is abundant multisensual imagery to ground the poem in the literal activity the title names. And a student who goes no further than that literal meaning should not be faulted as a reader.

But it can be about more than apple-picking. "Approaching the Reading" questions 3 and 4 (p. 476) send students in that direction. Apple-picking is an autumnal activity, and autumn is a traditional archetype for old age and approaching death. Sleep, likewise, is a traditional metaphor for death (especially in the archetypal phrase "winter sleep"). A variety of details in the poem point to old age and the end of life — ask students to pick some out (such as "Toward heaven," "I am done with apple-picking now," "I am overtired," "whatever sleep it is"). The final lines use metaphor to inquire into the nature of this approaching "sleep": Is it more like hibernation or just ordinary human sleep?

PAIR IT WITH   Joseph Awad, "Autumnal" (p. 574).

Anita Endrezze

The Girl Who Loved the Sky   (p. 476)

STARTER   Ask students to make a list of comparisons and contrasts in the poem.

ENTRY POINTS   This is a very teachable poem, one that students find appealing for its subject matter. It's a poem rich in figures of speech (Chapter 13 draws on it several times for examples). In this chapter, however, since figures haven't been explained yet, our focus needs to be on images. The poem uses images throughout, but relies on them especially in the opening sections — students like the imagery used to describe the school. Ask the class to point out examples they think are particularly evocative and effective.

Contrasts and comparisons can be used as a way of approaching the poem (the contrast between the narrator and the blind girl, between their ways of knowing or apprehending, between the two of them as outsiders and the other girls; the comparison to which the poem builds, between the departure of the narrator's father and the departure of the blind girl, which leads to the anger and bitterness she expresses at the end).

The "Approaching the Reading" section (pp. 477–78) provides other useful topics for discussing the poem.

PAIR IT WITH   Louise Glück, "Parable of Flight" (p. 659).

Louise Erdrich

A Love Medicine   (p. 478)

STARTER   Ask students to explain what "love medicine" is, from indicators in the poem.

ENTRY POINTS   The title of the poem connects to the title story in Erdrich's short story collection *Love Medicine* (1984), which traces the intertwined histories of Chippewa and mixed-blood families in North Dakota over more than fifty years.

The poem uses the same setting and the same kind of personal conflicts, but through a narrower lens, focusing on sisterhood and family. Students may have difficulty following the details in the poem (wondering if it means the sister drowned in the flood). Asking students to clarify its movement may be valuable in clarifying the physical abuse — apparently part of a recurrent pattern since the narrator has had to find and help her sister numerous times in the past.

"Love medicine" in the novel plays off two meanings: a traditional native potion thought to create or sustain love, and love as a medicine that heals and restores. The poem seems to apply the latter sense; the final line suggests the kind of patient, enduring, inclusive affection and caring with which the narrator nurtures her hurting sister.

PAIR IT WITH   Philip Levine, "What Work Is" (p. 681).

Cathy Song

Girl Powdering Her Neck   (p. 480)

STARTER   Encourage students to search for Utamaro Kitagawa on the Internet to see a wider representation of his work in color.

ENTRY POINTS   One way to introduce the poem is as an example of the many poems written in response to paintings or other art (see Chapter 2, "Responding Through Other Art Forms," p. 46). You might ask students to reflect on what would draw a poet to write about a painting — what is the appeal, what are the satisfactions? The footnote on page 480 gives a brief introduction to Utamaro Kitagawa. His print is a study of a geisha engaged in the daily ritual of preparing her body for her day's work. Rather than the full-length view typical of his earlier prints, this study is a close-up, bestowing erotic attention on her neck.

Song's poem follows the Utamaro print closely, including the emphasis on the girl's neck. The prompts given in "Approaching the Reading" (p. 482) offer some discussion topics that can be used for approaching the poem. As a further step in exploring it, you might ask students if they sense any difference in effect between the two depictions of the young woman. Is Song attempting only to replicate the print in words? Or is she trying to go beyond the print? Is the young woman in the print an individual, or an example from a type? Is Song's poem able to achieve more of an individual quality than the print? Notice the lines near the end referring to speech — the physical print renders the young woman silent; is Song's poem an attempt to give her voice, to make her a person rather than an object, to enter the life of someone who has been dead for two hundred years? Perhaps the closing haiku-like three lines admit the impossibility of doing so — though past and present lives may touch, they inevitably drift apart again.

PAIR IT WITH   W. H. Auden, "Musée des Beaux Arts" (p. 600).

Voice, Tone, and Sound

Li-Young Lee

Eating Alone   (p. 486)

STARTER   As a connection to and reinforcement of Chapter 10, ask students to pick out and comment briefly on three words or phrasings they found particularly striking or effective for their denotations or connotations, or the images they convey.

ENTRY POINTS   The chapter provides an extensive discussion of "Eating Alone." Li-Young Lee's father often comes into his poems (see "Visions and Interpretations" as well). His father was personal physician to Mao Tse Tung but fell into disfavor, and the family had a harrowing escape to Indonesia, where the father was placed in a concentration camp under Sukarno. He escaped, and he and the family fled to the United States where the father became a Presbyterian minister in a small working-class town outside Pittsburgh.

Li-Young Lee's poems reflect the Chinese respect for and closeness to ancestors and the sense of the continuing presence of the dead, as both of his poems in this book illustrate.

PAIR IT WITH   Li-Young Lee, "Visions and Interpretations" (p. 680).

Charles Bukowski

my old man (p. 488)

STARTER Ask students to write a paragraph (to hand in or use in class) on the effect of the short lines in the poem, especially their effect on voice.

ENTRY POINTS Bukowski was a hard-bitten, hard-drinking, gruff, tell-it-like-it-is writer. The kind of semi-autobiographical narrative in "my old man" is typical of his style and approach. One way to approach the poem is by thinking of it in terms of a short story by Ernest Hemingway. Bukowski used Hemingway as a macho role model and was influenced by his spare, terse, experimental writing style. That voice comes through in Bukowski's poems and is likely to be appealing to some students, and decidedly unappealing to others. Try to get them to see and say why, in either case.

PAIR IT WITH Sylvia Plath, "Daddy" (p. 705).

Theodore Roethke

My Papa's Waltz (p. 492)

STARTER Ask students to write a paragraph on what the poem is about immediately after reading it twice, before reading the "Approaching the Reading" section and the discussion on page 493 (or ask students not to read those pages until after the class discusses the poem).

ENTRY POINTS This is a good poem for discussion: It often yields sharply different readings, as described in the chapter. You might use this poem to discuss the extent to which the background students bring to a poem influences what they find in it: their attitude toward drinking, for example (or, more specifically, toward a parent's drinking); the degree to which they avoid displeasing their mothers; their own memories of romps with father, or physical abuse by father. For a discussion of a reader-response approach to the poem, see Bobby Fong, "Roethke's 'My Papa's Waltz,'" *College Literature* 17.1 (1990): 79–82.

PAIR IT WITH Robert Hayden, "Those Winter Sundays" (p. 462).

Marge Piercy
Barbie Doll (p. 494)

STARTER Ask students to come to class ready to discuss the associations Barbie dolls have for them and how those associations relate to the poem and its tone.

ENTRY POINTS Students may need to have the poem discussed section by section to understand the various uses of irony and satire. The verbal irony in the final line, saying the opposite of what is meant, is pretty obvious. But other ironies are less easily categorized: that in lines 1–4, in the contrast between the realistic nature of some toys and games girls are given and the unrealistic nature of others, like Barbie dolls; the irony of the word choice in line 5 — *magic* is inappropriate to the context, whereas one having an opposite meaning (*cruelty*, for example) would fit better; the exaggeration in line 10 (her feeling apologetic, or inadequate, emphasized by turning it into a verb); the satire on "practical" advice for "catching a man"; and the ironically poignant metaphors of sacrifice in lines 17–18.

A useful topic for discussion is the value or practicality of satire and irony. Ask students to consider and talk about whether Piercy's biting critique is more likely to be heard and remembered than a straightforward magazine article on the same subject. Ask if they think satiric writing actually accomplishes what it's intended to, or is mostly a way for an author to vent feelings that will be applauded by those who are already convinced.

PAIR IT WITH Janice Mirikitani, "For a Daughter Who Leaves" (p. 693).

Sekou Sundiata
Blink Your Eyes (p. 496)

STARTER Begin by reading the poem aloud so students will hear its rhythms and sounds, or arrange for a good student reader to read it.

ENTRY POINTS This poem is examined in detail in the chapter. It would probably be worthwhile to reinforce what is said there by asking students to point out and comment on examples of various poetic elements covered in the chapter.

The poem also invites discussion of the role and value of poetry. Racial profiling is a significant and serious problem. Is poetry a good way to call attention to and protest against the practice? Is this poem an effective way of doing so? Why and how?

PAIR IT WITH Langston Hughes, "Good Morning" (p. 1256).

Wilfred Owen

Dulce et Decorum Est   (p. 503)

STARTER   Ask a student to do some research on World War I and make a brief report on the kind of tactics used (the trench warfare and use of nerve gas). Suggest that all students reread the brief background description of World War I on page 125.

ENTRY POINTS   This poem and the next deal with the effect of war on combatants. Both (like Tim O'Brien's short story, "The Things They Carried," on p. 327) give an unvarnished, unromanticized account of what ordinary soldiers experience, not the heroic account given by political officials.

The poem is pretty straightforward. One way to approach it in class is to ask what it does say, and doesn't say, about war. For example, does it say that war is wrong or unnecessary, or that it is not fitting for a person to support or participate in war? Or does it limit itself to saying only that those responsible for conducting wars should not glamorize and romanticize them and the act of participating in them?

You might suggest that students consider the final line, and the poem as a whole, in the context of the Horatian ode Owen draws on (Book 3, ode 2). Horace's ode is about what a Roman boy needs to learn to be a good citizen and soldier: "To endure poverty happily, / riding against fierce Parthians / spreading terror with his sword, / and living in danger under the open sky." In that context the ode asserts that it is sweet and honorable to die for one's country. What seems to anger Owen is that Horace uses the idea like a slogan on a recruiting poster. Invite students to discuss the two words Horace uses: *sweet* and *honorable*. As David West writes in *Horace Odes III: Dulce Periculum* (Oxford UP, 2002), readers have long objected to the sweetness: "Honourable, yes [or, 'perhaps'?]. Sweet, no. . . . Horace's sentiment is a romantic view of war, which would not survive much close fighting" (25–26).

PAIR IT WITH   Yehuda Amichai, "Wildpeace" (p. 771).

Yosef Komunyakaa

Facing It   (p. 505)

STARTER   Show pictures of the Vietnam Veterans Memorial in class (or ask students to find pictures of it in books or on the Internet) to help them visualize the imagery in the poem.

ENTRY POINTS   The first three "Approaching the Reading" questions (p. 505) offer ways to initiate discussion of the poem. For some students, the main difficulty of the poem is the meaning of some phrases (such as "hiding inside the black granite," "I'm inside / the Vietnam Veterans Memorial," "Names shimmer on a woman's blouse," "I'm a window," "He's lost his right arm / inside the stone").

Ask students to compare and contrast "Facing It" and "Dulce et Decorum Est" (p. 503) in effect and theme. To what extent are they treating the same points and concerns? To what extent are their emphases different?

PAIR IT WITH   Tim O'Brien, "The Things They Carried" (p. 327).

Elizabeth Bishop

In the Waiting Room   (p. 506)

STARTER   Ask students to write a paragraph (to hand in or use in class) on the effect of the short lines, especially their effect on voice. If they have also read "my old man" (p. 488), ask them to compare and contrast the handling and effect of short lines in the two poems.

ENTRY POINTS   This poem and the next deal with growing up. In this poem, a seven-year-old reaches a moment of epiphany when she suddenly realizes that she is a person, an *I*. Students often are confused by lines 46–47 ("it was *me*; / my voice, in my mouth"), asking if the speaker actually does cry out. It may help to ask students to do some line-by-line explanations of the middle part of the poem, where the speaker is working out her sense of identity as an individual and her connection to humanity as a whole.

PAIR IT WITH   Julia Alvarez, "How I Learned to Sweep" (p. 560).

Audre Lorde

Hanging Fire   (p. 509)

STARTER   Ask a student — preferably a young woman with some dramatic talent — to prepare to read the poem aloud to the class. You might ask the student to rehearse it with you before class, giving attention to where phrases run pell-mell together and where a change of voice is needed to signal that the speaker is rushing on to a new (unrelated) subject.

ENTRY POINTS   This poem and the next one are character studies. Lorde's poem describes an adolescent girl who pours out the difficulties and frustrations she faces over the unfairness of life and her sense of isolation: No one understands or cares. Ask students to discuss if this is a fair and accurate depiction of adolescent angst. Ask too whether it is a sympathetic picture (does the poem lead them to care about and empathize with the speaker?), a comic sketch (poking fun at the things she is concerned about), a combination of the two, or something else.

PAIR IT WITH Joyce Carol Oates, "Where Are You Going, Where Have You Been?" (p. 75).

Robert Browning

My Last Duchess (p. 511)

STARTER Ask students to write a brief description of what the Duchess was like, or to be ready to describe her in class.

ENTRY POINTS This poem evokes lively discussion in most classes, regarding what happened to the Duchess and why. Students often need help with the dramatic situation implied by the Duke's words. Ask students to point out specific lines or phrases that indicate who the Duke is talking to (a representative sent to negotiate terms of his next marriage); where they are talking (a second-floor gallery or corridor, where the valuable painting of his last duchess is protected from the light by drapery in front of it); the occasion (a reception or dinner for the representative); how the Duke treats the representative (the gesture of acceptance and equality when the representative intends to follow him respectfully down the stairs and the Duke says, "Nay, we'll go / Together down, sir" [ll. 53–54], that is, side by side).

A good topic to discuss is why the Duke says what he does. Some students may say he gets caught up in the moment and reveals more than he intends to. Others may reply that the Duke doesn't seem the sort of person ever to do something unintentionally or uncalculatedly. Push them on this: What is he up to? (Perhaps he is sending a message to his next father-in-law and bride about what he expects in a wife?) The name-dropping and verb *taming* in the last two lines seem to reveal a lot about him.

Discussion of the poem needs to include the character of the Duke. That usually proves pretty straightforward: Students can readily describe his arrogance, possessiveness, and brutality and point to supporting evidence. They may debate whether he had his wife killed (and if so, how he could get away with it, even in sixteenth-century Italy); other students may suggest that she may have died of a broken spirit rather than being killed. The Duke and the poem leave that deliberately ambiguous.

Describing the character of the Duchess often proves less decisive than describing the Duke. Language such as "she liked whate'er / She looked on" (ll. 23–24) and "all and each / Would draw from her alike the approving speech / Or blush, at least" (ll. 29–31) suggests to some students that she was flirtatious, or even unfaithful to her husband. Others will reply that the language can be taken equally well as evidence of her innocence, the pleasure she takes in little things (not just expensive ones), and the way she treats everyone in an open, friendly way (in contrast to her husband). Pushing the Duchess too far in the direction of flirtation and infidelity risks changing the direction of the poem; giving the Duke some grounds of justification for what he felt and did turns the poem into a rather conventional marital conflict instead of a unique character study of a despicable human being.

PAIR IT WITH   Taslima Nasrin, "Things Cheaply Had" (p. 780).

CHAPTER 12 Form and Type

Gwendolyn Brooks

We Real Cool (p. 516)

STARTER Have the class try reading the poem in unison, as a rhythmic chant, two or three times, with lots of emphasis on *We*, thus creating a pause.

ENTRY POINTS The most striking feature of the poem, and a good way into it, is its form, as discussed in the chapter. If you use the Starter above, you might have the class also chant the rewritten version on page 517 and note the difference in effect caused by the change in form.

Another way to approach the poem is through "Approaching the Reading" question 4 (p. 517). Ask students to comment on what makes the last line effective; the poem "works" because of the ending. (Some possibilities are the switch in content, from things the Pool Players *do* to something that will happen to them; the way the last words *imply* rather than spell out; the use of internal rhyme and lots of alliteration to weave the lines together tightly; and the *brevity* of the line, missing a last syllable we expect to hear — thus making it sound incomplete, the way their lives are.)

PAIR IT WITH "Sir Patrick Spens" (p. 598).

Countee Cullen

Incident (p. 519)

STARTER Ask students to try singing this poem, the way a ballad singer would sing a sad story. What does doing so bring out about the poem?

ENTRY POINTS   Despite its apparent simplicity, this is a powerful poem, one that countless readers have found deeply moving. Ask students to account for its power. What makes the poem so effective? (Some possible explanations: the way it captures the thought and voice of a boy; the way it understates and makes the reader fill in the boy's pain and lasting emotional impact; the striking use of the ballad stanza, traditionally used to sing sad tales, as the poem's form. See if the students come up with others.)

PAIR IT WITH   Sandra M. Castillo, "Exile" (p. 618).

William Shakespeare
That time of year thou mayst in me behold   (p. 521)

STARTER   Explain to students that "thou mayst" was a conscious use of old-fashioned diction. Ask them to assess and be ready to comment on (or write a short paragraph on) its effect in the poem. How would the effect differ if the first line read, "That time of year you may in me behold"?

ENTRY POINTS   The important thing for students to notice, formally, is the sonnet's handling of quatrains and couplet. The chapter outlines this and the progress of the thought. Checking that the form and thought are clear might be worthwhile.

The most striking aspect of the poem might be its reliance on archetypes, especially seasonal archetypes. Ask students to point out similarities in the handling of archetypes and the development of ideas between it and the Joseph Awad poem, with which we've paired it.

PAIR IT WITH   Joseph Awad, "Autumnal" (p. 574).

Claude McKay
If we must die   (p. 523)

STARTER   The poem seems like an inspirational speech, a rallying cry. Read it aloud, or have a student do so, to bring out its oratorical tone and manner.

ENTRY POINTS   Students are generally struck by the aggressive call to action in the poem and surprised to find it in a sonnet. It is clearly not a typical subject for a sonnet, and students may find it incongruous to find a black poet using this quintessentially white poetic form to advocate active resistance to white oppressors. That can be a good way into the poem: Why would McKay write *sonnets* at all, and especially on a subject like this? If using traditional poetic forms was the only way to gain recognition and acceptance as a writer, was he selling his soul to gain such acceptance?

Another way into the poem, and a different slant on use of the sonnet, is to look at the oratorical devices it employs. Do those devices fit the sonnet form well? Might they perhaps be more effective in this constrained form than they would have been in a free verse poem? Could he be using the sonnet form (despite its white origins) because he recognizes that it intensifies the power of what the poem says?

PAIR IT WITH Richard Lovelace, "To Lucasta, Going to the Wars" (p. 683).

Gerard Manley Hopkins

God's Grandeur (p. 524)

STARTER Suggest to your students that they look for environmental themes in this poem. Ask them to prepare a list of "Hopkins Environmental Issues" touched on in the poem to be handed in or used in class.

ENTRY POINTS The poem is first and foremost a song of praise to God, akin to some of the biblical psalms, such as Psalm 19: "The heavens declare the glory of God; and the firmament [the sky, the heavens] showeth his handiwork" (King James Version; likewise Psalms 104, 148). Setting the poem in the context of the psalms might clarify the kind of vision Hopkins had for his poem.

The poem can also be approached as an environmental poem and may as such be meaningful to some students. The second quatrain issues a strong and moving indictment of the misuse of the earth through industrialization and reckless use of natural resources. Comparing it to, or discussing it with, another environmental poem, such as William Stafford's "Traveling through the Dark" (p. 554; especially ll. 15–17) or William Wordsworth's "The world is too much with us" (p. 755) can help open this aspect of the poem.

PAIR IT WITH Wole Soyinka, "Flowers for My Land" (p. 732).

Helene Johnson

Sonnet to a Negro in Harlem (p. 526)

STARTER Ask students to pick out (and write down to hand in or be ready to present in class) some juxtapositions in the poem that surprised them, that maybe don't seem to fit together well (for example, "perfect" and "pompous").

ENTRY POINTS This is a poem of paradoxes. One way into the poem is to ask students to identify surprising, seemingly incongruous juxtapositions in the poem and then explain how those incongruities can be reconciled to create a striking effect. Some of the juxtapositions are within the man (or woman?) described in the poem ("Disdainful and magnificent"). Others are between the standards and expectations of conventional white society and the nonconformity of the person being described ("incompetent" at doing what society expects, "barbaric song" in "civilized" society, and so on). The result is a complicated picture of a black person, one who resists the usual stereotypes. See if students respond favorably to that complexity and richness, or find it disconcerting and problematic.

PAIR IT WITH Langston Hughes, "When Susanna Jones wears red" (p. 1268).

Leslie Marmon Silko

Prayer to the Pacific (p. 529)

STARTER Line 5 calls the ocean "Big as the myth of origin," and the poem goes on to recount such a myth. Ask students to name other myths of origin (remind them that in this usage, *myth* means a narrative dealing with ultimate concerns, without any judgment on the truth, accuracy, or validity of the account).

ENTRY POINTS To make sure that students are following the thought of the poem, ask them to explain why the narrator has traveled to the Pacific, what she (assuming the narrator is or resembles Silko herself) did when she got there, and why her doing so is significant and meaningful to her (presumably a way of honoring the place of origin by returning to it and performing a ritual of gratitude and petition, asking the Ocean to continue sending the rain clouds the people depend on).

Students may inquire about the title. At first glance, the poem may seem to be a prayer. But the narrative form negates that. The key word to note is *speak* (to the Ocean) in line 12. Lines 13–16, then, are the prayer, and the speaker accompanies the verbal prayer with the action of giving four stones, for the Ocean to suck and taste.

PAIR IT WITH Linda Hogan, "The History of Red" (p. 670).

Nikki Giovanni

Nikka-Rosa   (p. 534)

STARTER   Ask students how they respond to Giovanni's phrase in line 25, "Black love is Black wealth" (could be a written assignment or something to be ready to discuss in class).

ENTRY POINTS   One way into this poem is to recognize that it is partly a memory poem and partly a poem *about* memory poems. Invite students to point out parts where the poem celebrates memories from childhood, and other parts where Giovanni analyzes how biographers will misunderstand and misinterpret those memories. (*Why* will they misunderstand and misinterpret?)

Other ways into the poem are suggested by questions 1 and 3 in "Approaching the Reading" (p. 535). You might ask about the title — the poet's name with its ending changed to agree with the Spanish *rosa* (meaning "rose").

PAIR IT WITH   Robert Hayden, "Those Winter Sundays" (p. 462).

David Mura

Grandfather-in-Law   (p. 535)

STARTER   Ask students to write down the six words they feel best describe Mura's grandfather-in-law.

ENTRY POINTS   This poem is mainly a character sketch of a rather eccentric and unpredictable man. Looking back at him, now deceased, the narrator portrays him in a lovable way. Have students discuss both attractive and not-so-attractive characteristics.

The most difficult parts of the poem are the last seven lines. Students may want to go through those slowly. They indicate that the narrator changed after (and because of?) his marriage. Ask students to pick out what he was like before (ll. 18–20), then explain how the narrator believes he would have remembered his grandfather-in-law if he hadn't married the granddaughter (ll. 21–23) and finally how he now remembers the grandfather-in-law (l. 24).

PAIR IT WITH   Cornelius Eady, "My Mother, If She Had Won Free Dance Lessons" (p. 642).

Joy Harjo
She Had Some Horses   (p. 537)

STARTER   You might begin discussion by asking students if they can think of other examples of a litany (a repetitive or incantatory recital).

ENTRY POINTS   The suggestions students come up with for the starter might provide a good way into the poem. Some possibilities might be prayers (formal ones from a prayer book, especially), or some of the biblical psalms, or Martin Luther King's "I Have a Dream" speech. The cheers used at some sports events take the form of a litany. Ask what is appealing, even powerful, about the litany as a form and why people would use it.

On the basis of their answers, discuss the effect of the litany in "She Had Some Horses." See if they agree that the litany form gives it power. If so, what kind of power? Is it a prayer? Is it an affirmation of belief? Is it an assertion of being and presence? What else might the poem be? What does the poem do? How do they respond to it?

In the first line and in the other refrain lines, the horses simply seem to be horses. But in most other lines, they are used as metaphors or are personified. Have students look at and comment on specific lines that are about people (such as ll. 38–42 and 44–47). What is the effect of expressing the points through horses instead of stating them directly? Who is "she"? Try substituting a word for *horses* (she had some *friends* or *classmates* or *fellow human beings* who . . .). Does it work? What is better about using *horses*?

PAIR IT WITH   Jayne Cortez, "Into This Time" (p. 626).

James Wright
A Blessing   (p. 539)

STARTER   Ask your students if they have ever had a romantic "moment of bliss," the kind of experience William Butler Yeats describes in his poem "Vacillation," as he sat in a coffee shop gazing at a busy street and his "body of a sudden blazed," so "great [his] happiness." If they have, ask them to write a brief account of their experience or to describe it in class, and compare it to what the speaker in "The Blessing" experiences. (The Yeats passage continues, "so great my happiness, / That I was blessèd and could bless.")

ENTRY POINTS   Discussing this poem together with the next one works well: both use the word *blessing* (a favor or gift, especially one bestowed by God, thus bringing happiness), and both deal with nature and the spiritual (specifically mystical, in this poem) experience it can at times create in people who are particularly attuned to it.

The narrative part of this poem is straightforward, and students usually don't need help with it. One line that can cause confusion is, "There is no loneliness like theirs" (l. 12), where loneliness seems to have a positive overtone (students often think loneliness can only be negative) and where it may seem surprising to call the horses lonely when they are together. The use of *loneliness* here might be compared to the use of the word in line 22 of Li-Young Lee's "Eating Alone" (p. 486).

Students also find the last three lines difficult and may struggle both with the concept of a near-mystical experience that the lines attempt to put into words and with the images used in the lines to describe such an experience.

PAIR IT WITH Elizabeth Bishop, "The Fish" (p. 608).

Galway Kinnell

Saint Francis and the Sow (p. 540)

STARTER Show in class a picture of St. Francis surrounded by animals (or ask students to find a picture of him in a book or on the Internet), and ask someone to explain briefly who St. Francis was.

ENTRY POINTS Students find this poem a bit more difficult to follow than "A Blessing" (p. 539), which complements it well. Working through the poem to help clarify its words, syntax, and choice of images is worthwhile. Both poems deal with "blessing" ("blessings of earth on the sow" — l. 15). "Self-blessing," in this poem, is the sense of favor or satisfaction or happiness a living thing bestows upon itself by recognizing its own inherent worth and beauty. St. Francis affirmed that beauty, the last line's "perfect loveliness" in all things — even such a seemingly unlovely one as a sow.

After students are clear about what the poem is about, ask them to compare and contrast it with "A Blessing"; see if they find a similar affirmation of the beauty of nature and its effect on those who are open to it.

PAIR IT WITH Mary Oliver, "Goldenrod" (p. 699).

Figurative Language

CHAPTER 13

Langston Hughes

Harlem (p. 546)

STARTER Suggest that students make a list of a half dozen things they dream of having or attaining (or, less personally, of the dreams people generally tend to pursue), then reflect or write a comment on what effect delay after delay would have, always seeing the goal put off into the future (especially if other people are attaining their goals).

ENTRY POINTS The chapter discusses "Harlem" in terms of its form and use of figures. Discussion of the figures — the implications and effects of the comparisons Hughes sets up — is a good way to explore the poem. Also, you might have students focus particularly on the verbs (all forceful, unpleasant, and evocative). Consider also the effect of only asking questions, not answering them or making statements: The poem depends on active reading, provoking readers to think out the implications and arrive at their own conclusions.

PAIR IT WITH Toi Derricotte, "A Note on My Son's Face" (p. 633); August Wilson, *Fences* (p. 1186).

Dennis Brutus

Nightsong: City (p. 548)

STARTER Suggest that students listen for the sounds of this "nightsong" and jot down or be ready to point out what they find.

ENTRY POINTS   The "Approaching the Reading" section (pp. 548–49) provides several effective ways to approach this poem. An alternative way is to look at its handling of sound. Students should come up with many examples of assonance (such as "*creaking iron-sheets / violence like a bug infested rag is tossed*"), some alliteration, and rhyme. Ask them to discuss the effect of sound in the poem (contributing to the songlike qualities of its title, connecting words with related terms in this tightly constructed piece, and so on).

PAIR IT WITH   Garrett Kaoru Hongo, "Yellow Light" (p. 473).

Angelina Weld Grimké

A Winter Twilight   (p. 550)

STARTER   Bring to class (or ask students to find) a painting or photograph of a winter landscape, with trees silhouetted against the sky.

ENTRY POINTS   The chapter discusses the poem in terms of its reliance on personification, which provides a good entry point to the poem. Another way to approach it is to compare its verbal image as a whole to a painting or photograph of a winter landscape. You might ask students to compare the verbal work and the visual work. What do they have in common? What can each do that the other can't? What does personification add to the verbal? (Perhaps a way to bring the scene "to life"? Does visual art have an equivalent technique by which to bring a scene to life?)

PAIR IT WITH   John Keats, "To Autumn" (p. 677).

Edwin Arlington Robinson

Richard Cory   (p. 552)

STARTER   One way to introduce the poem is to play Paul Simon and Art Garfunkel performing Simon's ballad "Richard Cory" (from their album *Sounds of Silence*).

ENTRY POINTS   The "Approaching the Reading" section (p. 553) can be used to initiate class discussion, as can the Simon and Garfunkel recording, if students have a copy of Simon's text to compare to the original. Invite students to point out differences; then use the differences to determine what the original poem was getting at (Simon's version changes "We" to "I"; it turns Cory from a quiet, sophisticated, wealthy businessman to a rich playboy; it changes the effect of the last line by following it with the refrain — even after hearing about Cory's suicide, he still wants to be Richard Cory and enjoy his kind of life for as long as it lasts). Ask students to state the theme of the poem (perhaps "appearances can be deceiving" — the way someone looks on the outside can be very different from what the person feels inside; or even that a combination of good looks, education, manners, and great wealth do not necessarily bring happiness) and then to state that of the ballad.

Some critics suggest that the name Richard Cory may allude to Richard Coeur de Lion, king of Britain, 1189–1199. That allusion, if it seems convincing, would add to the dignity and stature of Richard Cory, and it would connect with the imagery of royalty in the poem ("crown," "imperially," "glittered," "richer than a king").

PAIR IT WITH   Nikki Giovanni, "Nikka-Rosa" (p. 534).

William Stafford

Traveling through the Dark   (p. 554)

STARTER   Ask students to reflect on "I thought hard for us all" (l. 17). What does the narrator think hard about? Who is meant by "us all"?

ENTRY POINTS   The narrative in the poem is quite clear and is summarized in the paragraph following "Approaching the Reading" (p. 555). Students frequently express confusion about exactly what happened: For example, did the speaker's car hit the deer? ("Found" in line 1 suggests not.) Were other people in the car with him? (No others are indicated. He refers to "our group" in line 16, but it seems more meaningful to think of that as the speaker, the dead deer and still-living fawn, and the car.) Why didn't the speaker try to save the fawn? (Probably a practical impossibility. He'd have needed to lift a heavy deer into his car and find a veterinarian willing to do a C-section before the fawn expires; it appears that he has no alternatives, so regretfully — "my only swerving" (l. 17) — he does what he has to do.)

Invite students to consider the poem as an environmental poem. Ask what details might connect meaningfully. They might reply, for example, that the woods have been invaded by roads and cars that destroy wildlife and natural habitats (the dead deer is, in one sense, a synecdoche for nature generally; and the fact that the deer is pregnant means the next generation is affected as well). The wilderness *listens*, as if it's a person, wondering what this man will do with the deer, and wondering what humans generally will do to nature. The speaker "thought hard" in line 17: about all these issues, perhaps — what humans are doing to the world around them. And the speaker thinks hard "for us all," maybe for the wilderness as well as humanity and what the future holds for all living things.

PAIR IT WITH   e. e. cummings, "pity this busy monster,manunkind" (p. 630).

Thylias Moss

Tornados   (p. 556)

STARTER   One way to introduce the poem in class is to show some clips of tornados, the kind frequently shown on the Weather Channel or included in the movie *Twister!*; the Internet also has many sites with dramatic still shots of tornados. The clips or photos may help students visualize the images Moss uses in the poem.

ENTRY POINTS   This is a playful poem, which relishes the various, highly imaginative connections it can make between whirling winds and details in the speaker's life. The texture of the poem is quite dense, and students may need some help to work through the figures and descriptions. Ask students if they find an underlying seriousness beneath the playfulness. Could the church references in stanza 2, carried over into stanza 3, indicate that the speaker finds in tornados something akin to the divine presence and glory in nature that Gerard Manley Hopkins (p. 524) and James Wright (p. 539) celebrated in their poems in Chapter 12?

PAIR IT WITH   Victor Hernández Cruz, "Problems with Hurricanes" (p. 628).

Judith Ortiz Cofer

Cold as Heaven   (p. 558)

STARTER   Ask students to make a list of images associated with *cold* in the poem.

ENTRY POINTS   The "Approaching the Reading" section (pp. 558–59) provides varied approaches to the poem. The literal and metaphorical implications of weather get at the heart of the poem. One way to start is to ask students to list images dealing with cold and ones dealing with heat.

The poem offers crisp, clear examples of various figures: *simile* — the title, the clock in lines 7–8, "wrapped like mummies" in line 13 (the "wrapping" is a straightforward comparison, but it's surprising to compare mummies to living persons, just as it's surprising to compare adults to toddlers in line 15, even though both take similar "hesitant steps"); *metaphor* — "enveloping" (l. 9), "pouring" (l. 23); *metonymy* — "dripping minutes" (l. 24); *synecdoche* — "snow" (l. 4). Asking students to find these examples can be a good review of figures.

Ask students to work out the implications of the last four lines and to comment on the form (the short lines) of the last two lines.

PAIR IT WITH   Helen María Viramontes, "The Moths" (p. 391).

Patricia Goedicke
My Brother's Anger   (p. 559)

STARTER   Ask students to pick out one difficult figure of speech in the poem and write a brief explanation (to be used in class) on how the figure "works" and why it is effective. An alternative plan is to identify key figures yourself and assign them to various students to assure wider coverage.

ENTRY POINTS   Students find the subject matter of the poem intriguing, but some have difficulty understanding the figures. Working through the poem together, with students explaining how various figures work and fit in, can help them with the poem and with figures generally.

To approach the poem as a whole, ask someone to describe the character of the speaker (what does she mean that she's "too heavy"? Too heavy for what? Heavy as a result of what? Why does she have only a sieve to offer? What does she mean by that?) and to describe what seems to be troubling her siblings and their friends. We've paired the poem with "Hanging Fire," and one approach to the poem would be to ask students to compare the two poems. Do they seem to deal with similar situations or quite different ones?

PAIR IT WITH   Audre Lorde, "Hanging Fire" (p. 509).

Julia Alvarez
How I Learned to Sweep   (p. 560)

STARTER   Ask students to write a brief summary of what the speaker learns, or experiences, in the episode the poem describes.

ENTRY POINTS   This poem, like several other works in this textbook, depicts an epiphany experience in which a young person becomes aware that evil and death are a part of the world they inhabit. If the Starter above is assigned, ask students to report in class what they wrote. You'll probably get a variety of responses that in different ways will get at the point that the speaker was learning more than how to sweep a floor (which her mother didn't teach her anyhow). Bring in, if students don't on their own, the way sweeping becomes an apt, contrasting image for the reality the speaker is confronting.

PAIR IT WITH   Alice Walker, "The Flowers" (p. 20).

CHAPTER 14 Rhythm and Meter

e. e. cummings
Buffalo Bill 's   (p. 566)

STARTER   Some students may not have a clear sense of how famous Buffalo Bill was or of his status as myth or icon. Starting with some images from books or the Internet (of him and his Wild West Show) might be helpful in clarifying the background cummings is drawing on.

ENTRY POINTS   The "Approaching the Reading" section (pp. 566–67) and the discussion of it (p. 567) focus on form and rhythm. These provide good ways into the poem. Reading it aloud — in its original form and in the regularized form on page 567 — would seem important.

Another way to approach the poem might be to ask about its tone. Is cummings celebrating the Western hero or deflating the Western icon? Consider the denotations and connotations of the word *defunct* (why not *deceased?*). What tone should be used in reading the concluding question? How do "blueeyed boy" and "Mister Death" affect the tone?

PAIR IT WITH   Emily Dickinson, "Because I could not stop for Death" (p. 635).

Paul Laurence Dunbar
We Wear the Mask   (p. 570)

STARTER   Ask students to mark the stressed syllables in the first three lines of the poem and to label the predominant meter and line length.

ENTRY POINTS The tightly closed form is perhaps this poem's most prominent feature — in stanzas, meter, and rhyme (the only lines that don't rhyme are those ending in "mask"). The prompts and discussion following the poem on pages 571–72 focus on rhythm and meter and offer a good place to begin a discussion, which eventually should consider the reasons why Dunbar, as a black poet protesting the oppression of his race, would adopt constraining forms developed by the oppressor.

Students also might want to discuss the validity of the poem's argument. If they read Ellison's "Battle Royal" earlier, they will have found the same position advocated by the narrator's grandfather, which other members of the family regarded as appalling and dangerous. Was it a suitable method of resistance a century or half century ago? Has the need for it, or value of it, disappeared today?

PAIR IT WITH Ralph Ellison, "Battle Royal" (p. 237).

Lucille Clifton

at the cemetery, walnut grove plantation, south carolina, 1989 (p. 573)

STARTER Ask students to mark the stressed syllables in lines 1–5 and decide if the lines are in a regular meter (and, if so, what kind).

ENTRY POINTS The prompts following the poem raise questions about the rhythm of the poem and about whether the poem is metrical. Ask students where in the poem they hear a regular beat (if at all) and where an irregular beat. We find a regular meter in parts of the poem. The first five lines, for example, establish an expectation of metrical regularity:

aMONG the ROCKS
at WALnut GROVE
your SIlence DRUMming
IN my BONES,
TELL me your NAMES.

The next six lines are less regular, almost nonmetrical, but returning to a regular beat frequently enough to remind us of the opening lines. The final section of the poem slips into a litany for the deceased (see the discussion of litany on p. 73 of this manual, in the discussion of Joy Harjo's "She Had Some Horses"). These lines are metrical — though at times irregular — and the beat reinforces the rhythms of the litany.

PAIR IT WITH Thomas Gray, "Elegy Written in a Country Churchyard" (p. 660).

Joseph Awad

Autumnal   (p. 574)

STARTER   Ask students to read the first nine lines several times and to be ready to explain the effect — on rhythm and meaning — of the short sentences and their frequent periods.

ENTRY POINTS   The "Approaching the Reading" questions (p. 575) deal mostly with the poem's rhythm and how it is controlled. Reading the poem aloud, so students will hear its rhythms, would be valuable.

Asking students to compare the poem to "After Apple-Picking" and "That time of year thou mayst in me behold" can lead into a good discussion of the poem. Like them, "Autumnal" relies on seasonal archetypes. Like "After Apple-Picking," it uses imagery of frost and raises the question of accomplishments in life, as in the haunting words of lines 10–16. Like Shakespeare's poem, it deals with love between old persons and brings out the depth and beauty of mature love, valued all the more because they know their remaining time together is limited.

PAIR IT WITH   Robert Frost, "After Apple-Picking" (p. 475); William Shakespeare, "That time of year thou mayst in me behold" (p. 521).

Lorna Dee Cervantes

Freeway 280   (p. 575)

STARTER   Because of the poem's mixture of English and Spanish words, it would be valuable for students to hear it read aloud. Read it yourself or ask for a volunteer who is fluent in both Spanish and English to prepare to read it to the class.

ENTRY POINTS   This poem and the next one are about returning — going back to a place that once was home and finding that it has changed (or hasn't changed?) and can no longer be home. Both poems are also about *self*, as are the final four poems in the chapter. They can be used as a group to discuss the relationships between place, self, and identity.

In "Freeway 280," the narrator returns to the neighborhood where she grew up but finds a freeway has replaced much of what was there before. She walks through the trees and empty spaces that remain, hoping to find something of the person she used to be, in hopes that it will help her understand better who she is now.

The "Approaching the Reading" section (p. 576) offers several ways to approach the poem, through its theme, diction, rhythm, use of figures, and title. It is a good poem to discuss on its own or in combination with other poems in this chapter.

PAIR IT WITH   Julia de Burgos, "Returning" (p. 773).

Jim Barnes
Return to La Plata, Missouri   (p. 577)

STARTER   Ask students to paraphrase lines 1–3 (that is, to put the lines into their own words in a way that helps make their meaning clearer).

ENTRY POINTS   While the speaker in the previous poem returns to her old neighborhood with feelings of nostalgia, the speaker in this poem remembers his earlier anger and bitterness and concludes that his hometown remains a repressive place where he cannot stay. The "Approaching the Reading" questions (pp. 577–78) provide several ways to approach a discussion of the poem: through rhythm; the use of the second person (in contrast to Cervantes' first person in the previous poem); the closed form (terza rima, a traditional form with a long history, but handled in an unusual way because the lines do not have regular meter — though many of them seem to come close); and the content.

You might ask students to discuss whether the poem says more about the speaker or about the town. For example, lines 1–2 bring up "the hard rage / you felt in the heart of the town." Was it *his* rage, experienced while living in the heart of the town? Or was he sensing a rage present in the heart of the town itself? To what extent is what the speaker attributes to the town something projected by the speaker (then or now) onto the town from within himself?

PAIR IT WITH   Julia de Burgos, "Returning" (p. 773).

A. K. Ramanujan
Self-Portrait   (p. 578)

STARTER   Ask students to listen carefully for meter and rhythm in the next four poems —"Self-Portrait," "I'm Nobody! Who are you?," "Speaking," and "Wishes"— and to be ready to indicate which are in meter and which are not (and why they concluded that, in either case) and to discuss the poems' rhythms (and the way meter contributes to rhythm, for the ones in meter).

ENTRY POINTS   This poem is nonmetrical. The rhythms are rather choppy and broken, because of the short lines and the use of commas, to fit the complexity of the issue the poem is dealing with.

Invite students to discuss the meaning of the poem, which seems to be about thinking there is a self when actually all there is is what is reflected back to us in any form (the father signs it because he made the speaker, conceptually [pun?]).

PAIR IT WITH   Octavio Paz, "The Street" (p. 782).

Emily Dickinson

I'm Nobody! Who are you?   (p. 578)

ENTRY POINTS   This poem is metrical. The second stanza is a ballad stanza, iambic lines alternating between tetrameter and trimeter. The first stanza disguises the ballad stanza form by numerous variations from the pattern that has not yet been established in our ears. The first line lacks a middle accent ("i'm NObody! WHO are YOU?"), as does the second, which also has two stressed syllables in succession: "Are YOU – Nobody – TOO?" The third line has regular iambic meter but only three feet, whereas the ballad stanza would call for four: "Then THERE'S a PAIR of US?" That is reversed in the fourth line, which has four feet rather than the usual three (iambic following after an initial spondee): "DON'T TELL! they'd ADverTISE – you KNOW!"

It's a poem many readers enjoy and relate to. Suggest that students try comparing it, like the poem above, to Paz's "The Street," with its haunting focus on *nobody*.

PAIR IT WITH   Octavio Paz, "The Street" (p. 782).

Simon J. Ortiz

Speaking   (p. 579)

ENTRY POINTS   This poem is not metrical. It relies instead on the rhythms of the terse precise speech of someone who listens more than he talks. The tight, restrained style is suggestive rather than expansive. The reader fills in the implications about the close interaction between father and nature and between child and nature.

Although Savageau's "Bones — A City Poem" is not about a child or speaking, it can be valuable to consider it together with Ortiz's poem because it conveys the same intimacy with nature and the same sense that various parts of nature are closely interrelated.

PAIR IT WITH   Cheryl Savageau, "Bones — A City Poem" (p. 719).

Georgia Douglas Johnson

Wishes   (p. 579)

ENTRY POINTS   This poem is metrical. It mixes iambic and anapestic feet in lines of seven feet, with the two lines in each couplet falling into the same pattern:

> i'm TIRED of PACing the PEtty ROUND of the RING of the THING i KNOW —
> i WANT to STAND on the DAYlight's EDGE and SEE where the SUNsets GO.

> i WANT to SAIL on a SWALlow's TAIL and PEEP through the SKY'S blue GLASS.
> i WANT to SEE if the DREAMS in ME shall PERish or COME to PASS.

> i WANT to LOOK through the MOON'S pale CROOK and GAZE on the MOON-man's FACE.
> i WANT to KEEP all the TEARS i WEEP and SAIL to some UNknown PLACE.

The anapests give the poem a swinging rhythm, reinforced by the sounds of the internal rhymes, end rhymes, and prominent alliteration. These are wishes not for the American dream, but for a world of fantasy and magic that will lift the speaker from her mundane everyday life and from her painful, difficult life, in which she has shed enough tears to fill an ocean she can sail across.

Students find it interesting to discuss this poem with Hughes's "Dream Variations" because of their similar content and their similar mixing of iambs and anapests.

PAIR IT WITH   Langston Hughes's "Dream Variations" (p. 1257).

CHAPTER 15 Writing about Poetry

Just as many students lack confidence for reading poetry, so do many of them lack confidence for writing about poetry. This chapter tries to develop their confidence and give them specific ideas for preparing, planning, starting, developing, and supporting a short paper about poetry. The chapter emphasizes that proper preparation is crucial, that students should begin reading the poem or poems for the paper a week before they begin writing, and should reread the poem or poems numerous times, preferably once or twice each day until they begin to write. You could encourage them in this by including readings to be used for the paper in the class assignments a week and a half or two weeks before the paper is due (just assigning them to be read, not talking about them in class), and encouraging students to follow up with regular rereadings.

For development, a new approach — explication — is added in this chapter. You can help students understand this approach by modeling it in class a couple of times, calling attention to the approach before you use it. That doesn't require spending the whole class period on explication — selecting a short segment for detailed close reading, perhaps spending ten minutes on it, can be very effective. Another way to prepare students for a poetry paper and to build their confidence is to assign them to write a one-page sample paper (perhaps an explication of a poem or segment of a poem); you might then write brief comments on each paper on what is done well and what could be better, or you might go over a couple of the papers in class, pointing out strengths and weaknesses.

We think it is important for students to read this entire chapter, but especially the paragraph on page 586 discussing and illustrating the use of allusions. Of course, stories and plays use allusions too, but they often seem especially important in poetry. It might be helpful not to leave this paragraph until the end of the poetry unit. Ask students to read it earlier and begin pointing out allusions (or ask students if they notice them) as examples come up in poems discussed in class.

The chapter aims to give students practical advice by sprinkling in many ideas for topics, within its paragraphs as well as in the formal lists at the ends of sections, and by the sample paper at the end of the chapter. Encourage your students to read the sample paper carefully, perhaps even twice, and to read the "Student Writer at Work" comments leading into it (p. 591). There is no substitute for studying a model of what a good paper looks like and does.

A Collection of Poems

Ai

Why Can't I Leave You? (p. 596)

WORKS WELL FOR Voice; images.

ENTRY POINTS After even just one reading, the poem presents its subject clearly. The words are direct, the speaker readily identifiable. However, there can be more than one possibility for why she can't leave him. Talk about what those reasons might be. What keeps her in this relationship?

After reading the poem, begin a discussion with the line "There is safety in that" (line 20). This can show students that after getting a sense of what a poem is dealing with, it is possible to reenter the poem at a place other than the beginning in order to open it to further insights and to reveal its richness and complexity.

Notice the lines: how direct they are, how they tend to end on a meaningful word, how each is a unit unto itself. What is revealed about the speaker in the way the lines are constructed?

Discuss whether the speaker is addressing the man directly. If she is, what effect does that have on your reading and on your feelings for her? If students think she is not, talk about what that says about her and what the impact is of her not talking directly to him.

PAIR IT WITH Kamala Das, "In Love" (p. 632).

Agha Shahid Ali

I Dream It Is Afternoon When I Return to Delhi   (p. 597)

WORKS WELL FOR   Magical realism.

ENTRY POINTS   Have the students discuss the "logic" of a dream. What makes this poem feel like a dream? Then talk about why using "dream logic" is an effective approach to the poem.

Discuss what the speaker is experiencing, both in his inner world and the outer world. What about this experience is particular to the setting of the poem, and what is common to anyone who would experience something like this?

Ask students to talk about the final stanza, especially the change in tone that occurs with the word "Suddenly" (l. 37). What is suggested by the beggar women offering him money and weeping for him? See if they think a comparison with "Half a Day" is appropriate and illuminating.

PAIR IT WITH   Naguib Mahfouz, "Half a Day" (p. 435).

Anonymous

Sir Patrick Spens   (p. 598)

WORKS WELL FOR   Ballad; ballad stanza.

ENTRY POINTS   This poem provides a good example of the popular folk ballad — in its sad tale with a tragic ending, sketched out in broad details with abrupt transitions and little attention to characterization or motivation, and its use of ballad stanza. It originated as a ballad to be sung, and recordings of it being sung can be found. If you have a student with musical talent who likes this sort of music, you could invite her or him to sing it to the class.

Typical of ballads, "Sir Patrick Spens" leaves significant gaps for the reader to fill in. You might start by asking someone to summarize the story, pointing out where the gaps are and indicating how they might be filled.

Ask students to discuss what (little) we can tell about the character of the king and Sir Patrick (they should at least note the contrast, that the king stays home in comfort drinking wine while sending out someone he doesn't know or care about on a dangerous — and unspecified — mission). Students may ask about stanza 4, where Sir Patrick wonders who has it in for him. This can be read as if the mission, and the selection of Sir Patrick to undertake it, is a way to get rid of him. But stanzas 1 and 2 suggest that Sir Patrick is chosen because he is the best sailor available. Stanza 4 could then be a way of expressing frustration rather than a question to which he expects an answer.

You might ask students to discuss whether Sir Patrick should have undertaken the mission. Why did he undertake it? (Presumably loyalty to the king.) In accepting it, he puts his men in danger. Did he have a loyalty to them as well? Which loyalty should have taken precedence?

PAIR IT WITH   Dudley Randall, "Ballad of Birmingham" (p. 708).

Susan Atefat-Peckham

Dates   (p. 599)

WORKS WELL FOR   Images; tone.

ENTRY POINTS   Ask students, after they have read the poem and understand what is happening, to consider the "positioning" of the speaker, how the somewhat distanced perspective actually creates a deeper intimacy and connection to all that is going on. Talk about all that is having an impact on the speaker. (A lot is.)

The speaker has returned to her homeland. In what ways can you discern how much she remains connected to her place of origin, and in what ways does she now seem somewhat removed, less a part of her culture?

The poem is rich in sensuous material. Discover the images that are particularly so and notice how the poem could be seen as a tapestry of the senses. Discuss the effects of this rich assemblage of images and the juxtaposition of such with the poem's focus on death. Atefat-Peckham was also an accomplished visual artist, a painter. Where can you see this influencing her poem?

Have a conversation about different cultural ways of dealing with the death of a loved one. Some students in the class may be living in two or more cultures. Have them talk about what that is like for them, how they must adapt, even change, as they move from one culture into another.

PAIR IT WITH   Mark Doty, "Tiara" (p. 639).

W. H. Auden

Musée des Beaux Arts   (p. 600)

WORKS WELL FOR   Classical allusion; irony; tone.

ENTRY POINTS   It might be helpful to use the Brueghel painting to begin a discussion. Note the narrative content and have the students talk about how it connects to the poem.

This is an interesting poem to use to discuss tone. What are the attitudes revealed by the speaker? You might even have the class discuss the poem's tone or tones and compare it/them to the "tone" of the painting.

This poem has a direct statement in the first line. Discuss how that affects the rest of the poem. Discuss too what effect it has on the students as readers when they read such a pronouncement at the beginning.

The poem can be seen as an "essay poem." Have the students talk about why the essay is usually thought of in terms of prose and what differences in impact there may be depending on which genre is used to bring about the essay's point.

Have the class come up with a list of contemporary examples from their own lives of situations similar to that in the poem. For example, perhaps someone had a close family member die on the day of a major news event.

You might invite students to write their own poems or prose in response to a painting of their choice, or each could select a painting. Perhaps bring in some prints and have the students each select one and write in response to it as Auden did.

PAIR IT WITH   Eavan Boland, "The Pomegranate" (p. 613).

Jimmy Santiago Baca

Family Ties   (p. 601)

WORKS WELL FOR   Figurative language; images.

ENTRY POINTS   You might start by talking about the poem's the title. What ironies are revealed?

The poem lends itself to discussing the issue of how you maintain your cultural ties when you have, through one means or another, changed fundamentally from the way you were "brought up." Many students experience this, especially first-generation college students. A discussion of this reality in light of or sparked by the poem could be valuable.

Have the students identify and list the variety of images in the poem. Discuss what associations and implications they connect with. In what ways are potential cultural collisions and fusions embodied in these images?

Discuss the poem from the point of view of the generations in the poems. What are the clashes, potential clashes, causes for such, and differences in values, economics, and ideas?

Focus on the speaker. Have the class discuss the complexity of feelings, the ambiguities and internal conflicts the speaker is experiencing. What makes this particularly poignant and provocative? His feelings are never stated outright. What are the moments, observations, and images that enable the reader to recognize these feelings?

What is implied by the poem's ending?

PAIR IT WITH   Jim Barnes, "Return to La Plata, Missouri" (p. 577).

Amiri Baraka

AM/TRAK   (p. 602)

WORKS WELL FOR   Rhythm; sound.

ENTRY POINTS   Begin a discussion not by asking what this poem is about, but by having the students either write down or state their reactions and impressions. See how varied they are as well as what they have in common. Then do the same for any of the sections of the poem. Discuss how this range of reactions is fitting for this poem and why.

The poem is highly influenced by jazz. Discuss in what ways the poem is like jazz music and in what ways it differs. Then discuss how the principles of jazz can be applied to things other than music. Ask the students to talk about when they might feel as if they must perform as if they are jazz musicians.

The poem is assertive, abrasive; it doesn't hold back its anger, hostility, or frustration, and is willing to confront and attack. Have the students find the places where this is particularly so. Discuss what lies behind the speaker's invective, stance, and attitude.

The poem is filled with "riffs of language." Have the students pick out several and discuss these in terms of sound, rhythm, plays on words, mixtures of diction, phrasings, and so on. Discuss their effectiveness in the poem.

Ask the students what they think this poem is about. If you discover that there is a multiplicity of ideas, ask them if all are appropriate. Discuss whether the poem has a single theme or central idea or many. Then have a discussion that focuses on whether discerning what the poem is about is more important than other things about the poem. If some feel that the poem has other valuable effects, discuss why they feel that way and open up a conversation about challenging the traditional definition of a poem's subject, what it is "about."

Ask the students to state whom they think might be offended by this poem. Perhaps those they list are implicated by the poem or can be seen as an implied part of the poem. Discuss audience in terms of those who would be affirmed by the poem and those who would be offended by it.

PAIR IT WITH   Sonia Sanchez, "An Anthem" (p. 717).

Gerald Barrax

Dara   (p. 607)

WORKS WELL FOR   Lines.

ENTRY POINTS   Ask students to discuss what makes this "birth of a daughter" poem distinctive. This is the kind of subject that easily could be treated sentimentally. What keeps the poem from lapsing into sentimentality?

Discuss the cultural implications of this poem. Consider that this experience is archetypal: Everyone is born! Talk about whether the poem, therefore, is limited by its being clearly about the birth of an African American child or whether this particularity adds to the effectiveness of the poem (and how this particularity is ironically applicable to the birth of any child).

Discuss the tone of the poem and what it reveals about the attitude of the speaker toward the birth of his daughter, toward his wife, toward the world.

Discuss the ending, particularly the last six lines.

This is a poem of address. What, if any, difference does that make in the effects of the poem on the reader?

PAIR IT WITH   Simon J. Ortiz, "Speaking" (p. 579).

Elizabeth Bishop

The Fish   (p. 608)

WORKS WELL FOR   Figurative language; imagery.

ENTRY POINTS   This poem has been well established as one of the "chestnuts" of poetry. Have the students speculate on why the poem has been so acclaimed by critics and general readers. Encourage differences of opinion.

When in college, one of the authors of this textbook had to break up a potentially violent argument between two fellow students who lived in the house where he did. The conflict was over line 49 from the poem "— if you could call it a lip —"; one person claimed it could not be called a "line of poetry," while the other affirmed that it could. Invite students to stage their own argument over the line and/or discuss what is considered valid for a "line of poetry."

Bishop was fascinated by the discovery of beauty in the most unexpected of places. Discuss this in light of the poem.

Discuss the diction in the poem. Bishop's diction here is very clear, down to earth, direct, uncomplicated. What makes that effective and appropriate? Talk about how such common language can create such intensity.

Focus on the speaker. Try to list all the feelings and emotions the speaker experiences. Talk about what triggers them. Talk about what makes this particular experience emotionally universal.

Naomi Shihab Nye has said that to the poet everything is significant. Bishop celebrated the most commonplace of experiences; she was mesmerized by detail. Talk about this poem in relation to both poets' stances.

The poem contains several figures. Point them out and then discuss what they do in the poem.

Have students select something seemingly insignificant from their daily lives and list their discoveries about it that reveal that what they selected is indeed significant after all.

PAIR IT WITH Galway Kinnell, "Saint Francis and the Sow" (p. 540).

William Blake

The Chimney Sweeper (p. 610)

WORKS WELL FOR Irony; naïve speaker.

ENTRY POINTS You may need to fill in some background for the poem (or ask a student to do some research and make a brief report). In the eighteenth century small boys, perhaps as young as four years old, were used to clean chimneys by climbing up the flues and brushing the soot into bags. The boys often were sold into service by their parents or guardians and were treated badly by their masters. Working conditions led to disease, injury, and deformity.

Ask someone to summarize the content. Tom's dream may need clarifying — it may not be all that realistic as a dream, but it gives Blake a way to bring in the religious establishment and chide it for relegating the boys to the next world instead of addressing their horrid situation in this world. (The coffins of black are simple, direct symbols — almost closer to metaphors for the chimneys the boys' lives are trapped in.)

One way to approach the poem is to focus on power: Many types of power come to bear on the situation. Ask students to identify some, such as the power parents have over their children (they can even sell them, or rather their services; the children may not technically have been slaves, but the effect was nearly the same); a variety of forces, likewise, have power over the parents — landlords, employers, businesspersons, the government (situations of need and opportunity for profit grow out of and create economic power relations); and the power of the church, for good or ill (the words in Tom's dream when the angel tells him in lines 19–20 that "if he'd be a good boy / He'd have God for his father, and never want joy" are surely ones he has heard when he was awake, perhaps from his employer or in church; Blake is exposing and challenging the way religion has been and can be used to validate and continue economic exploitation).

The poem is filled with irony — ask students to point out examples (the richest, and most poignant, appearing in the final line). That line, and the poem as a whole, depends on the use of a naïve speaker who doesn't realize the implications of what he is experiencing and saying. The power of the poem comes in part as readers are hit with understandings the speaker himself is unaware of.

PAIR IT WITH Langston Hughes, "I Dream a World" (p. 1256).

Peter Blue Cloud

Rattle   (p. 610)

WORKS WELL FOR   Structure; myth.

ENTRY POINTS   Have students read the poem aloud as a collective experience. Assign various parts of it. Or have two students read it aloud, one reading the section on the right, the other the left. Discuss various ways of reading the poem both down the page and across the page. What effects are caused by having two or more voices read the poem? Discuss what multiple voices bring to the possible meanings and impact of the poem.

Discuss the poem in light of the idea of incantation, prayer, or chant.

What does the poem ask to be restored? Discuss the impact on the reader of reading the poem or hearing the poem in a variety of contemporary contexts.

Rhythms play a very important role in the poem. Much will be lost if the reader does not experience, feel, and understand the influence of the rhythms. Discuss their role in the poem and the impact on the reader.

Discuss the poem's tone and what it reveals about the attitude of the speaker.

Talk about what students think is meant or implied by the ending lines, "Let us / shake the rattle / always, forever."

PAIR IT WITH   Sherman Alexie, "That Place Where Ghosts of Salmon Jump" (p. 1325).

Eavan Boland

The Pomegranate   (p. 613)

WORKS WELL FOR   Archetypes; myth; classical allusion; lines.

ENTRY POINTS   The poem works with archetypal material. Ask students to identify and discuss the archetypes in it and the way Boland works with them in the poem. What makes this an effective way to express the poem's theme?

Discuss the speaker in terms of how she feels about being a mother, her concerns and feelings for her daughter, the ways she feels about the impact of the world and life itself on her daughter.

The poem is from Boland's collection *In a Time of Violence*. Have the students discuss the ways reading the poem in that context affects its impact on them.

Boland is from Ireland and writes often about the effect of violence within a culture on women's lives. Discuss the ways her concern shows itself in this poem.

Discuss the possibilities for the pomegranate as a symbol. What meanings might ripple out from the image? Why is it appropriate for this poem?

Ask students to discuss what they think about the speaker's ending the poem by saying, "I will say nothing."

Have the students talk about the ways they can relate their own lives to the poem. In the midst of what violence must they live? What impact does that have on them?

PAIR IT WITH Judith Ortiz Cofer, "Not for Sale" (p. 134).

Anne Bradstreet

To My Dear and Loving Husband (p. 615)

WORKS WELL FOR Form (heroic couplets); figurative language (conceits).

ENTRY POINTS This is a poem of address and a love poem, written by a Puritan wife, the first female poet in the American colonies. She writes in the heroic couplets that were the predominant verse form in England at the time, but with imagery and figures more typical of the earlier metaphysical strain of John Donne and George Herbert.

Poets writing love poems face the difficulty of finding a way to put the depth and breadth of their feelings into words that are likely to seem inadequate, and perhaps hackneyed. Ask students to consider Bradstreet's effort. How well does she succeed in describing her love in a convincing and adequate way? Get them to focus on the comparisons she makes: What kind of values do they reveal? What is suggested about her and her culture by the economic imagery she uses? You might have students compare this poem with Elizabeth Barrett Browning's sonnet, written to her husband a century and a half later, "How do I love thee? Let me count the ways" (p. 617).

Ask the class to work out the meaning of the final two lines. When she writes, "we may live ever," does she mean in heaven? Or in their love? Or in this poem? You might have the class compare these lines to the final six lines of Edmund Spenser's sonnet, "One day I wrote her name upon the strand" (p. 735). Does Bradstreet's poem convey a similar point? The final two lines differ from the first ten by the inclusion of an extra syllable. Ask students to assess the effect of the longer lines.

PAIR IT WITH Elizabeth Barrett Browning, "How do I love thee? Let me count the ways" (p. 617).

Gwendolyn Brooks

the mother   (p. 615)

WORKS WELL FOR   Tone; structure (parallelism, lists).

ENTRY POINTS   The poem lends itself to a discussion of the issue of abortion, especially given its first line. This can lead students to see how easily they can draw an unsupported moral conclusion because of how they impose their views on a line or on the whole poem.

Ask students to talk about the title in relation to the poem. Why "the" mother, for example? The poem is written in first person. Why the shift?

Discuss how this poem could be appropriated by differing sides of the abortion debate to support their view. What cautions does this raise in the students?

Bring the cultural background of the poem to bear on a reading. Perhaps have the students discuss what influence their own backgrounds had on their reading of the poem.

What is the effect of the blunt, direct voice of the poem?

Have a discussion about the relation of the speaker to the poet herself. What issues and misunderstandings and insights arise?

PAIR IT WITH   Michael S. Harper, "Nightmare Begins Responsibility" (p. 664).

Sterling A. Brown

Riverbank Blues   (p. 616)

WORKS WELL FOR   Rhythm; the blues.

ENTRY POINTS   The title says outright that this poem is an example of the blues. What connections to blues music can be seen in the poem? Ask students to discuss what the effect is, on reading the poem, of immediately knowing that it is to be read in the context of the blues aesthetic.

Have the class read the poem out loud, either dividing up the class or having different students read the whole poem. Discuss what happens when one hears the poem.

Discuss how many of the images not only describe but also evoke feelings, and also suggest the feelings of the speaker; the speaker is perhaps projecting feelings onto the surroundings.

Discuss what role — other than making similar sounds — rhyme plays in the poem.

Have students listen to some classic blues and compare the music to the poem. Point out to them that "muddy waters" is in the poem.

PAIR IT WITH Langston Hughes, "The Weary Blues" (p. 1266).

Elizabeth Barrett Browning

How do I love thee? Let me count the ways   (p. 617)

WORKS WELL FOR Abstract language; sonnet.

ENTRY POINTS This poem is widely known and loved. Students who don't know much other poetry may be familiar with it and like it because it is clear, eloquent, uplifting, and sincere. You might ask how many students know it and like it. Then ask what are the qualities and characteristics they like in it.

It is, of course, often cited as an example of how not to write a love poem. It lacks concrete images; it is sentimental; it's a "one-size-fits-all" poem — anyone can use it because it contains no individual characteristics about a specific person. To say all this to students who finally have found a poem they like can discourage them.

Perhaps a better strategy is to pair it with another love poem, such as Gary Miranda's sonnet, and ask students to compare the two — how are they similar, how are they different, what do students like about each, which poem would they rather have had written for them as a love poem (the one-size-fits-all type, possibly being recycled from a previous relationship, or the type that is clearly meant for a certain individual). In the end, they may continue to like "How do I love thee" better, and that's okay: It's not a bad thing for them to feel deeply about a famous poem, any famous poem.

It's a poem that can work well with biographical criticism, as the sonnet sequence of which it is a part — *Songs from the Portugese* — played a significant part in the love story of Elizabeth Barrett and Robert Browning.

PAIR IT WITH Gary Miranda, "Love Poem" (p. 693).

Sandra M. Castillo

Exile   (p. 618)

WORKS WELL FOR Diction; figurative language.

ENTRY POINTS Here's a poem that lends itself to discussions of language, of the effects of combining dictions. The discussion could focus on what the combinations reveal simply by being juxtaposed in the poem, on the effects of this mix of dictions, on what such a mix can imply and embody, and on when using combinations from different languages is and is not effective.

Ask students to discuss the relationship of the poem to the epigraph. Talk about the "function" of an epigraph. A poem can be an "embodiment" of the meaning of the epigraph, it can emerge out from the epigraph, it can be the result of the epigraph's being a trigger, it can be a reaction or response to the epigraph, or any combination of these.

Enter the poem through the experience of the speaker. What has she gone through? What are the differences in attitude between the speaker, the person in the poem, and the poet?

This is a good poem to use to discuss the purposeful use of stanzas. Review the meaning of stanza as "room" and review the various uses of a stanza. Apply these to the poem and talk about why it was wise and effective to use a stanza structure.

Talk about the ways this poem is both "culture specific" and also "human specific," that is, connects to most everyone. Discuss whether the experiences in the poem are archetypal.

Students might write their own similar experiences and then compare them with one another and with the poem. This could lead to a conversation about how an effective poem can explore a theme applicable to most while at the same time affirming the particular.

PAIR IT WITH   Judith Ortiz Cofer, "Silent Dancing" (p. 1295).

Rosemary Catacalos

David Talamántez on the Last Day of Second Grade   (p. 620)

WORKS WELL FOR   Lines; tone; irony.

ENTRY POINTS   Start off by asking how the students relate to the poem. This could lead to discussing the value of such a poem and also what one must be careful about when a poem so closely connects to one's own experience, how one can easily project into such a work things that are not there.

Ask students how the poem reveals what is being valued in the school's culture and what then by implication, by "absence," is not being valued, and then to discuss the effects of this on David Talamántez.

Ask students to discuss how they feel toward David. Have them point out what precisely in the poem leads them to feel as they do. Encourage them to notice nuance and subtleties as well as the obvious. Talk about whether they feel their "emotional buttons" were being pressed by the poet or whether their feelings were touched authentically.

The poem lends itself to students getting in touch with their own experiences similar to David's. They might write an anecdotal account of what happened to them in school and then compare. A profitable discussion about the impact of a dominant culture on one's education could result.

PAIR IT WITH   Toni Cade Bambara, "The Lesson" (p. 183).

Marilyn Chin

Turtle Soup   (p. 622)

WORKS WELL FOR   Conflict; juxtaposition.

ENTRY POINTS   A valuable discussion about different generations can come out from reading this poem, how those from one generation see the world differently from another, what conflicts and clashes ensue, if there is any way to reconcile the differences, if there is any way to live together within such conflicts.

Chin uses *you* in a way that some students may be less familiar with. Discuss this usage, what it does in the poem, how if affects the reader.

Have a discussion about two people from the same family and from the same culture now living in a new culture: how they "adapt," how their ways of living within a foreign culture differ, what the consequences are, what is gained and what is lost.

Talk about "turtle soup." What makes it a powerful image? Is it a metaphor? A symbol? For what? Why would Chin select that image and also make it the poem's title?

Focus on the speaker. Discuss her attitudes, what she is like, what the students think of her. Then discuss her in light of her mother. Does thinking of her as a daughter affect one's prior considerations?

The final stanza opens the particulars in the poem out into a wider set of considerations. Read the stanza again and talk about why it is an appropriate outgrowth from what has come before in the poem and about all it leads the students to reflect on.

> Is there nothing left but the shell
> and humanity's strange inscriptions,
> the songs, the rites, the oracles?

PAIR IT WITH   Nelli Wong, "Grandmother's Song" (p. 754).

Samuel Taylor Coleridge

Kubla Khan   (p. 623)

WORKS WELL FOR   Images; sounds.

ENTRY POINTS   The notes on page 623 fill in background for the poem — that the poem came to Coleridge during an opium-induced reverie, that it's unfinished because he was interrupted while writing it and the remainder of the poem did not come back to him, and that the historical Kublai Khan (1215–1294) was the founder of the Yüan dynasty and overlord of the Mongol Empire.

The poem is best approached as a feast for the senses: It's a description of a "pleasure dome," after all. Ask students to pick out and discuss imagery of sight, sound, and smell — and images that convey emotions (especially the tumult of lines 14–24). How does the imagery contribute to the dreamlike, almost trancelike qualities being related in the poem? You might also ask students to discuss how sound techniques contribute to the effect of the imagery and the dreamy aura of what is being described.

At a further level, the poem — like Percy Bysshe Shelley's "Ode to the West Wind" (p. 721) — may be about the power that makes it possible to write poetry. You could ask students to pick out and explain images that would work at this level.

PAIR IT WITH   Agha Shahid Ali, "I Dream It Is Afternoon When I Return to Delhi" (p. 597).

Billy Collins

Marginalia   (p. 624)

WORKS WELL FOR   Lists; humor; speaker.

ENTRY POINTS   One way to start with this poem is to simply ask the students if they can relate to it. Then talk about how the poem suggests other things about human behavior. What is ironic about "marginalia" in light of the works being read? Ask the students to think about possible broader implications of the idea of marginalia.

The poem's structure is a list, a list made up of lists with lists in the lists. Discuss the effectiveness of this approach. Go back to the section on lists as structures (p. 532) and connect the poem to what is discussed there and to other poems that use lists, or catalogs. How would one explain that this is not just a list? What makes the poem more than clever?

Billy Collins has said that something he loves about writing a poem is when it suddenly "makes a turn." Where in this poem does that occur? In what ways does that turn change not only the direction of the poem, but the heart of the poem as well?

The poem lends itself to a discussion of allusion. What are the effects in the poem and on the reader of using them? Of using them in this poem? Are there allusions that must be understood? Can one "get" the poem without knowing the allusions? What are the possible liabilities of using them? Have the students talk about which allusions were especially effective for them.

The poem can lead to a discussion of humor in poetry. Why is it relatively uncommon? What makes it difficult to discuss? Why is humor difficult to write, to create? Why is it so often not taken seriously, treated as separate from the serious?

Discuss the speaker's feelings throughout the poem. What does the speaker portray as to what he is feeling? See if the students think that he may be covering what he is deeply feeling. If they think that he is, where in the poem do they get that sense?

The poem offers an opening to talk about the printed word: about the sense of authority and approval given instinctively to words; about cultural implications of that (who has the power to get their words into print, who doesn't); and about others who are marginalized, who write in or from the margins, about what authority their words do or don't have.

PAIR IT WITH   Marianne Moore, "Poetry" (p. 694).

Jayne Cortez

Into This Time   (p. 626)

WORKS WELL FOR   Rhythm; structure (line, parallelism, lists); tone.

ENTRY POINTS   Have the students read the poem aloud. Work to get the rhythms and pacing to be effective. Then ask students to discuss why talking about a poem without including the impact of the poem's rhythms can lead to an incomplete understanding of the work. The rhythm is crucial to this poem. Discuss what it embodies and evokes.

The poem uses litany. Discuss the effectiveness of this structure in light of the poem's subject and its impact on the reader. Ask what the students think about the way a litany can make them feel.

The poem gives the opportunity to discuss the incorporation of unsettling material, disturbing images and their effects, why some people would say this is not appropriate for poetry, and what saying that might reveal about the reader, about culture, about the purpose of poetry or any art.

Juxtaposition is prevalent throughout the poem. Discuss the power of these combinations and collisions. What do they reveal about the speaker's experience? In what ways do they embody the culture milieu?

The poem's impact greatly depends on its tone. Have the students describe the tone. Make sure they catch the rich mixture of feelings that lead to the speaker's tone. What attitudes do the students feel the speaker holds toward everything talked about in the poem?

Discuss ways this poem speaks to those within its culture and also to those of other cultural backgrounds.

Discuss the title. What is "this time"? What does it mean to say "into" this time? What effect does the title have on one's reading the poem?

PAIR IT WITH   e. e. cummings, "pity this busy monster,manunkind" (p. 630).

Victor Hernández Cruz

Problems with Hurricanes   (p. 628)

WORKS WELL FOR   Irony; juxtaposition.

ENTRY POINTS   Here's a poem that can lead to an enjoyable discussion of irony. Simple as that. Then the students might create their own "Problems with _____" poem and enjoy one another's work.

Implication is central to this poem, giving the class a good opportunity to get a better grasp on how implication works in a poem, how the material must be what it is while also suggesting something more or other. In this case, there is a lesson to be learned. But what do the students think that lesson is?

Yes, the poem is funny. But what exactly makes it funny and makes us laugh or smile knowingly?

Notice the line breaks, especially the words they break on. Have the students discuss the effects of breaking lines on these words.

Describe the speaker. What is his attitude? His tone or tones? Why does his "teaching us a lesson" not put us off?

Ask students what they make of the last three lines: the juxtaposition of noise, water, and wind with mangoes; why we are told to "beware" of beautiful and sweet things (does the poem open up here?); why it says to beware of "all such" things.

PAIR IT WITH   Thylias Moss, "Tornados" (p. 556).

e. e. cummings

in Just-   (p. 629)

WORKS WELL FOR   Structure (free verse); rhythm; sound.

ENTRY POINTS   This is one of cummings's "Chansons Innocentes," little songs for children. It celebrates spring and children by invoking a classical allusion most children won't recognize but adult readers are expected to. The "goat-footed / balloonMan" (ll. 20–21) alludes to Pan, the merry and playful half-man/half-goat Arcadian shepherd god whose music on his pipes accompanied the return of Persephone from the underworld (see the note on page 613), which turned Demeter's winter-long mourning into rejoicing and led to the coming of spring (this is "Just-spring," the very beginning of it — but have students try out other definitions of "just" as well).

This is a good poem to work with for understanding the effects of "white space," variations in speed of reading, playfulness of language, innovative use of word combinations. There is a kind of kinetic energy especially apparent in the poem. Have at least three students read the poem aloud and then discuss the ways they interpreted these various effects in their readings. Notice how "spring" is emphasized by its placement; similarly with "whistles" and "far and wee" (the latter is spaced differently each time, leading to different rhythms, especially as in the final three lines it seems to fade away into the distance). Notice also how names are crammed together, the way the children themselves would say them.

Students are often attracted to cummings's poems because "he doesn't worry about punctuation." Have a discussion about punctuation and lack of punctuation as meaningful rather than as following rules or not caring about rules. Point out that in order for cummings to work as he did, it was necessary for him to thoroughly understand the rules of grammar.

PAIR IT WITH   William Carlos Williams, "Spring and All" (p. 753).

e. e. cummings

pity this busy monster,manunkind   (p. 630)

WORKS WELL FOR   Tone; voice; structure.

ENTRY POINTS   The poem lends itself to a discussion of syntax for effect. Have the students talk about what cummings creates by his use of fractured, distorted, disjointed syntax in the poem. The poem is a good one for leading students to see that a writer can use sentence structure itself to evoke meaning, feeling, and energy.

Begin a discussion of the poem by focusing on it as a political poem, a protest poem. What is being protested, and what is valued? Have the students discuss the differences between a poem that has a political purpose and one that includes the political but not for its primary purpose.

William Stafford said that all his poems were protest poems, implying that all poems are protest poems. Ask students to reflect on that idea and discuss it as a position, and then relate it to several poems, including this one.

Talk about how cummings creates words from joining words and adding suffixes and prefixes. Build a discussion around how this affects a reader, about its effectiveness or lack thereof in the poem.

Have one group in the class prepare an argument that the poem is hopeful, another group that the poem is despairing. Ask the two groups to discuss what they found.

Build a discussion around the idea of pity in the poem. Why does cummings use the word *pity*? Does the word shift in meaning or in tone throughout the poem? Are there ironies in its use? Is it sincere? Pity is often something we are asked not to do because it is seen as demeaning or condescending. Have the students talk about these issues and also discuss the concept in terms of what cummings is asking the reader to pity.

PAIR IT WITH   Percy Bysshe Shelley, "Ozymandias" (p. 721)

Keki N. Daruwalla

Pestilence   (p. 631)

WORKS WELL FOR   Images; figurative language.

ENTRY POINTS   The title tells the reader what the poem is dealing with. Ask students to discuss the value of knowing right away what the poem is going to focus on. In what ways does the title intensify the experience of the poem?

Focus on the speaker. Discuss what the speaker is feeling, what the tone or tones of voice reveal. What is the impact on the reader of listening to this voice against the background of the pestilence?

The poem uses a variety of words not often found in poems. Have a discussion about the risks taken when using this diction and on its effectiveness.

Discuss the central image of feet. What makes that image arresting, appropriate, effective, and powerful?

Discuss the lines "but memory like a crane-arm / unloads its ploughed-up rubble" (ll. 37–38).

PAIR IT WITH   Wislawa Szymborska, "The End and the Beginning" (p. 784).

Kamala Das

In Love   (p. 632)

WORKS WELL FOR   Figurative language.

ENTRY POINTS   Among the most challenging poems to write is a love poem. As some might say, "They've all been written," or "There are so many terrible love poems." Ask students to talk about how they feel about this one. Discuss what makes it fresh, effective, provocative, convincing.

The title likely draws out certain assumptions and expectations for what follows in the poem. Discuss which of these, if any, are fulfilled by the poem.

A powerful way to enter this poem is by focusing on the speaker. Ask students to discuss what the speaker is going through, feeling, experiencing. What conflicts, both inner and outer, is the speaker dealing with? In what ways do the lines themselves, both in content and in structure, embody the speaker's inner experience?

Have the students reflect on and speculate about what the cultural context is for this poem and this speaker.

Discuss why the speaker ends the poem saying, "This skin-communicated / Thing that I dare not yet in / His presence call our love." Discuss what is implied or suggested by the speaker's watching the crows. Discuss whether the speaker and the poet are one and the same.

PAIR IT WITH   Elizabeth Barrett Browning, "How do I love thee? Let me count the ways" (p. 617).

Toi Derricotte

A Note on My Son's Face   (p. 633)

WORKS WELL FOR   Tone; imagery.

ENTRY POINTS   The students may want to start right in with a discussion of the social/political/cultural issues in the poem. As the discussion takes place, encourage them to support what they are concluding with evidence from the poem.

Ask students to discuss the use of sections in the poem. What do the separate sections signal or indicate? Discuss why it is an effective strategy for the poet to separate the poem into three sections.

Have the students reconsider the poem in light of the last two lines. Talk about how this ending hit them the first time and how reading the poem again in light of the ending changes their experience. This can lead into a discussion of reader-response theory's affirming the importance of both a first reading and subsequent, and repeated, readings.

Discuss the speaker. What is she experiencing, thinking about, realizing, going through?

Toi Derricotte has written and spoken extensively about what it has been like for her, an African American, to be taken for white. Does that information affect the reading of the poem? Why or why not?

PAIR IT WITH   Jayne Cortez, "Into This Time" (p. 626).

Emily Dickinson

Because I could not stop for Death   (p. 635)

WORKS WELL FOR   Irony; figurative language; structure.

ENTRY POINTS   One place to start discussion of this poem is point of view: The speaker is dead, has been dead for some time (for centuries), and is looking back at the time of her or his death.

Ask students to summarize the way the speaker's passing is described: a gentleman giving a lady a carriage ride, maybe even a suitor picking up his love for an afternoon drive. Have them point out details and images that establish the overall metaphor. Have them point out details and images that take on double meanings (the personification of Death, "And Immortality" [personified], "I had put away / My labor and my leisure too," "We paused before a House that seemed / A Swelling of the Ground," "Were toward Eternity").

Ask the class about tone: Do they sense a change ("quivering and chill") as the carriage goes past the sun? Is that the point at which the speaker realizes this isn't just an ordinary Sunday drive? Does the speaker fear death? Notice the reversal of form in lines 13–14 (4-3 turns into 3-4) — why? What's the effect? What is the tone in the final stanza?

Ask students to comment on the various implications in the first two lines: "Because I could not stop for Death" (too busy even to think about dying?), "He kindly stopped for me" (why kindly? Is it ironic? Why "stopped for me"? Who is in control?).

PAIR IT WITH   A. E. Housman, "To an Athlete Dying Young" (p. 672).

Emily Dickinson

Much Madness is divinest Sense   (p. 636)

WORKS WELL FOR   Paradox; form; sounds.

ENTRY POINTS   Many students love this cryptic, tightly knit poem that affirms their nonconformity. Ask the class to work through the paradoxes and clarify the meaning and implications of what is being said: What kind of madness makes sense? To what kind of "discerning" eye? What kind of sense is madness? What is the poem saying about the majority?

Ask students to focus on the structure and form. They should notice (or you should point out) the parallelism and reversals in lines 1 and 3 and 6 and 7; the symmetrical organization of a three-line sentence, a two-line sentence, and another three-line sentence; the center section (the middle sentence, the heart of the poem thematically) being made up of two trimeter lines, though tetrameter would be expected in line 5; the *ababcdcd* rhyme scheme (counting "Eye" and "Majority" as slant rhymes, or perfect rhymes if Dickinson still ended the latter with a long *I* sound); the use of alliteration and assonance to create unity across the sentences (*m* and *s* in lines 1–4, *a* and *d* in lines 5–8).

PAIR IT WITH   Cornelius Eady, "My Mother, If She Had Won Free Dance Lessons" (p. 642).

Ana Doina

The Extinct Homeland – A Conversation with Czeslaw Milosz (p. 636)

WORKS WELL FOR Speaker/voice; myth.

ENTRY POINTS The students will benefit from knowing about Czeslaw Milosz. Point them to the biographical sketch on p. 1446. They should at least know that he is a Nobel Laureate from Poland who has lived in the States and who has written extensively about the effects of living in two cultures and of being both homeless and deeply connected to his homeland while also making other countries his home.

What is a homeland? Have students write down their own definitions of home. Discuss the differences in their definitions. Relate their definitions to those in the poem both stated directly and implied. Ask students what they consider their homeland. Discuss if they even feel they have one in the deepest sense. Do any feel they have an "extinct homeland"? Discuss what that could be both in a physical and emotional or spiritual sense.

This is a very dense poem. Even the lines are heavily weighted both in subject and in construction. Discuss how this affects their reading. Some may feel that the poem reads like prose. Discuss what makes this a poem and also if any feel it would be more effective if written as prose.

The epigraph considers home as "this world." Discuss the poem in light of the epigraph. What is the relationship of the poem to the epigraph? Tie the relationship into the reference in the title that this is a "conversation." In what ways do the students see the poem as a conversation? How does that affect their interpretations? Discuss the dynamics of being a reader who is listening in on a conversation.

The poem is rich with figures. Ask students to pick out some examples and discuss their effectiveness, their role in the poem, what they create, their impact on the reader.

Talk about the speaker. How would the students describe the speaker? What tones/attitudes can the students discern? After doing so, discuss the last stanza, how the speaker describes herself. What can one make of these descriptions? For example, what is implied by her saying, "I am my own myth" (l. 70)?

Discuss various takes and views of the directly bold statement at the start of the last stanza: "There is no homeland."

This poem was anthologized in a collection edited by Virgil Suárez and Ryan Van Cleave entitled *American Diaspora*. In what ways does the poem embody that title?

PAIR IT WITH Bharati Mukherjee, "Orbiting" (p. 315).

John Donne

A Valediction: Forbidding Mourning (p. 638)

WORKS WELL FOR Figurative language (conceit); tone.

ENTRY POINTS Students enjoy the intricacy of the argument in this poem, once they can follow it. But they might well need help following its thought, partly because some of the connections between thoughts are associative rather than direct and logical. You could ask the class to try working through the steps of the poem, but you may need to be ready to help out:

(1) The extended simile in stanzas 1–2 proves difficult to many students: the speaker and his love must accept their separation the way a virtuous person faces death — calmly, quietly, with equanimity (the conceits "tear-floods" and "sigh-tempests" may be confusing initially).

(2) The flood and tempest imagery leads the speaker's thoughts to jump to earthquakes and the damage they can cause — the way separation damages the relationships of ordinary lovers. The separation of the speaker and his love, though of much greater consequence because their love is so much greater, causes no more damage than a movement in the heavenly spheres does on earth.

(3) The metaphors "profanation" and "laity" in lines 7–8 move their love into the higher realm of religious devotion, which other people, ordinary people, won't be able to understand because their relationships rely on the physical and separation weakens the bonds, as stanzas 4 and 5 explain.

(4) The metaphor "refined" in line 17 sets up the conceit in stanza 6: Their souls are one, unified at such a level that, though their bodies separate, their souls remain together, the way gold remains united even though stretched to the thinness of a long, fine wire.

(5) Or, if the souls must be considered as two, they still are unified, the way the two legs of a drawing compass are one instrument — one foot staying fixed and forming the stable center of a perfect circle, the other moving away but still grounded in its home.

PAIR IT WITH Gary Miranda, "Love Poem" (p. 693).

Mark Doty

Tiara (p. 639)

WORKS WELL FOR Juxtapositions; irony; figurative language.

ENTRY POINTS   The poem offers a way to discuss assumptions about funeral practices and behavior at funeral services. The students might want to discuss what the cultural assumptions are in relation to death and treatment of the dead, and how they are not appropriate for all cultures. This can lead to insights into the differences among cultures in their attitudes toward death and the dead.

Discuss the speaker's attitude toward Peter, society, this occasion, death, heaven. What assumptions and cultural ideas does the speaker challenge? Have the students discuss their own responses to the speaker's points of view.

The poem lends itself to noticing juxtapositions, some direct and some very subtle. Have the students identify as many types of juxtaposition as they can and then discuss what these reveal, what insights they open us up to, how they alter preconceptions and perceptions, what effects they create in the poem.

Mark Doty often reveals beauty that is usually overlooked, never seen, disregarded, or dismissed. In what ways does he do that within this poem?

Discuss the structure of the poem: what makes it effective, what it adds to the poem, why it is appropriate, how it works with the subject material, what its effects are on the reader.

The poem takes some surprising turns. Note these and ask the students what they make of these in terms of the speaker and how they affect their own thinking and considerations.

PAIR IT WITH   Leslie Marmon Silko, "The Man to Send Rain Clouds" (p. 377); Susan Atefat-Peckham, "Dates" (p. 599).

Rita Dove

The Satisfaction Coal Company   (p. 641)

WORKS WELL FOR   Structure (lines); tone.

ENTRY POINTS   Because this poem gives information in rather indirect ways, students may want to talk about what is going on in the poem. There is a narrative underlying this poem. One could even say the poem embodies this narrative lyrically. Have a discussion about "the story" that the poem comes out from. The students may have a number of possible stories or there may in fact be a number of stories.

The speaker's attitudes are well worth exploring. Have the students list them. Discuss what they reflect about the times, about conditions, about work and daily living. Discuss too why the speaker thinks and feels as she or he does and how this might differ today or even be criticized.

Ask students what they make of the beginning of section 3 where the speaker says, "They were poor then but everyone had been poor. / He hadn't minded the sweeping, / just the thought of it — like now / when people ask him what he's thinking, / and he says, I'm listening."

This poem is rich with sounds. Ask students to point out some different types of sound elements in the poem and talk about what they add to the piece.

PAIR IT WITH   Gary Soto, "The Elements of San Joaquin" (p. 729).

Cornelius Eady
My Mother, If She Had Won Free Dance Lessons   (p. 642)

WORKS WELL FOR   Speaker; figurative language; line breaks.

ENTRY POINTS   Students may start out feeling confused about what the poem is saying. Ask someone to initiate a summary and then ask others to join in and help clarify it. Ask what students think the speaker means by saying "if she had won free dance lessons" and what he means by calling her a "crazy lady" in line 11. Ask them to discuss what the poem implies about the relationship between son and mother, and about the effect of the mother on the son. Ask if they think he might be talking as much about himself as about his mother.

The poem is a memory poem and a poem about separation — leaving and coming back. Ask students to focus particularly on the meaning of "any child who wakes up one day to find themself / Abandoned in a world larger than their / Bad dreams" (ll. 17–19) and relate them to the larger separation motif.

Why is "dance" an appropriate subject and perhaps metaphor for the poem?

What do the students make of the speaker in the first line of stanza 4 referring to his reflection as "a small thought"?

Ask students to work out the meaning of the final stanza. How can a phone ring like a suitor? How can an invitation arrive in the mail "Like Jesus"? What's the point of introducing a religious figure at the end? Why close with "extending a hand"?

PAIR IT WITH   Sherman Alexie, "Father and Farther" (p. 1326).

T. S. Eliot
Journey of the Magi   (p. 643)

WORKS WELL FOR   Archetypes; allusion; imagery.

ENTRY POINTS   This poem will be clearest for students who are familiar with Christianity and the post-Christmas coming of the Magi, or wise men.

Eliot retells the story from the perspective of one of the Magi, using a first-person speaker who can recount what happened but does not fully understand its implications.

All students, however, can relate to the archetypes that give the poem its structure: the journey into experience or understanding, the deadness associated with winter and night, and the life and birth associated with spring and light.

Many of the details in the opening section are Eliot using imaginative license to fill in details not included in Matthew 2:1–12 — what the journey from the East to Bethlehem was like. Although some details in the middle section are similarly "realistic" (the running stream, the water-mill, the tavern and vine-leaves), others are allusive: the "three trees" foreshadow the three crosses on Calvary (Luke 23:32–33); the old white horse alludes to the horse ridden by the conquering Christ (Rev. 19:11–16); "dicing" alludes to the soldiers at the crucifixion gambling for Jesus' tunic (John 19:23–24); and "pieces of silver" suggests the thirty pieces of silver Judas received for turning Jesus over to the authorities (Matt. 26:14–15).

The part of the story focused on in the Bible — the arrival in Bethlehem, honoring the baby and presenting him gifts — is reduced in the poem to the understatement (and situational irony) of "it was (you may say) satisfactory" (l. 31). Ask students to explain the effect of handling it this way (for example, it might be the appropriate response for a king visiting a child not in a palace but in an ordinary house in a village; and it ties in with the speaker's inability to comprehend what he had experienced).

Many students find the last section difficult. It is set up by mixing allusions to the crucifixion story with the Christmas story. The speaker tries to make sense of the effect that what he saw had on him. He was changed by the journey and seeing the child — he no longer is comfortable (at ease) in his old country; he even refers to his own countrymen as "an alien people" (l. 42). The poem seems to use birth and death at two levels: When the words are not capitalized, they refer to physical birth and death; when they are capitalized, they refer to Jesus' birth and death, or to a spiritual experience (spiritual rebirth). Thus the speaker says an encounter with the child Jesus, who would later die a sacrificial Death, led to a rebirth in his life that makes him eager for his physical death and passing on to the next, spiritual, life.

PAIR IT WITH   David Henry Hwang, "As the Crow Flies" (p. 903).

T. S. Eliot

The Love Song of J. Alfred Prufrock   (p. 645)

WORKS WELL FOR   Dramatic monologue or interior monologue; allusions; sounds; lines; irony.

ENTRY POINTS   This is a difficult poem for students, but a rewarding one for them once they begin to grasp what's going on in it. One way into the poem is by examining the character of the speaker. Some other facets of the poem may need to be dealt with before the whole of Prufrock's character becomes reasonably clear, but it's an important question to put in front of students and have them keep in mind.

In getting at his character, consider the narrative approach. The poem is presented either as a dramatic monologue (see p. 491) or an interior mono-logue (p. 97). Have students review the two terms and discuss which best fits the poem. That requires deciding whether Prufrock is addressing an actual person when he says "Let us go then, you and I," the way the Duke does in Robert Browning's "My Last Duchess" (p. 511) or Ulysses does in Alfred, Lord Tennyson's "Ulysses" (p. 739), or if we are reading what Prufrock says to himself, or what he plans to say given the opportunity, the way the mother does in Tillie Olsen's "I Stand Here Ironing" (p. 353).

The title also comes to bear on the assessment of his character. Is the poem the love song of J. Alfred Prufrock? If so, what does that mean? In what sense is that the case? Or is the poem about J. Alfred's love song, or his at-tempts to choose or sing such a song to another person? Where does love appear in the poem?

The first part of the poem focuses on the "overwhelming question" (l. 10) Prufrock is about to ask, or tries to ask, or perhaps intends to ask on his visit, at the social occasion he attends or thinks about attending. Ask students to talk about the question: What is the question? (Will you marry me? What is the meaning of life? Other possibilities?) Of whom does he intend to ask the question? Why is it so difficult to ask it? Answers to what the question is and why it is so difficult to ask bear directly on Prufrock's character, of course.

Up to line 84, the poem deals with the difficulty, even agony, of finding the courage to ask the question. From line 84 on, it is clear Prufrock has decided not to ask the question (or, without deciding, recognizes his inability to do so). In the rest of the poem he rationalizes, explaining that it was no use anyhow and reflecting on what the rest of his life will be like (since his failure to ask the question signals that his life will go on as it has; asking the ques-tion — whatever it is — might have led to a change in his life).

In addition to Prufrock himself, get students to talk about Prufrock's world. What kind of society or culture does he inhabit? Is it a vital world with signifi-cant values, or a sterile and lifeless world? Ask them to relate the epigraph to the poem — does it apply to the poem's world? Is Prufrock in a living hell?

The poem is filled with allusions. Ask students to identify ones they rec-ognize (they should at least be able to identify Michelangelo and Hamlet, and perhaps John the Baptist) and to discuss how they relate to the poem (as contrasts to Prufrock and/or his world, perhaps). They are less likely to recog-nize verbal allusions; you might point out a few such examples (perhaps the one to Andrew Marvell's "To His Coy Mistress" in lines 92–93, if the class has read that poem), just to make them aware of that way of texturing the poem.

Finally, you might direct attention to the form and style of the poem. It's not the free verse Eliot often uses: This poem uses rhyme and alternates between metrical and nonmetrical verse. It is rich with assonance, alliteration, and a variety of figures of speech.

PAIR IT WITH   Edwin Arlington Robinson, "Richard Cory" (p. 552).

Martín Espada

The Saint Vincent de Paul Food Pantry Stomp   (p. 649)

WORKS WELL FOR   Tone; speaker; sounds.

ENTRY POINTS   Ask someone to sum up the speaker's attitude, tone, and situation, and to describe him as a person.

Discuss *stomp* as a metaphor. Why is it appropriate? What does it suggest or reveal?

Discuss whether "Madison, Wisconsin" has any effect on the students' reading of the poem.

The speaker implies several things concerning both Christianity and charity. Ask students to discuss what they think these implications are and what they themselves think of them. Have them reflect on what would lead the speaker to use the phrase "Christian suspicion" (l. 2).

Ask students what they make of the ending image, "the salsa band / of the unemployed."

PAIR IT WITH   Sherman Alexie, "The Business of Fancydancing" (p. 1323).

Sandra María Esteves

A la Mujer Borrinqueña   (p. 649)

WORKS WELL FOR   Structure; repetition; parallelism.

ENTRY POINTS   A starting point for this poem is its speaker. Ask students to discuss what the speaker is like, what qualities she conveys. Ask to what extent she seems to be an individual and to what extent a representative of the women of Puerto Rico. Bring up the title: *la Mujer* is singular — could its effect be plural (or representative)? Ask if "To the woman" in this case seems to make it a poem of address, or is it a poem dedicated to the women of Puerto Rico?

Ask about the nearly flat, straightforward, discursive style and voice. Do the students think it effective or ineffective? Why?

Ask students to discuss "My eyes reflect the pain / of that which has shamelessly raped me" (ll. 28–29). What do the lines mean? Is she referring to a literal or a figurative rape?

Discuss the repeated lines "Our men . . . they call me negra because they love me / and in turn I teach them to be strong."

PAIR IT WITH   Jamaica Kincaid, "Girl" (p. 283).

Carolyn Forché

The Colonel   (p. 650)

WORKS WELL FOR   Prose poem; rhythm; images.

ENTRY POINTS   This is a prose poem. Have the students talk about why it is a poem even though it is written in the structure of prose. Remind the students that line is but one element of poetry; it does not constitute whether a work is a poem. Ask how they would respond to someone who argued that prose poetry is not poetry.

Prose poet David Young has said that one way of considering a prose poem is to think of it as a novel on a postage stamp. Ask students to consider if that description applies to this poem. If so, have them explain why.

What is the speaker's situation? Discuss her reactions. What alternatives, if any, do any of the students think she could have taken? What complex moral issues and dilemmas does the speaker face? Have the students consider what they might have done in this situation, or if they have been in a similar moral dilemma, have them relate it to the poem and talk about what it was like for them.

This poem has been controversial in light of the poet herself. Many have strong feelings against turning horrible facts into works of art. Others feel the "poem of witness" is a very important calling for a poet. Invite students to discuss this issue. Include in the discussion the colonel's saying, "Something for your poetry, no?"

Have the students discuss whether it matters to them if the poet was indeed there or instead has written the poem thirdhand, having not experienced the horror of this situation or the immediacy of the suffering — especially in light of the first two sentences: "What you have heard is true. I was in his house."

The poem has an imagistic structure. Discuss the range of images, their impact, what they create individually and as a whole.

Discuss what is suggested by the last sentence: "Some of the ears on the floor were pressed to the ground."

PAIR IT WITH   Wole Soyinka, "Flowers for My Land" (p. 732).

Robert Frost

Mending Wall   (p. 651)

WORKS WELL FOR   Blank verse; synecdoche.

ENTRY POINTS   It is easy for students to miss the complex ironies in many of Frost's poems. This is certainly one of them. Not only does he often say one thing *in order* to mean another, but often there are many other things that could be meant. This gives the students an opportunity to realize that to be effective ambiguities must first of all be clear. In this poem the ambiguities of things being positive or negative or both can be discovered and discussed. Examine such lines as "Something there is that doesn't love a wall," "set the wall between us once again," "'Stay where you are until our backs are turned!,'" "It comes to little more," or, the most recognized, "'Good fences make good neighbors.'" Such lines lend themselves to a discussion about the complexities of effectively used ambiguity.

Discuss the word *mending* in the title. The word describes what they are doing. Some people think it is describing the wall. How might the students articulate the distinction?

When characterizing himself as a poet, Frost often referred to himself as a "synecdochist." Discuss the uses of synecdoche within the poem and the poem itself as a synecdoche.

How would the students describe the speaker? What are his attitudes? Compare the speaker with his neighbor. What distinguishes them from one another? If students feel they embody different "American icons" or American values or philosophies, have them discuss these.

The poem is written in blank verse. Review blank verse (p. 527) and discuss why it is effective and appropriate for the poem.

Discuss "mystery" in relation to the poem.

Discuss line 24, "He is all pine and I am apple orchard."

Discuss what the something is that doesn't love a wall.

PAIR IT WITH   August Wilson, *Fences* (p. 1186).

Robert Frost

The Road Not Taken   (p. 652)

WORKS WELL FOR   Form; sound.

ENTRY POINTS   This is among the most widely known and most misunderstood of Frost's poems. Encourage students to talk about what makes this poem so enigmatic and easily turned into whatever the reader wants it to mean. You might approach this by setting up a debate. Have one side argue that the poem is about not going with the norm. Have another side argue that the poem is about how no matter what choice one makes, it is what one does not choose that one thinks about always. Have another side argue that the poem is about the ways the speaker figures out how to rationalize whatever decision is made. And have yet another side argue that it's about the speaker devising a way to explain and rationalize the choice to those who question taking the common way and to those who question taking the uncommon way.

Talk about the structure of the poem, the five-line stanzas, the metric patterns, the rhymes and rhyme scheme. What effect does the form have on the reader? What role does structure play in the poem? Can the patterns and rhymes be read ironically?

Focus on the speaker. Discuss the speaker's situation, tone, attitude, and character, making sure that students bring out details to support their points.

The poem is rich with assonance. Discuss what the use of sound adds to the poem and why assonance is appropriate for this poem.

Discuss what the speaker means by saying, "I shall be telling this with a sigh / Somewhere ages and ages hence" (ll. 16–17).

Suggest that students try writing their own personal piece about a time they found themselves in a circumstance similar to the speaker's.

PAIR IT WITH   William Stafford, "Traveling through the Dark" (p. 554).

Richard Garcia

Why I Left the Church   (p. 653)

WORKS WELL FOR   Magical realism; form (lines).

ENTRY POINTS   Ask students why the speaker left the church. The poem lends itself to a tangential discussion that draws on students' similar experiences, if not with the church then with another institution. Have them tell their stories and draw parallels to the poem.

Many of the students probably have experienced something similar to Sister Mary Bernadette's order, "'Out! Come back / when you're ready'" (ll. 23–24). Ask them to discuss why this kind of thing is especially problematic to a person this age.

If students have read an example of magical realism, such as Gabriel García Márquez's "A Very Old Man with Enormous Wings" (p. 415), Helena María Viramontes's "The Moths" (p. 391), or Agha Shahid Ali's "I Dream It Is Afternoon When I Return to Delhi" (p. 597), ask if this poem could be another example of the type. What in the poem would support categorizing the poem as such (for example, when in lines 25–27 the speaker "rose from my chair / and kept rising / toward the ceiling")? Does seeing it that way help to understand the poem? Ask students what they make of this. What "reality" does its nonrealism suggest or embody?

Ask students to discuss the comic elements of the poem. What do they add? Why are they appropriate? What do they say or suggest? Or have the class discuss what makes this kid so likeable.

Discuss the poet's feelings toward what happened. What might be some of the things he feels compared to what the kid felt?

Discuss the last line — "I'll have to make something up." Ask students to think of it in relation to the events in the poem, to the poet himself, and to the art of poetry or any creative writing.

PAIR IT WITH Elizabeth Bishop, "In the Waiting Room" (p. 506).

Christopher Gilbert

Horizontal Cosmology (p. 654)

WORKS WELL FOR Images; rhythm.

ENTRY POINTS Consider ways the poem combines the natural world, domestic life, black culture, jazz, singing, and reflection. Ask students to discuss what the poem suggests by combining these. What do these have in common, and in what ways do they amplify or enrich one another? What is the relevance of the meaning of the words in the poem's title?

Ask students to describe or characterize the speaker. In what ways is the speaker talking to himself? Is this a dramatic monologue? Yes? No? Why? Why not? Is the speaker trying to talk himself into something? To support what he is thinking? If so, what speculations can be made about what he's concerned about and what his situation is?

Consider the possible associations, meanings, and implications connected to "the saxophone" and how they apply to section 4 of the poem.

Give some background to the class on Charlie Parker if students are not familiar with him. In what ways does having this information affect the students' reading of the poem? Invite discussion of why Charlie Parker is an appropriate allusion for the poem. What is it that Charlie Parker's playing does for the speaker?

Discuss lines 26–27, "what you're afraid of / facing, *Living is intense.*"

Discuss the simile in lines 28–29, "I am bad from note to note / like god's nostril."

Discuss why the speaker connects feeling in the world to "the technology / bigger than the ear" (ll. 33–34).

What do the students make of the ending of section 4, "you must be- / hold enough to play"?

PAIR IT WITH Kazuko Shiraishi, "Dedicated to the Late John Coltrane" (p. 724).

Allen Ginsberg

A Supermarket in California   (p. 656)

WORKS WELL FOR   Form (lines); allusions.

ENTRY POINTS   As background to this poem, ask students to read the excerpts from Walt Whitman's *Leaves of Grass* in the textbook and refresh the class's memory about Whitman and his view of America. Ask them to read this poem in that context and have them discuss the differences and similarities between Whitman's and Ginsberg's visions. Ask them to discuss how the context of reading and understanding Whitman affects their reading of the poem. How may Whitman's vision be considered a part of this poem? Whitman proclaimed that he was speaking in his time for those without a voice. Discuss whether the students feel that Ginsberg is doing the same for their time.

T. S. Eliot and Ezra Pound often said that art comes from other art. In what ways is that notion applicable to this poem?

Characterize the speaker. What are the speaker's attitudes, complaints, hopes, laments? In what ways is the speaker marginalized? How do we know?

In what ways is the poem ironic? In what ways is it a celebration? In what ways is it both? What is funny about the poem? What incongruities strike the students as comic?

Why does the speaker include Lorca?

Ask students what they make of the last paragraph, the rich complexity of that final image. Ask how they respond to line 11, "Will we stroll dreaming of the lost America of love . . ."

PAIR IT WITH   Walt Whitman, *Song of Myself* (p. 748).

Diane Glancy

Battery   (p. 657)

WORKS WELL FOR   Figurative language; form.

ENTRY POINTS   The note on page 657 provides some background for the poem. Fill in more if the students need it. What gaps must the reader fill in? What makes having to do so detract from the poem? What does doing so add to one's reading of the poem? Then consider with them the speaker's attitude, views, ideas, judgments, and conclusions about David Koresh.

Ask students to talk about what they think the speaker's views are of this form of religious belief. Does knowing Glancy is Native American make any difference? Discuss whether students feel the poet and the speaker are the same or whether the speaker is a voice for the poet.

Talk about the use of traveling to the site in the poem. Is it an archetype? If it is, for what? If not, why not?

Ask the students to list the ironies in the poem and then discuss their impact on the speaker and on the reader.

The poem's descriptions are vividly apocalyptic in many ways and on many levels. Discuss how the speaker's vision of the common surroundings is affected by the events at Waco.

PAIR IT WITH   Flannery O'Connor, "A Good Man Is Hard to Find" (p. 341).

Louise Glück

Parable of Flight   (p. 659)

WORKS WELL FOR   Images; symbol.

ENTRY POINTS   This is a rather elusive poem. Ask students if they find themselves drawn to it even though it is "difficult to get a handle on." Each stanza seems to leap away from the one before it. One's usual expectations for transitions or connections are not fulfilled. Have the students discuss what is disconcerting and fascinating about this use of stanza structure.

The poem fuses the inner and outer worlds. Discuss what this implies about the self. Discuss the ways this poem reveals that there is no separation between the human and the natural worlds, between the inner landscape and the outer landscape.

Discuss what the speaker seems to be trying to come to terms with about mutability. In what ways does the poem reveal or embody the view that mutability *is* reality?

Discuss the integration of questions in the poem. What do they create? Why are they important? What do they say about the speaker? About our own lives?

Why would the speaker say about the birds, "Does it even matter / what species they are?" (ll. 13–14)? What does that question reveal about the speaker and about what the speaker is feeling? Why would the speaker say in line 15 that the point is "They [the birds] leave here"?

Discuss the tone of the poem, the hushed, muted, quiet voice and what it creates in the poem and in the reader.

The title says that the poem is a parable. Discuss in what ways this poem is a parable. What type of lesson is to be learned from a parable? How does it differ from the usual ways of "learning a lesson"? What might be the lesson or lessons one could learn from this poem?

PAIR IT WITH   David Hernandez, "The Butterfly Effect" (p. 668).

Ray González

Praise the Tortilla, Praise the Menudo, Praise the Chorizo   (p. 659)

WORKS WELL FOR   Diction; figurative language.

ENTRY POINTS   Discuss the "praise poem" as a genre. What makes it unusual? Ask students to discuss their own ideas as to why poems of celebration are uncommon.

This poem has layers of implications and irony. Ask students to find examples and discuss what realizations they had as they discovered and considered them.

Discuss the use of food images in the poem. Why are these effective? Why food? Why these foods? What associations do the students make with these images? Discuss what the foods are connected with in the poem. Why does the speaker make these particular connections? What meanings do they create or evoke?

Read the poem as a celebration of the senses. In what ways does the poem elevate the senses above the ordinary? What is really being celebrated in the poem?

Discuss the rhythms and sounds in the poem. What do they add or evoke? Why are they appropriate? Do the same for the poem's tonal qualities.

Invite students to write their own praise poem and then have them read their work aloud. Have a celebration of praise poems.

PAIR IT WITH   Alberto Ríos, "Nani" (p. 713).

Thomas Gray

Elegy Written in a Country Churchyard   (p. 660)

WORKS WELL FOR   Images; tone; personification; other figurative language.

ENTRY POINTS   This is one of the most widely read English poems of the eighteenth century, admired greatly by "ordinary people," a classic of popular poetry. Samuel Johnson, in his life of Gray (1781), wrote, "The Churchyard abounds with images which find a mirror in every mind, and with sentiments to which every bosom returns an echo. The four stanzas beginning 'Yet even these bones' are to me original: I have never seen the notions in any other place; yet he that reads them here, persuades himself that he has always felt them. Had Gray written often thus, it had been vain to blame, and useless to praise him."

The opening three stanzas sketch the scene, the sounds and sights of sunset, looking down on a rural church, with its "ivy-mantled tower," and churchyard. The lines are packed with images: ask students to pick out examples appealing to the different senses.

Lines 13–36 reflect on the people buried in the churchyard, not famous persons but ordinary folk, "rude [untaught] forefathers" of the village. It uses a list of "No mores" to describe what they did in their lives but now do no longer. You might ask students to pick out lines or phrases they like or find meaningful or moving. Also, you might discuss if the lines use sentiment effectively or are overly sentimental. The ninth stanza is famous for its expression of the inevitability of death.

Lines 37–40 introduce the theme of remembrance: These are not famous people who are remembered or who are in books. Yet, says the speaker, in lines 41–76, this is no reason to dismiss them — it was their situation, not their abilities, that determined their lives. They may have had as much potential to make an impact on the world, for good or ill, as famous people, but lack of opportunity left them unknown. Some of the lines may be difficult for students to follow: You might have the class go through them, rephrasing them and asking questions about them.

Lines 77–92, the stanzas Johnson commented on, attest to the longing for life and the desire to be remembered, and the attempt to preserve the memory of someone by erecting a gravestone. Read Johnson's comments to the class and ask students to discuss what qualities in them would account for his admiring them so much. Ask whether they agree with his assessment. Ask students also to consider the difference between the fragile words engraved on an inexpensive gravestone and the words that a poet writes. Many poems affirm the permanence, the immortality, of poetry (you might compare this with Edmund Spenser's sonnet "One day I wrote her name upon the strand" — p. 735); Gray might be making that claim, as a contrast to the weathering gravestones, and supporting it by the many allusions in the "Elegy" to earlier poems, which live on by being remembered and by being echoed in this poem.

Critics have differed about the "thee" in line 93 and the subject of the Epitaph in lines 117–28. We follow Richard P. Sugg's suggestion ("The Importance of Voice: Gray's *Elegy*," *Tennessee Studies in Literature* 19 [1974] 115–20) that the "thee" is the poet, the voice created by Thomas Gray, he who "in these lines" is being mindful of the unhonored dead. Some day a "kindred spirit" may wonder about the poet's fate and ask an elderly shepherd about him. Lines 98–116 relate the reply of the "hoary-headed swain," an engaging account (full of allusions to earlier literature) of the dreamy figure who used to wander about the neighborhood muttering poetic lines under his breath but who now is buried in the country churchyard.

Lines 117–28 of the "Elegy" can be seen as an epitaph to "the poet," that is, to poets generally. But there is also a sense in which the "Elegy" can be seen as Gray's own epitaph. As Sugg puts it, "Gray, by creating the independent voice of [the "poet" in] the *Elegy* to speak on the mortality of poets and the immortality of poetry, makes the *Elegy* his own 'Epitaph'" (120).

PAIR IT WITH   Benjamin Alire Sáenz, "Elegy Written on a Blue Gravestone (To You, the Archaeologist)" (p. 716).

Kimiko Hahn

When You Leave   (p. 664)

WORKS WELL FOR   Tone; myth.

ENTRY POINTS   This is a poem of address, yet the "you" is mentioned only in the title. Discuss the "you" in the poem. Who is the person addressed? What is the person's relationship to the speaker? Why, after being mentioned in the title, is the person never mentioned again? Why does the speaker tell this story to the one addressed?

Discuss the speaker's comparing the sadness to "a color" in line 1. Discuss the way the poet has structured the poem by extending the color image throughout the poem. What effects does this create? How does it draw in the reader? In what ways is the color explored, considered? What makes this use of color effective?

This poem lends itself to use of the theory of reader response. There are many gaps. Ask the students to mark the gaps and then discuss the various ways they filled them in. Talk about which gaps it was surprising for them to realize that they were indeed filling in.

Ask students to consider the tone of the poem. How could it be described or characterized? What does it reveal about the speaker and the speaker's attitudes toward the subject and the one addressed?

Discuss the ending. After the poem has been closely focused on the single color, it then opens out into timelessness. Discuss what the students make of this. What do they think it means to "open the color forever" (l. 18)?

PAIR IT WITH   Duane Niatum, "First Spring" (p. 696).

Michael S. Harper

Nightmare Begins Responsibility   (p. 664)

WORKS WELL FOR   Diction; figurative language; tone.

ENTRY POINTS   Focus on the speaker/father as he watches through the emergency room window while doctors attempt to save his child. He is obviously going through a lot. Ask the students to sort out all that he is feeling, experiencing, realizing, reacting to, and reflecting on. He himself is one of the things he thinks about. What does he reveal about himself?

The issues of race are made all the more complex and complicated by other issues within this poem. Ask students to sort out all the issues and then discuss how they intertwine. Touch on the resulting effects of these on the speaker as well as the reader. Ask them to bring in the title. What might the phrase in and of itself mean? In what ways does the poem embody as well as explicate the title? Ask the students to talk or write about a situation in their own lives where "nightmare began responsibility."

What gender issues are raised by the poem? In what ways do they differ from the more common gender issues one encounters?

Consider why the poem uses italicized words and phrases. What do the italics signify? What effects do they have? Discuss such lines as "distrusting white-pink mending paperthin" (l. 7) and "*distrusting-white-hands-picking-baboon-light*" (l. 11) and "my distrusting self" (l. 24).

"Pane" is both at the beginning and in the next-to-last line. Discuss how it is used and consider the use of a "serious pun." Notice the similar usage in Lucille Clifton's poem "at the cemetery, walnut grove plantation, south carolina, 1989" (p. 573).

PAIR IT WITH   Ben Jonson, "On My First Son" (p. 674).

Samuel Hazo

For Fawzi in Jerusalem   (p. 665)

WORKS WELL FOR   Form; sounds; tone.

ENTRY POINTS   Some students find parts of the poem confusing — the first few lines, particularly. You might start by asking if anything is unclear, and ask someone to give a brief summary of what happened. Be sure they are clear that the speaker is returning home from Jerusalem, not going to Jerusalem. He is leaving the Middle East ("a world too old to name" — line 1) and flying back to the United States ("Columbus' mistake" — line 4).

You might ask students to identify several levels of conflict, both interior and exterior.

This is a poem of address. What makes that approach to the subject more effective than writing it in, say, third person *about* Fawzi?

Ask students to describe Fawzi. What does he represent? What is he like? What is his experience both in the past and present? Why is the speaker so drawn to him, obsessed with him? Ask what students think are the reasons Fawzi "never kept / the coins I offered you" (ll. 16–17) and why, in the final stanza, the speaker says he lives Fawzi's loss. Why does the speaker refer to Fawzi as "my friend"?

Why does the speaker say in the last stanza, "But what could praying do?" (l. 41)?

Discuss what the speaker is experiencing as an Arab American, one who is a member of this cultural tradition but living in another country. Have any of the students who have had similar experiences talk about them and relate them to those of the speaker. Ask what makes this poem both timely and timeless.

The poem uses many traditional formal elements: rhyme, iambic tetrameter, regular stanza structure. Discuss what these add to the poem, what roles they play, what effects they have, and why they are appropriate.

PAIR IT WITH   Naomi Shihab Nye, "The Small Vases from Hebron" (p. 697).

Seamus Heaney

Digging   (p. 667)

WORKS WELL FOR   Images; sounds.

ENTRY POINTS   Here's a wonderful poem to discuss if you have students who are first-generation college students. Invite them to compare their experiences and the way they feel with that of the speaker. Ask them to consider what the speaker means by the use of the word *digging*.

Discuss the complexity of the relationship between the son and the father and also the grandfather.

Discuss the simile in the first couplet: "snug as a gun." What associations do students think can be made with that simile?

Ask what the students think the speaker implies by the last two lines when he says, "The squat pen rests. / I'll dig with it." Dig for what?

PAIR IT WITH   Li-Young Lee, "Eating Alone" (p. 486).

George Herbert

The Pulley   (p. 668)

WORKS WELL FOR   Form; word play.

ENTRY POINTS   Ask the class to summarize the little creation myth Herbert has devised and to give several reasons why God might not want to give humans rest. See if anyone notices a variation on Pandora's box — in this case, something being deliberately left in the glass instead of something inadvertently escaping from the box.

It is striking that nowhere in the poem is a link to the title suggested. Make sure students understand what a pulley is. Then ask students about its relation to what the poem is about.

Notice the pun on "rest" and "restlessness" in lines 16 and 17.

PAIR IT WITH   T. S. Eliot, "Journey of the Magi" (p. 643).

David Hernandez

The Butterfly Effect   (p. 668)

WORKS WELL FOR   Humor; irony; figurative language.

ENTRY POINTS   Students may need to be told about the idea that weather in one part of the world, for example, can be affected by the simple flapping of a butterfly's wings in another part of the planet. After doing so, discuss the use of this idea in the poem as well as what metaphorical implications the students may discern from this idea.

Invite students to consider the speaker's use of the "butterfly effect" in various ways: as explanation, excuse, blame, reason, self-acquittal, realization, permission, liberation.

Ask them to discuss whether the poem is comic, serious, comically serious, seriously comic, or some other weaving of attitudes. What leads them to think one way or another? What makes deciding difficult or impossible?

The speaker's tone is richly ironic. This can be difficult to describe other than saying that "the speaker's tone is ironic." Billy Collins suggests that an ironic tone means that the speaker is feeling many or at least several things at once, some of which are contradictory. Have the students list what they think the speaker is feeling, and also what they think his attitudes are toward everything he attends to in the poem. Then ask them to discuss what in the poem supports their conclusions.

Discuss what the speaker means when he says in lines 15–17, "when I rewind my life, / starting from a point when my heart / was destroyed, I see the dominoes rising."

Contemporary writers often lament that it is all but impossible to write a love poem: so many have been written. How can one find a fresh approach? Students, however, listen to love song after love song. Have them discuss this observation. Then discuss what makes this poem fresh.

Discuss what makes the poem's last moment so wonderfully absurd and believable.

This poem should connect well to the experience of many in the class. Have the students relate their own "butterfly effect stories." Or use this as a writing assignment.

PAIR IT WITH   Thylias Moss, "Tornados" (p. 556).

Robert Herrick

To the Virgins, to Make Much of Time   (p. 669)

WORKS WELL FOR   *Carpe diem*; figurative language; sounds.

ENTRY POINTS   This is perhaps the most famous poem of the *carpe diem* tradition in English. Students have probably read, if not studied, it before and are likely to enjoy rereading it. Invite students to talk about what makes it so memorable and successful. Is it the way the advice is expressed? Or is it the advice itself? (Is what the poem asserts true, that life goes downhill after thirty, or after twenty? Some other folks would contest that assertion vigorously). What does the poem advise: Live it up while you're young?

In Herrick's day, marriage was the most sensible and practical thing for which a young woman could aspire. Things are much different today. Does the poem adapt to new situations? Does its central meaning have universal significance or application?

A. E. Housman in "To an Athlete Dying Young" uses "rose" in a key line about the fleeting nature of time: "And early though the laurel grows / It withers quicker than the rose." Herrick uses "rosebuds" in line 1. Ask students to discuss the difference in meaning and effect. (The race imagery in line 7 also links Housman's poem to this one — Herrick's refers to the sun, but the journey archetype carries the significance over to humanity.)

Have the class consider the organization of the poem's content. Is the arrangement of the stanzas important? What would happen to the effect if the stanzas were switched to a different order?

PAIR IT WITH   Audre Lord, "Hanging Fire" (p. 509).

Geoffrey Hill

In Memory of Jane Fraser   (p. 669)

WORKS WELL FOR   Structure; figurative language.

ENTRY POINTS   This can be a useful poem for discussing the subtleties in a work. The tone is muted. The images are quietly evocative. Understatement appears throughout the poem. The class could talk about the effects of those approaches, what makes such usage powerful in this poem, what makes it appropriate. What do the images evoke in the reader, what associations cluster around each?

Ask students to identify gaps that they filled as they read. Which gaps are particularly subtle? Have the students explain how they did so.

Focus on the speaker. Discuss the complexity of the speaker's voice and tone. Is there any way to discern and articulate what the speaker is feeling?

What in the poem could be used to support conclusions about the speaker's feelings, attitudes, voice, and tone?

Rhyme is especially important in this poem. What is its purpose? What meaning could one give to it? What does it suggest in relation to what the speaker must be feeling and going through? Ask students to explain what makes the rhymes seem particularly striking, appropriate, and effective.

There is one off rhyme, in the final stanza. Ask students what they make of it. Why does it seem striking, unsettling, and appropriate?

What makes this poem so cold? Yes, the snow, but what else? And what meanings might be aligned with such cold?

Discuss whether the students think that "pane" is a play on words. Do they find it distracting or effective?

The poem ends on a stunningly stark final line. Discuss what that causes in the reader and in the poem itself. Ask students how they reacted to the last line and how they would explain it in a way that relates to the poem as a whole.

The poem is written in iambic tetrameter. This is an excellent poem to show students the way meter and rhythm work together, are different and yet coordinated. Ask several students to read the poem aloud giving attention to but not overemphasizing its metrical quality. Then discuss with them what the meter adds to the poem.

PAIR IT WITH   Judith Ortiz Cofer, "Cold as Heaven" (p. 558).

Linda Hogan

The History of Red   (p. 670)

WORKS WELL FOR   Myth; imagery; lines.

ENTRY POINTS   Many students initially find this a difficult poem. You may need to work through it with them, clarifying the movement of its thought. Lines 1–23 deal with origins and birth, which keep recurring in imagery throughout the poem; 24–36 deal with hunting; 37–55 deal with medicine; 56–66 deal with war, again, and death and survival; 67–90 deal with love and fire and home (the cave — that is, tent — of bison skin in which the speaker lives). Each topic relates in one way or another to various examples of "red."

One way to approach this is to ask about various ways Hogan looks at red. What is it about red that makes it particularly appropriate for what she has to say? What ironies do the students discern in relation to the color and its use in the poem? Which of Hogan's visions of red are ones that strike the students as a new way of perceiving or as particularly provocative?

Suggest that students consider the violence in the poem. So much is made of the use of violence in contemporary culture. Ask them to discuss what distinguishes Hogan's use of violence, why it is effective, important, and necessary. Discuss how she handles it. Why is it not gratuitous?

Throughout the poem, Hogan gives the reader powerfully graphic depictions. She then ends with a terse, straightforward assertion. Discuss what the speaker is saying as well as the speaker's tone and attitude. What does the speaker stand for? What does the speaker mean in the last three lines by "This life in the fire, I love it, / I want it, / this life"?

The poem combines personal history with personal mythology, affirming one's own history instead of giving the usual attention to "big history," and seeing one's own life in mythic terms. Have the students read the poem in this light. Then discuss the ways Hogan weaves history and mythology together as well as what makes this weaving effective and appropriate.

What makes this poem's coming out from a native culture so important? How does knowing the history and experience of native peoples impact and affect the students' reading of the poem? Discuss whether it is possible to read the poem without that context.

PAIR IT WITH   Adrienne Rich, "Diving into the Wreck" (p. 710).

A. E. Housman

To an Athlete Dying Young   (p. 672)

WORKS WELL FOR   Archetypes; sounds; meter.

ENTRY POINTS   Many students find this poem appealing, perhaps because it deals with an athlete. Ask students to respond to its central point, the ironic claim that the young athlete who died is fortunate because he did not outlive his fame. Do they think outliving fame is a significant problem for famous athletes or pop stars?

The poem works so well in part because of its use of archetypes. Ask students if the poem's effect would change if the young man had been a cricket player or rugby player instead of a runner. They may suggest that a runner is important because it connects to the "journey" archetype, particularly in the way line 5 universalizes the experience: "the road all runners come." See if they conclude that "runners" there refers not just to all athletes but to all human beings.

Ask students to focus on repetitions within the poem (such as "shoulder-high" in lines 4 and 6, "town" in line 1 and "Townsman" in line 8, "shady" in line 13 and "shade" in line 22, "threshold" in line 7 and "sill" in line 22) and comment on their effect (unifying the two parallel situations of cheering the winner and mourning the fallen).

The most famous lines in the poem are 11–12, "And early though the laurel grows / It withers quicker than the rose." Ask students to discuss the pairing of "laurel" and "rose" — what does each suggest in itself? What do they convey together?

PAIR IT WITH   Geoffrey Hill, "In Memory of Jane Fraser" (p. 669).

Lawson Fusao Inada

Plucking Out a Rhythm (p. 673)

WORKS WELL FOR Images; lines; rhythm.

ENTRY POINTS This poem gives advice or instructions. Ask students to discuss whom they think the poem is addressed to and why they think the speaker is giving these instructions. What do they think would be the result of following such instructions? Do they think these instructions apply to more than one person who wants to play jazz?

Ask students to identify ironies in the poem. To what degree are we to take the poem seriously? Do any of the students think that the speaker is putting on the one addressed? If they do, what would be the speaker's purpose in doing so?

W. H. Auden said that for art to be effective it must never be sincere. Ask the students to discuss that idea in light of this poem and the attitude of the poem's speaker. This can give the opportunity to discuss the importance of attending to tone in a work.

Discuss the structure: how the poem is laid out in tight, straightforward stanzas with the lines and sentences being blunt, stark, at times disjointed and dissonant. What effects does that create? Discuss why this style is appropriate for this poem.

Suggest that students look for painterly qualities in the poem as well as cinematic qualities. It might be interesting to see the poem in light of several art forms: visual art, cinema, music. What musical instruments and what kinds of jazz does the poem make the students think of?

Discuss the "figure" in the poem. What is the point of saying that "The figure is in disguise"? Why is it that "the figure / comes to life" (ll. 19–20)?

Look at ways the poem leads one to think about what is "really life," "really alive," the relationship between art and "real life." Think about art itself as "real life" and "real life" as that which distracts from the real. What paradoxes does the poem put the reader in touch with? Discuss them.

PAIR IT WITH Ishmael Reed, "Poetry Makes Rhythm in Philosophy" (p. 709).

Ben Jonson

On My First Son (p. 674)

WORKS WELL FOR Epigraph; heroic couplets.

ENTRY POINTS Jonson's brief epigraph is a moving expression of a father's grief. It may be useful to inform or remind students that the mortality rate for infants and children was high in years before antibiotics were available. It was common for parents to guard themselves from becoming too attached to their children, lest they be hurt too much if a child should die. "Sin" in line 2 may mean "mistake," rather than indicating that Jonson felt he caused the son's death by loving him too much.

The metaphor of business in lines 3–4 is important. Ask students to discuss those lines: In what sense was the son "lent" to him?

Lines 5–8 are complex, in thought and syntax. Ask students to work through their meaning. They should be able to catch that he wishes he could give up his parental feelings. But they may find it less clear when he shouldn't be grieving over "the state he should envy" (for Jonson as a Christian, death means moving on to a better place, heaven, and it means his son has escaped life's diseases and the problems associated with old age; thus his faith and his intellect tell him he should rejoice for his son, but his emotions don't allow him to do so).

It is a poem of address to the departed son. Thus, the first part of line 9 is spoken to the son, telling him, if he is asked [who he is, presumably], "Here doth lie / Ben Jonson his best piece of poetry." Ask students to explain the line. Notice that if the quotation stops after six syllables, it answers by giving the boy's name, which was the same as his father's. If the quote goes on, it answers by affirming that this boy was the finest work created by Ben Jonson (using the Renaissance commonplace of a poem as something made; *poem* derives from the Greek *poiein*, "to make").

Ask students to explain the final line. It seems to convey the sense of emotional guardedness mentioned above, through a pun on "like": The father vows not to "want (or wish for)" too much the things he loves, and (drawing on an archaic meaning) not to let those things be too pleasing or too agreeable.

PAIR IT WITH   A. E. Housman, "To an Athlete Dying Young" (p. 672).

A. Van Jordan

The Journey of Henry "Box" Brown   (p. 675)

WORKS WELL FOR   Imagery; narrative.

ENTRY POINTS   Here's a poem rich with provocative images. They are visceral, sensuous, textured with all the senses. Ask students to consider and talk about what makes these images so strong in the poem, what it is about them and the way Jordan combines them that makes them so striking. Then discuss why they are especially appropriate for the subject matter Jordan is dealing with.

Talk about the way the poem begins, how the first line emerges from something not in the poem. Ask students to list what they think may have led to the speaker's first line and the whole poem.

Ask students to identify juxtapositions and combinations in the poem, and references to history, religion, commerce, and slavery. Why would the speaker connect these to Brown? Why does it make sense that Brown would be thinking of such references?

Discuss the violence in the poem. Why is it effective? What makes it complex rather than gratuitous? What is it about the writing that makes the reader feel the violence?

Consider why the speaker is so moved by this story. What difference does it make whether he knows and tells the story?

Direct attention to the line breaks. Notice what words Jordan places at the ends of lines. Why would Jordan emphasize these words?

Direct students' attention to the "box." Is it a symbol? If so, a symbol of what? Ask students what they associate with "box" as it is used in the poem, what ways this image adds layers of meaning to the poem.

Have the class consider different ways the ending can be read: "and his voice trembled — / asked, *Is all right within?* to which Henry, / in a trumpeted tone, replied, *All right.*"

PAIR IT WITH   Sterling A. Brown, "Riverbank Blues" (p. 616).

John Keats

Ode on a Grecian Urn   (p. 676)

WORKS WELL FOR   Ode; images; tone.

ENTRY POINTS   Discussion of this poem should start with the object it describes, an urn. It's a good idea to show the class a photo of a Greek vase (or better still an actual Greek urn, or a reproduction), so the students can visualize more readily what Keats is describing.

One definition of an urn is "a large or decorative vase, especially one with an ornamental foot or pedestal." The fact that Keats wrote "Grecian Urn" rather than "Grecian Vase" points toward a second definition, "a vessel for the ashes of the dead." Though the urn is a work of art, it was intended for a practical purpose, not as art for art's sake. Thus, the poem deals with art (the urn as a work of art, and the next-to-last line) and with death. Ask students to talk about the way the two come together (the circularity suggests the unity of art and the endlessness of eternity, for example).

The speaker addresses the figures depicted on the urn — the youths, trees, musical instruments, altar, priest, and heifer. Ask students to discuss the speaker's attitude toward those figures: Why is the speaker drawn to them? What does the speaker admire in them? He seems intrigued with their permanence — that they are unchanging, eternal. Why? What's the appeal? He calls them "forever warm . . . forever panting" (ll. 26–27). Yet in line 45 he says "Cold Pastoral!" How do the two correlate?

The most controversial aspect of the poem involves the final two lines: who speaks them and to what effect. The note on page 677 lays out different alternatives and provides a good place to start a discussion of them.

PAIR IT WITH   Benjamin Alire Sáenz, "Elegy Written on a Blue Gravestone (To You, the Archaeologist)" (p. 716).

John Keats

To Autumn   (p. 677)

WORKS WELL FOR   Personification; archetypes; imagery.

ENTRY POINTS   The poem is addressed to autumn: that autumn could receive such an address is the first evidence of personification. Ask students to point out other details that develop autumn as a person (especially in stanza 2 — have students work through the details to make sure the imagery is clear). Ask also what else is personified. (The sun as a bosom-friend of autumn is personified; spring is personified as a singer; the small gnats mourn.)

The poem depends on archetypes for part of its effect. Ask students to point out where archetypal symbols are used and to explain their effect (they should notice the seasonal archetypes of autumn and spring; they expand the poem from being just about seasons to apply to human life — the last stanza affirms that autumn — and old age — are, or can be, a rich, fruitful, satisfying time of the year and of life; spring and youth are not the only desirable ones).

The poem is rich with imagery. Have students point out examples (mostly sight imagery in stanzas 1 and 2, but predominantly images of sound in stanza 3).

PAIR IT WITH   Angelina Weld Grimké, "A Winter Twilight" (p. 550).

Etheridge Knight

Hard Rock Returns to Prison from the Hospital for the Criminal Insane   (p. 679)

WORKS WELL FOR   Narrative; details; lines.

ENTRY POINTS   Ask someone to explain what's going on in the poem. It's pretty straightforward, but some students find it tricky. Then ask students to discuss the speaker, his attitudes toward Hard Rock and the world, his tone, his language, what makes him convincing. In what ways do the students find themselves liking and not liking him? What elicits their understanding and empathy? What leads them to wonder about his credibility?

The poem's descriptions are particularly graphic. Ask students what is effective about them? Why are they not gratuitous? What about these descriptions draws in a reader rather than putting off a reader? Discuss the irony of the descriptions, their odd beauty.

If any students are acquainted with Ken Kesey's 1962 novel *One Flew over the Cuckoo's Nest*, or the 1975 film directed by Milos Forman, have them discuss the similarities and differences between it and the poem. Does the genre make a difference to any students? If so, in what ways?

What leads the reader not only to respond to the poem as an anecdote but also to sense that the poem is leading one to realize its connection to a variety of issues? In what ways is this situation metaphorical?

Discuss what the poet does to make readers care about Hard Rock besides telling us what happened to him. Do the students think one should care? Why or why not?

Discuss the impact of having the speaker tell the story about Hard Rock. The poem could have been voiced by someone distanced from the situation. What is the effect of having the speaker be an inmate?

Knight spent time in prison. Discuss if knowing that affects the students' responses to the poem. Discuss the ways the students might consider the prison a metaphor in their own lives.

PAIR IT WITH   Nazim Hik et, "Letters from a Man in Solitary" (p. 776).

Li-Young Lee

Visions and Interpretations   (p. 680)

WORKS WELL FOR   Form; images; figurative language.

ENTRY POINTS   This poems works well in class, and students find it intriguing, though difficult. A good place to begin is by asking the class to work out what's going on in the poem. Ask them to divide it into sections (to make sure they notice the change from four-line stanzas to three-line to two-line — the changes in form signal a change in subject; and to make sure they pick up on the transitional words "Truth is" in line 17 and "Even this" in line 29) and explain what is talked about in each.

As students look at stanzas 1–4, have them also look back at Li-Young Lee's poem "Eating Alone" in Chapter 11 (p. 486) and ask them about similarities. In both poems the speaker sees his father, who is no longer living. In discussing "Eating Alone" earlier in this manual (p. 61), we mentioned the Chinese cultural respect for and closeness to ancestors, and the sense of the continuing presence of the dead. That seems to inform both poems. Bring up the title: How is the speaker to interpret the experience? Was it a vision when he saw his father coming down to him? In lines 15–16 the narrator says he saw a vision — how is he to interpret it?

Ask students what "Truth is" means in line 17 (is it that the speaker is stepping back and trying to reach a more accurate and adequate description of the experience?). Interpretation (of visions and experiences generally) is difficult and complex, as line 27 admits. Again there is a vision — "dreamed / a dream" (ll. 25–26), which neither of them understood. What was the dream? Why don't they understand? Ask students why the poem laves a gap here: Are we supposed to focus not on what the dream was but on the difficulty of *understanding* (both it and many things)?

Still another attempt at understanding and explanation begins at line 29. Ask students how lines 29–40 differ from 1–16 and 17–28. (The earlier sections are narrative, with characters and a sequence of events; narrative does not seem adequate or appropriate to communicate the essence of the experience. So lines 29–40 resort to images, and interpretation is left to the reader.) Ask students what they make of lines 29–40, especially the "two griefs," the tree, the chrysanthemums, and the "old book." (They will probably want to explain these in narrative terms; you may want to suggest that they settle for feelings or emotions associated with images, even though they can't explain the story that lies behind or connects the images.)

The poem leads the reader to reflection. Discuss what the students are led to reflect on by the next-to-last stanza: "and all of my visions and interpretations / depend on what I see," and also what the image of "rain" in the last couplet leads them to think about or feel.

Lee has said that poems are about silence. Apply that idea of his to this poem. What does it reveal?

Discuss why the speaker says in line 29, "Even this is not accurate." Why would the poet write something that is not accurate? What effects does this moment have on the reader? How does it affect a reader's feelings about the speaker?

PAIR IT WITH   Sherman Alexie, "Father and Farther" (p. 1326).

Philip Levine

What Work Is   (p. 681)

WORKS WELL FOR   Lines; speaker.

ENTRY POINTS   Levine became well known for his hard-hitting, working-class poems. Ask students what in "What Work Is" exemplifies this? Ask the students to look for both direct and subtle indications.

You might introduce this poem by having each student each write down a definition of work. Then ask them to write down what they believe the speaker thinks work is. Invite various students to read what they put down and ask the class to discuss various answers. Do any ironies emerge in how the poem deals with what work is?

Have the students characterize the speaker. Describe the speaker's tone. What does it indicate about his attitude toward each thing he talks about in the poem?

Discuss the way Levine uses *you* in the poem. Who is *you*? What does this usage add to the poem? What difference would it make if Levine used a different point of view?

Ask students about the relationship between the speaker and his brother. Then ask about the relationship of the speaker to the poet. In what ways does this complicate the reading of the poem?

Why in the end does the speaker say that he does not know what work is?

PAIR IT WITH   James Baldwin, "Sonny's Blues" (p. 138).

Timothy Liu

Thoreau   (p. 682)

WORKS WELL FOR   Allusion; juxtaposition, tone.

ENTRY POINTS   If the students are not familiar with Thoreau, you will need to fill in some information about him. But after you do so, they may wonder what that has to do with the poem. The juxtaposition of the title and the poem could lead to an interesting discussion. What are the ironies both subtle and obvious in the poem? How do those relate to the reference to Thoreau?

Discuss the relationship of the speaker to his father and to his mother as well as the relationship of the father/son to the mother. What makes these all the more complicated? What might be implied by the poem's first line, the speaker's saying, "My father and I have no place to go"?

This poem lends itself to a valuable discussion of the results of different cultures interconnecting, the ambiguities and realizations that can result. The poem combines the Yankee Puritan tradition, the tradition of American rugged individualism, Asian American culture, the gay community, the culture of AIDS, and traditional Japanese. Ask students to reflect on and discuss the complexities that result from such interconnectedness.

The poem makes a sudden and surprising turn just after the quote from Thoreau. Have the students discuss what they make of this turn, why the speaker suddenly has this reflection, what it reveals about what the speaker is realizing, what it suggests about a change in his feelings.

PAIR IT WITH   Julia de Burgos, "Returning" (p. 773).

Richard Lovelace

To Lucasta, Going to the Wars (p. 683)

WORKS WELL FOR Figurative language; puns; paradox.

ENTRY POINTS This poem, like John Donne's "A Valediction: Forbidding Mourning" (p. 638), is a poem about separation, in this case a soldier departing for war. Its tone, however, is very different.

Note the pun in line 1, "unkind" as "inconsiderate, cruel, harsh" and "unnatural" (see the note to Sir Thomas Wyatt's "They flee from me," p. 756). The second meaning is important: his leaving her to go to war and protect her is a natural act.

Ask students to discuss the imagery of "nunnery," "chaste," and "quiet" in lines 2 and 3. What is implied in the contrast with "war and arms" in line 4? What is the effect of that imagery in relation to the metaphor of the "new mistress" in line 5?

What is the meaning and effect of "a stronger faith" in line 7? What is implied by bringing in the religious term *faith*? Faith in what? Stronger than what?

Ask students to resolve the paradox in the last two lines. What do the lines mean? How does his love of honor enhance his love for her? Does "adore" in line 10 seem justified?

PAIR IT WITH Nahid Rachlin, "Departures" (p. 371).

Robert Lowell

Skunk Hour (p. 683)

WORKS WELL FOR Form (lines, stanzas); images; tone.

ENTRY POINTS Lowell was one of the most prominent of the poets often referred to as confessional poets, implying that they were, like a penitent in the confessional booth, revealing the most troubling sides of themselves. Ask the class to pick out aspects of the poem that align with this idea.

Focus on the speaker and ask the class to consider the relationship of the speaker to the poet himself. Are there any indications that they are the same? Does it matter? Discuss the speaker's character. Discuss the tone and what it reveals about the speaker's attitudes.

Suggest that students think of this as a quintessentially American poem. What part of America is being focused on? How can you tell? What attributes often associated with the United States are evident in the poem? What are the speaker's attitudes toward these? What underlying criticisms of the culture does the poem reveal?

Discuss the image of the skunk and the term *skunk hour*. If these are metaphorical or symbolic, discuss what they refer to and what further meanings they suggest.

Direct the class's attention to the famous lines "The season's ill — " and "I myself am hell" (ll. 13, 35). What might lead the speaker to say these things? What do they say about the speaker's feelings?

Discuss the speaker's relationship to his surroundings. In what ways is he commenting on the culture and in what ways is he projecting his own feelings about himself onto his surroundings?

PAIR IT WITH   T. S. Eliot, "The Love Song of J. Alfred Prufrock" (p. 645).

Heather McHugh

What He Thought   (p. 684)

WORKS WELL FOR   Narrative; speaker; irony.

ENTRY POINTS   Ask someone to describe the setting of the poem, the speaker's situation within the setting, and what happens. In what ways does this setting affect the speaker? Discuss the speaker's characterizations of the others in the group. What is the speaker's attitude toward each? How can you tell? How do you feel about her attitudes?

When asked what is the truth, the speaker blurts out in lines 40–41, "'The truth / is both, it's both,'" and then acknowledges "But that / was easy. That was easiest to say" (ll. 41–42). Why does she realize this? What makes that easiest to say? Ask students to discuss the speaker's answer in light of their own experiences in such settings, especially in academic settings.

Use this poem about poetry as an opportunity to initiate a discussion of poetry itself: the essence of poetry, the necessity of poetry, its role, its purpose, what it can say that nothing else can.

Have a student describe the way the poet has written the poem. Then ask the class to discuss what makes it a poem rather than an anecdote broken into lines.

Ask students to discuss what they make of or think of the ending of the poem, "poetry is what / he thought, but did not say," and how they themselves connect to it.

PAIR IT WITH   Marianne Moore, "Poetry" (p. 694).

Claude McKay

America   (p. 686)

WORKS WELL FOR   Structure (sonnet); figurative language; tone.

ENTRY POINTS   Ask a student to describe the speaker, paying particular attention to the tone and the heightened diction. What might these reveal about the speaker? Ask students to characterize and evaluate the speaker's attitudes toward America.

The poem is written by an African American and deals with his stance toward America. It is written in perhaps the most Anglo of forms, the sonnet. Ask students if they find something ironic about this. And ask them to come up with several reasons McKay might have had for writing the poem as a sonnet. (For example, he could have used the form as a metaphor for oppression or containment or the forces that restrain the voice of the African American. He could have been showing that a black poet can appropriate English forms. He could have been asserting his intelligence against those whose bigotry would deny that an African American is capable of writing a sonnet. Or he may simply have written the poem in sonnet form because that's what the material told him it wanted, without any deeper intentions.) Guide the class to consider such possibilities and ask how they lead to different readings of the poem and perhaps, as some would argue, to a different poem itself.

Discuss the last line. What are "like priceless treasures"? Why does the speaker see them "sinking in the sand"?

Look closely at the rhyming words. What can one infer from which words he chose to rhyme, from what the rhyming may suggest both ironically and straightforwardly, and from the fact that the rhymes are end rhymes putting even more emphasis on the word that appears at the line break?

The speaker says he has "not a shred / Of terror, malice, not a word of jeer" (ll. 9–10). Yet he says he does not have these because he stands as "a rebel fronts a king in state" (l. 8). Discuss the complexities of this statement, this stance and this idea.

PAIR IT WITH   Langston Hughes's "One Friday Morning" (p. 1249) or "Freedom's Plow" (p. 1258).

Clarence Major

Young Woman   (p. 687)

WORKS WELL FOR   Speaker; tone; irony.

ENTRY POINTS   Ask someone to describe the relationship between the speaker and the "young woman." Why does he love her? In what ways does he praise her, support and affirm her? What is it about her that causes him to respect her? What does he hope for her?

Who is the *you* in the poem? Invite the class to discuss various possibilities for who or what the *you* could be.

There are several particularly alluring lines in this poem, lines that lead the reader to wonder. Ask students to respond to the following lines:

old people are spending their last days / deep in your life. (ll. 2–3)

What kind of lady can you become? (l. 11)

Who are you? Where can you live? (l. 15)

Husbands are wild and helpless! (l. 19)

Why is line 16, "*Remember your grandfather's mule?*," in italics? Why is that question asked? What does it mean to say something like this? Have the students write down an equivalent to that line from their own lives and family history, and ask them to comment on what the phrase or image they wrote means to them.

Invite students to discuss why the speaker says at the end, "Still I love you — / and want to marry you" (ll. 20–21)? How do the students read and react to the word *still*?

PAIR IT WITH Jamaica Kincaid, "Girl" (p. 283).

Christopher Marlowe

The Passionate Shepherd to His Love (p. 687)

WORKS WELL FOR Sounds; images; *carpe diem*.

ENTRY POINTS Students generally like this light, beautifully written love poem. It illustrates well the uses of imagery, sound, and meter, blending them into a melodious song that appeals to the romantic in almost anyone. Invite students to pick out the features that make the poem effective at what it attempts to do.

It also illustrates nicely the pastoral tradition, with shepherds busy (or not busy) with almost anything except tending sheep. It draws on idyllic rural imagery that is thoroughly conventional, but in the context that is what seems called for and is what we expect. Note also that the poem is set in May, with its associations of birth, newness, and growth.

PAIR IT WITH Sir Walter Ralegh, "The Nymph's Reply to the Shepherd" (p. 707).

Andrew Marvell

To His Coy Mistress   (p. 688)

WORKS WELL FOR   Denotation and connotation; figurative language; rhythm; allusion; *carpe diem.*

ENTRY POINTS   This is a beautifully structured poem. Begin by asking students to describe the point of the poem as a whole (presumably they will recognize it as a seduction poem) and then to summarize the content and logic of its three sections (one hopes they will recognize it as a tightly knit argument in three steps — "Had we," "But," "Now therefore" — and be able to explain the speaker's point in each step).

Focus on rhythm and tone in each section. Ask students to characterize the rhythm in each section and to point out techniques that affect the rhythm and the attendant tone (the first slow-paced and low-keyed; the second faster and more intense; the third still more rapid and urgent). Have them notice syntax and punctuation, as sentences get longer and caesuras less frequent in the second and third sections and commas replace the semicolons of the opening section.

This is an effective poem for studying denotation and connotation, and for exercises on using the *Oxford English Dictionary.* Students could be asked to find contemporary usage of "mistress," "complain," "quaint," and "transpires," for example, and to consider connotations of many words in the first section, including the juxtaposed "Ganges" and "Humber."

It's also a good poem for allusions, both classical (the allusion to Helios behind "Time's winged chariot") and biblical (in the final line).

And you might ask students to discuss their reaction to the poem's argument (and method of argument). It is a playful, amusing poem in many respects; but see if some students find it at least slightly offensive as well, perhaps because of the aggressiveness and brutality — physical and intellectual — of the final section.

PAIR IT WITH   Kamala Das, "In Love" (p. 632).

Orlando Ricardo Menes

Letter to Mirta Yáñez   (p. 690)

WORKS WELL FOR   Images; lines; tone.

ENTRY POINTS   While this poem is a "letter" addressed to Mirta Yáñez, there is a sense that it is an "open letter," meant for others as well. What in the poem gives this sense? Ask students to discuss to whom, and about what, they think the speaker is talking, and what the speaker feels is "incredibly ironic" about the title *Some Place in Ruins.*

Ask someone to explain what the speaker is so distressed about and cares about (and how we can tell). Ask someone to describe the tone of voice. What supports that description? What does the tone reveal about the speaker's attitudes?

Consider the difference between the classical idea of ruins and a place that is now in ruins. Why does this difference matter to the speaker?

The poem juxtaposes ideas of beauty and ugliness. What are the speaker's ideas of each? Make sure to think about both the inner and outer worlds.

Ask students to discuss the last section of the poem where the speaker says, "The world / has scarcely noticed / your destruction, / invisible behind bars / of sugar cane." What does the metaphor "bars / of sugar cane" suggest?

PAIR IT WITH   Ricardo Pau-Llosa, "Years of Exile" (p. 700).

Czeslaw Milosz

It Was Winter   (p. 691)

WORKS WELL FOR   Myth; archetype; tone.

ENTRY POINTS   The poem is very complex in the way it weaves together various events both historical and personal. Invite students to discuss why they think these are placed together in the poem and what the resulting effects are. You may need to explain the story of Donner Pass (or ask if a student can tell it): a group of eighty-nine farmers and adventurers left Independence in April 1846 to go to California, but were stranded by early storms in the Truckee basin of the Sierra Nevada mountains; a few got out through what is now known as Donner Pass, but by the time they could return with help, only forty-eight were still alive, having subsisted on what provisions they had left, hides from their oxen, and eventually the bodies of their dead friends and relatives.

Consider the profound depth of connections that the speaker feels. Pay particular attention to the tonality of the poem. How would students describe it? Try asking them to compare it to a type of music or musical instrument.

There is a mythic quality to this poem. What gives it that resonance? Ask students to discuss the significance of the season of winter as a central image in the poem. Does it carry archetypal significance?

The poem has an inner structure that is richly imagistic. Ask students to list the range of senses invoked in the poem. Ask them to discuss what that range suggests about what the speaker values and what it evokes as one reads the poem.

The speaker identifies with certain people in the poem. Which? What does that suggest about what the speaker cares about?

Ask students to discuss the speaker's sense of the place of human beings in the world. How can we tell from the poem what the speaker considers the human condition? Consider the idea or theme of exile. From what is one exiled in this poem? What is an exile? Ask why the speaker feels grateful in lines 50–51, "I feel grateful / For every pebble."

PAIR IT WITH   Reza Baraheni, "Autumn in Tehran" (p. 772).

John Milton

When I consider how my light is spent   (p. 692)

WORKS WELL FOR   Form (sonnet); allusions; figurative language; speaker.

ENTRY POINTS   This poem can be discussed apart from its biographical context, but doing so costs it much of its power. Milton went blind in 1652, in his mid-forties, perhaps from congenital reasons, or perhaps (as he thought) from putting in so much time as spokesperson for the government that came to power after the execution of Charles I. For a person who had devoted his life to reading, writing, research, and scholarship — that "one talent" he possessed now rendered "useless" — the loss of sight was a devastating blow. This poem is part of his reaction.

The poem opens with a striking metonymy — "light" substituted for "sight" — which sets up the "dark" of line 2 — darkness of blindness, yes, but also the darkness of the world about him. He saw the world divided sharply into the darkness of the repressive monarchy and constraining Church of England, and the light of the republic established after the Civil War and the replacement of the Church of England by the Presbyterians as the dominant church. But Milton was aware that the political and religious causes in which he had invested so much of his time and himself were also flawed: He had fought against narrowness and repression, but the side he supported was now turning narrow and repressive.

Milton was a deeply religious person, deeply Christian despite arguably unorthodox positions on some doctrinal issues. His response came in biblical terms, drawing on the passages cited in the footnote on page 692. A personified patience replies to his fears and complaints that God does not need him and does not depend on his efforts. Although he can no longer travel widely as God's courier, others are available to fill such roles. He can instead serve as a footman, waiting to be told what to do. He must be patient and wait to be told what he is to do.

Ask students to look up the biblical passages and to discuss how Milton is using them and how they are meaningful and appropriate. Ask them also to discuss the use of figurative language and how it works in the poem.

PAIR IT WITH   Anita Endrezze, "The Girl Who Loved the Sky" (p. 476).

Gary Miranda

Love Poem (p. 693)

WORKS WELL FOR   Diction, figurative language; form (sonnet).

ENTRY POINTS   Dan Carter's student paper, "A Slant on the Standard Love Sonnet" (p. 592), discusses various "slants" in the poem: its unusual handling of sonnet form, its unique approach as a love poem, and its use of slant rhyme, for example. Emily Dickinson has a famous dictum about poetry, "Tell the truth, but tell it slant." You might ask students what her line might mean and how it applies to this poem.

Note the rhyme scheme. Ask students to discuss the words that rhyme, how emphasizing them through the rhyme itself as well as it being end rhyme adds to the poem. Consider the use of slant rhyme and how it is appropriate for the poem's take on love. What does the rhyme add to the reader's experience of the poem?

Ask the class to think about the possibilities for simile and metaphor in the poem. In what ways does that approach to the subject give the reader a fresh way of looking at and considering love? If one way of thinking of metaphor is that it "changes the world" by the slightest or grandest of gestures or realizations, in what ways does this poem fulfill that notion?

Invite the class to reflect on why the speaker loves the word *angle*. Extend the conversation to discuss words that students realize affect their own worlds. Have them make a list and then talk about these.

Another startling metaphorical moment is when the speaker realizes that listening to eighteenth-century dances makes him think of "you untangling / blueberries, carefully, from their dense branches" (ll. 13–14). Ask students to discuss this way of thinking of metaphor as an unusual connection and what that connection leads to. Have students record some moments when they have had such experiences and discuss these.

PAIR IT WITH   Kamala Das, "In Love" (p. 632).

Janice Mirikitani

For a Daughter Who Leaves (p. 693)

WORKS WELL FOR   Images; figurative language.

ENTRY POINTS   Ask someone to summarize what the poem is about and how the epigraph relates to the poem.

Ask if students think that the speaker is the same as the mother in the poem. What would support one's conclusion either way? Ask them to discuss the relationship between the mother and daughter and what the speaker is going through, paying attention to the rich mix of feelings embodied in the poem.

The title indicates that the poem is likely a poem of address. Is it? To whom? If so, what supports that conclusion? If not, why not, and why then that title?

There are many images and moments that lead one to fill in the gaps. Have the students point out which images and moments led them to respond in a way to fill in what is not there.

The images are particularly striking, luminous, and culturally connected. Discuss the various roles they play in the poem and the effect they have on the reader both individually and cumulatively. What changes in cultural ideas and conditions between the two generations are revealed in the poem? Discuss what supports what students notice.

There are several powerful tensions in the poem. List them and then discuss their impact and what they lead the reader to realize and reflect on.

Ask the students to think of a cultural artifact that is significant in the way or ways it links generations in their families. This could be an artifact from a recognized culture or one that is private. Have a conversation about the ways this artifact of theirs compares to that in the poem and also talk about the significance and the emotions connected with this artifact.

PAIR IT WITH Wang Ping, "Opening the Face" (p. 702).

Marianne Moore

Poetry (p. 694)

WORKS WELL FOR Structure (stanzas, lines); diction; images.

ENTRY POINTS This is a good poem for talking about poetry itself. Ask students to list some things that, according to the poem, are poetry or are characteristic of poetry. Then discuss what things are not. Talk about the speaker's tone and the attitudes revealed by the tone. Discuss what the speaker means by "genuine" in lines 3 and 29 and what the "raw material of poetry in / all its rawness" (ll. 26–27) is. Why would demanding these prove that one is interested in poetry? Ask how the class responds to a poet writing a poem about disliking poetry and discuss their reactions.

Ask students to pick out what for them are particularly provocative images and have them talk about what those images mean in light of the poem and the speaker. For example, talk about what it means to be "'literalists of / the imagination'" (ll. 21–22) and what "'imaginary gardens with real toads in them'" (l. 24) are.

The poem is structurally complex, with divisions into stanzas — some five lines, some six — and a variety of line lengths — some short, some very long. Ask students to reflect on and talk about the value and effect of the form in a poem about poetry. Discuss also the internal structure of the poem, including the role and effectiveness of the lists.

Moore revised this poem several times. One of its versions is composed of only the first three lines:

> I, too, dislike it: there are things that are important beyond all this fiddle.
>   Reading it, however, with a perfect contempt for it, one discovers in
>   it after all, a place for the genuine.

Talk about the differences in effect between the two versions. See if some of the students prefer one version over the other and talk about why.

PAIR IT WITH   Heather McHugh, "What He Thought" (p. 684).

Robert Morgan

Mountain Bride   (p. 695)

WORKS WELL FOR   Narrative; voice; irony.

ENTRY POINTS   This is a narrative poem. Have a student summarize the startling, unsettling tale. Ask students to consider what beyond shock is the effect of this poem.

Discuss the voice of the poem. What makes it appropriate? What prevents it from being a stereotype?

One could say this poem is an example of southern gothic. Ask a student to look up a definition and explain what makes the poem fit that category. It might be interesting to compare it to other southern gothic works, a Flannery O'Connor story, for example.

Ask students to comment on the stanza structure of the poem. What does it add to the poem? What difference would it make if the poem were not written in stanzas? How are the stanzas similar to and different from ballad stanzas? Does this poem fit in other ways to the ballad tradition?

PAIR IT WITH   Flannery O'Connor, "A Good Man Is Hard to Find" (p. 341).

Duane Niatum

First Spring   (p. 696)

WORKS WELL FOR   Figurative language; form.

ENTRY POINTS   Ask someone to sum up what the speaker is going through, what inner and external conflicts is he dealing with. Ask why the title is "First Spring." Why "first"?

The poem embodies a profound sense of unity, connection, oneness of the human and the natural world, even so far as to say that they are not distinct. And yet, there is great lament within the poem. There is not the celebrative tone usually associated with this way of being in the world. Ask students to discuss the speaker's concerns and attitudes, and the ironies in this depiction of the interconnectedness of all things.

What is the speaker's relationship to the past, to the elders, to the present, to his situation now compared to what it would have been before his culture was destroyed, to the natural world? What makes this poem an expression of native culture both present and past? Why is that central to the full understanding of the poem?

Ask about the speaker's relationship to his lost love. In what ways is that integral to the poem, to all that the speaker talks about, deals with? Discuss why the speaker says, "*Sorry, sorry, I'm too busy / with the friends still left. / I'll call you.*" (ll. 15–17).

Why does the speaker say, "Why tell her they're the sparrows at the feeder, / bees in the lilacs, roses, and plum trees, / books on the shelves and everywhere, / paintings on the walls, sculptures in the corners, / wind at the door and on the roof?" (ll. 19–23)? What is the "they"?

What is the "it" in the last seven lines of the poem?

This is a good poem for helping students discover metaphorical content that is not very obvious. Have the students point out the various figures and discuss their power in the poem and on the reader.

PAIR IT WITH   Jim Barnes, "Return to La Plata, Missouri" (p. 577).

Naomi Shihab Nye

The Small Vases from Hebron   (p. 697)

WORKS WELL FOR   Figurative language; form (external and inner).

ENTRY POINTS   Naomi Shihab Nye is Palestinian American. Her grandmother lived her whole life in the West Bank. Ask students whether that information affects their reading of the poem, and if so, how.

Nye says that most poems are political and that a person's carrying out her or his daily work in the midst of conflict is an affirmative political act. Invite the class to consider the ways her ideas are reflected in the poem.

The poem has several startling moments, arresting twists and associations. Ask the class to point them out and to discuss ways they affect a reader. There are two single line moments in the poem. Why are they singled out? Discuss their relationship to each other. The poem is set against the terrible situation in the Middle East. What does the poem affirm within these circumstances? Discuss whether these affirmations are rationalizations.

This poem is a good one to study inner structure. Trace the movement of the poem, how it begins with the beautiful, colorful description of the small vases and ends with the horrific and colorful description of the brothers. Discuss how the poet structures the varied images in the poem while at the same time maintaining a seamless movement.

Ask students to point out figures in the poem. What is their impact? Discuss whether that way of presenting the situation is more powerful and truthful than writing in a straightforward way. This could possibly lead the students to a discussion of the difference between the facts as given in the news media and the truths embodied in this poem or any poem.

Ask students to discuss lines 30–31, "a crushed glass under the feet / still shines."

PAIR IT WITH   Samuel Hazo, "For Fawzi in Jerusalem" (p. 665).

Dwight Okita

In Response to Executive Order 9066 (p. 698)

WORKS WELL FOR   Voice; speaker; tone; irony.

ENTRY POINTS   The class might need to be told about the internment camps. After explaining what they were, ask the students to discuss the use of "Relocation Centers" as a euphemism for the camps. Discuss why Denise would think that the speaker is "giving secrets / away to the Enemy" (ll. 18–19).

This poem gives an opportunity to discuss the handling of the speaker. Would it be fair to say it is akin to a naïve speaker in fiction? It is all the more complex given that the poet is male and the poem's speaker is a young girl. Ask someone to characterize her. What is gained for the poet by having the speaker be female and fourteen? What does the tone reveal about her attitude? Discuss what she cares about and if the poet uses these things to imply a political statement.

The poem also offers the opportunity to discuss the issue of whether the voice in a poem is that of the poet or is a way for the poet to state her or his feelings, views, ideas. In this poem, that could make a difference in how the poem is read. Discuss if there is any way to support the idea that the poet is using this speaker to voice his own feelings.

Ask students to discuss the last stanza — what makes it especially poignant? What is the effect of its returning to an earlier reference in the poem?

PAIR IT WITH   Countee Cullen, "Incident" (p. 519).

Mary Oliver

Goldenrod   (p. 699)

WORKS WELL FOR   Handling of words (word play); imagery; sound.

ENTRY POINTS   This poem is a fine piece to work with in examining various types of word play. Ask students to find and discuss unusual combinations of words, fresh uses of alliteration, and the prevalence of assonance and consonance. How do these enrich the poem? How are they appropriate to the tone and subject?

Consider the speaker's attitude toward the natural world and toward human consciousness, and the relationships between the two. Could the goldenrod be considered a synecdoche? Why or why not? It's somewhat uncommon for a speaker of a poem to come right out and say that she or he is happy, as this speaker does. Ask students why the speaker says it, and what makes saying it acceptable, believable in the poem? Discuss why this straightforward statement is not corny or sentimental. What does the speaker mean by saying, "And what has consciousness come to anyway, so far, / that is better than these light-filled bodies?" (ll. 28–29)?

Ask students to talk about the structure of the poem. Does the handling of lines and stanzas seem attractive and effective to them?

Discuss the poem in terms of audience. Is there a limited audience for such a poem as this? Why? Why not?

PAIR IT WITH   Gerard Manley Hopkins, "God's Grandeur" (p. 524); Xu Gang, "Red Azalea on the Cliff" (p. 785).

Michael Ondaatje

Biography   (p. 700)

WORKS WELL FOR   Form; images; sound.

ENTRY POINTS   The poem seems on the surface, at least, pretty straightforward. Ask someone to summarize the content. Then ask the class to discuss the title: the relationship of the title to the speaker and to the poet, or the possibilities for what the poem could be a biography of, or whether the poem is giving a definition of biography.

Discuss the relationship and comparison between the reality of dream life and waking life. Ask the students if they think the poem is also dealing with that relationship in a broader context than the dog and why. Could the poem be considered a synecdoche? Think of Robert Frost's saying that he considered himself a "synecdochist" (p. 552). How might his idea apply to this poem?

Ask students to discuss the line "tacked to humility all day" (l. 5) as applicable to the dog and to anything else they can see its being associated with.

Have students list and then discuss the ironies in the poem. In what ways do they extend beyond an application to the dog? Discuss the implications of the children being "unaware that she / tore bulls apart, loosed / heads of partridges, / dreamt blood" (ll. 9–12).

PAIR IT WITH   Dahlia Ravikovitch, "Clockwork Doll" (p. 782).

Ricardo Pau-Llosa

Years of Exile   (p. 700)

WORKS WELL FOR   Images; figurative language; magic realism.

ENTRY POINTS   For the poem to achieve its best effect, you should show students prints or images (available on the Internet) of paintings by Humberto Calzada, or ask them to find examples of his work themselves. In either case, ask someone to describe the connection between the paintings and the poem.

One way to enter and read a poem is by following what the speaker is going through. Ask students to try applying this idea to the poem. Consider who the *we* might be in the poem. How does water fit into things, and what is the relationship of the title to the body of the poem?

If students have read an example of magical realism, such as Gabriel García Márquez's "A Very Old Man with Enormous Wings" (p. 415), Helena María Viramontes's "The Moths" (p. 391), or Agha Shahid Ali's "I Dream It Is Afternoon When I Return to Delhi" (p. 597), ask if this poem could be another example of the type. What in the poem would support categorizing the poem as such? How does seeing it that way help in understanding the poem?

The poem is rich with figures. Have the students point them out and then discuss the role of each in the poem.

Discuss the lines at the beginning of the third stanza: "And we waited for the new day / when losses would turn to stories." Story is a way for the self to prevail over traumatic events. How does that idea connect with the lines mentioned in the previous entry point?

Ask students to list the realizations in the final stanza and discuss them in terms of the poem and in the ways the students relate to them.

One could say that this poem is an example of personal mythology, a work that transforms events from one's own life into mythic form. Ask students to discuss this idea as it applies to the poem and then suggest that they write their own personal mythology poem using a particular unifying image to represent what their experience was like.

Focus on the last sentence — "We create, we are free / now that we have lost count of everything" — and discuss it in terms of the poem, the speaker, and the students' lives.

PAIR IT WITH   Orlando Ricardo Menes, "Letter to Mirta Yáñez" (p. 690).

Gustavo Pérez Firmat
José Canseco Breaks Our Hearts Again   (p. 701)

WORKS WELL FOR   Form; figurative language (simile, synecdoche).

ENTRY POINTS   José Canseco, born in Havana in 1964, played major league baseball for seventeen seasons (1985–2001), the majority of them with the Oakland Athletics. Discuss why the poet chose him for the central image in the poem. What might he represent? You may need to give the students more information about Canseco or ask them to look him up on the Web, bring to class what they found, and apply the information to the poem. This would also give the opportunity to discuss the advantages and limitations of using allusion in a poem, especially an allusion that one can't assume is known by a wide audience.

Ask students to discuss the father/son relationship — what they think is implied about the quality of this relationship, what it is built on, and how Canseco's career and life apply positively or problematically to the relationship.

The poem has been anthologized in a collection of poems that deal with American diaspora. Discuss why this poem fits that context.

Ask students how they read lines 13–14, "(He had to be Cuban, that impossible man-child, / delicate as an orchid beneath the rippling chest.)." List those readings that the students come up with and discuss the ambiguities of the lines. Talk about which of them seem right for the poem and which could lead to a misreading of the poem as a whole.

Discuss why the speaker says at the end of the poem, "I'll keep my fingers crossed for next season / when José, like a certain country I know, / will break our hearts again." Ask students to discuss what they think the speaker is hoping for in terms of his son, his own life, and his native Cuba.

PAIR IT WITH   Virgil Suárez, "A Perfect Hotspot" (p. 381).

Wang Ping
Opening the Face   (p. 702)

WORKS WELL FOR   Images; form (lines).

ENTRY POINTS   One way to enter the poem is through a discussion of conflicts within the poem. Consider conflicts between cultural ideas, between people, between generations, between the speaker and this tradition.

Ask students to discuss the speaker's attitudes toward the "'lady of wholesome fortune'" (l. 3). Make sure they base their conclusions on material from the poem as well as on what some of them may know from their own experiences. Add to the discussion the students' ideas about the relationship between the speaker and the poet, if they feel that there is one. What is the speaker going through?

Discuss what it means to "open a face" and how that idea could represent other things besides a cultural tradition.

Ask students to discuss lines 20–22, "'Don't make a sound, girl,' she whispers / to my drenched face, 'not until you bear him a son, / not until you have grandchildren.'"

After reading the poem several times and exploring all its issues, discuss the possible feelings and thoughts the speaker might have about what she is told at the end of the poem: "'When he sleeps, put your shoes / in his boots and let them sit overnight. / It'll keep him under your thumb, forever.'" Notice the insertion of the comma between "thumb" and "forever."

PAIR IT WITH   Janice Mirikitani, "For a Daughter Who Leaves" (p. 693).

Robert Pinsky

Shirt   (p. 703)

WORKS WELL FOR   Form; allusions; details (images).

ENTRY POINTS   One way to approach the poem might be to say "What's the big deal? It's just a shirt" and ask students how they think the poem responds. Guide them to see that the poem shows how no artifact exists in a vacuum, that it has profound associations, even has a history, and that anything we own is the result of a complex situation involving many people, ideas, and forces. It also reveals that we cannot remove ourselves from the social, economic, and political implications connected to anything we own. Try to get them to discuss such issues as they get into the poem.

The quotation in line 25 is from Hart Crane's "To Brooklyn Bridge," the first section of his multisection poem "The Bridge" (1930), a stanza describing how a mad person (bedlamite) jumps to his death from a bridge tower: "Out of some subway scuttle, cell or loft / A bedlamite speeds to thy parapets, / Tilting there momently, shrill shirt ballooning, / A jest falls from the speechless caravan" (ll. 17–20).

Ask the class to consider the role of the inclusion of the 1911 fire at the Triangle Shirtwaist Factory (l. 10). A video account of the fire can be found in "The Power and the People (1898–1914)," episode 4 of the series *New York: A Documentary Film*. The Web site for the series is pbs.org/wnet/newyork/series/index.html.

It's a tightly structured poem: Ask students to discuss how the form fits the poem's subject. Ask them to look for ironies in the poem. (Make sure they talk about the juxtaposition of the horrific and the beautiful.)

Pinsky uses several lists in the poem. What do they add? What is their role? What impact do they have? Is where he places the lists strategic? If so, in what way?

Point out the allusions to the poets Hart Crane and George Herbert and ask what the references to poets contribute to the work. Why these two poets?

Discuss the implied criticisms in the poem. Ask the students to discuss whether they think that the speaker and by extension Pinsky implicate their own selves in the poem's subtle critique.

Ask the class to respond to the stanza beginning with line 40: "George Herbert, your descendant is a Black / Lady in South Carolina, her name is Irma / And she inspected my shirt."

PAIR IT WITH   Zora Neale Hurston, "Sweat" (p. 263).

Sylvia Plath

Daddy   (p. 705)

WORKS WELL FOR   Speaker; tone; diction; imagery.

ENTRY POINTS   This can be a difficult poem to deal with in class because of its subject matter and intensity. We have had success with reading the poem aloud first, to be sure students hear the simple but insistent nursery rhyme–type rhythms and sound combinations. Students are taken aback by the intensity of the poem and its subject matter. They want help in understanding what is going on — why the mixture of violence, Nazi references, and devil imagery. It will probably be of most help to show them the benefits of using a psychoanalytical, and specifically Freudian, approach to the poem (point them to the summary on p. 1483).

Plath herself claimed the poem is linked to Freud. Introducing the poem in a poetry reading for BBC radio, Plath said, "The poem is spoken by a girl with an Electra complex. Her father died while she thought he was God. Her case is complicated by the fact that her father was also a Nazi and her mother very possibly part Jewish. In the daughter the two strains marry and paralyze each other — she has to act out the awful little allegory once over before she is free of it" (qtd. by A. Alvarez in *The Art of Sylvia Plath: A Symposium*, ed. Charles Newman [Bloomington: Indiana UP, 1970] 65).

Walking students through a Freudian reading maybe help them grasp what is going on: The speaker in "Daddy," as a child, entered the stage of desiring her father — viewing him as everything, idolizing him (Electra complex). To pass beyond this stage, in sexual development, she needed to separate from her father (to give up, or "kill" [l. 6], her incestuous desire for him).

Before she was able to, however, he died (l. 7). And so the speaker is caught in a situation of conflict, anxiety, and guilt: Because her father is dead, she is unable to complete the natural process of separation from him and reach a mature daughter-father relationship with him; but the desire to have such a separation (to "kill" him) creates a sense of guilt — did she *cause* his death by desiring it? — from which she now cannot escape. Thus her father, both during his life (as an authoritarian figure) and after his death, exerted a confining influence on her life — she is trapped (stanza 1) inside her fixated relationship with him, imaged as the "black shoe," which later emerges as the boot that represents Nazi oppression and male dominance over women (ll. 48–50).

The speaker's anxiety and guilt are increased by the fact that her father was a German and a Nazi, while her mother was part Jewish. Thus, her unresolved attachment to her father identifies her with behaviors she finds repulsive: the oppression of Jews, the extermination of Jews in the death camps (l. 33), the underlying violence of the Nazi movement. Her unconscious desire for her father is imaged as a universal love for the force his politics endorsed: "Every woman adores a Fascist, / The boot in the face, the brute / Brute heart of a brute like you" (ll. 48–50). She feels simultaneous attraction and revulsion, sees her father simultaneously as god and as devil (ll. 8, 54).

The speaker sees her mother both as rival and as a representative of a victimized race. She identifies with the oppressed race: "I think I may well be a Jew" (l. 35). This leaves the speaker with a deep sense of guilt, torn between desire for her father and sympathy for the people he is oppressing. Her attempted suicide (l. 58), she says, was an effort to be united with her father; it could equally be an effort to escape the tension and conflict her feelings about her father and her sense of guilt impose on her.

The attempt at suicide proving unsuccessful (ll. 61–62), she got married (l. 67) and viewed the marriage as a fulfillment of her desire to unite with her father (she identifies husband with father — l. 64 — including the brutality and oppression she claimed to love — l. 65–66). But the marriage did not work out, so the speaker broke it off — "killed" it, "killed" her husband and in the process "killed" her father (ll. 6, 71). By ending her marriage, the speaker gains freedom from her father as well as her husband. The father-husband vampire finally is dead, and the speaker is released from the guilt, confinement, and tensions of her unresolved attachment to him/them: "Daddy, daddy, you bastard, I'm through" (l. 80).

Having been shown such a reading of the poem, with its references to suicide, students are likely to ask about the extent to which the poem is autobiographical. Some details regarding the speaker in "Daddy" are similar to Plath's own life. The speaker's father was born in Poland (l. 16); so was Plath's father, in Grábow. The speaker's father apparently was a teacher (l. 51); Plath's father taught biology and German at Boston University. The speaker's father died when she was ten (l. 57); Plath's father died when she was eight. The speaker attempted suicide ten years later (l. 58); so did Plath. The speaker married a few years after that (ll. 64–67); Plath married British poet Ted Hughes in 1956. The speaker's marriage lasted seven years (l. 74) and apparently has ended (l. 71); Plath and Hughes separated in the seventh year of their marriage. The speaker is thirty years old (l. 4); so was Sylvia Plath when she wrote the poem on October 12, 1962, the day after Ted Hughes moved out.

However, Plath and the speaker are not identical. Plath's father and mother were German immigrants; her father was not a Nazi, and there is no evidence that the ancestry of either included Jews (as Plath says the speaker's did). But many would say that the voice of Sylvia Plath *can* be heard through and around the speaker's voice (refer students to the discussion of voice in Chapter 11, p. 486). The speaker's need to, and inability to, separate from her father coincides with Plath's own need to do so. The speaker projects onto her father the guilt Plath seems to have felt over Nazi atrocities because of her own German ancestry, and she herself identifies with the Jews in an effort to alleviate that guilt. In a poem written as Plath's separation from Ted Hughes was becoming final, the speaker looks back on her marriage as an effort to achieve a relation to her father and identifies her husband with her father.

Plath herself said that her actual father was not to be confused with "Daddy," cruel, destructive, "the masculine principle gone mad" (Richard Ellmann and Robert O'Clair, *The Norton Anthology of Modern Poetry*, 2nd ed. [New York: Norton, 1988] 1417). In the poem, the speaker seems to initiate the break with her husband, thus also achieving the separation from her father, which was prevented by her father's death. In real life, it was Hughes who took the initiative, reenacting what the father did twenty years earlier. Thus, although Plath does not kill her father/husband through divorce (as *in* the poem), she could be said to do so *by means of* the poem. A psychoanalytical reading could suggest that the poem serves as Plath's ritual "killing" of father and husband, the violent imagery becoming the means of, as well as the reason for, her rejection of and separation from them. The poem itself could become a vehicle to and declaration of freedom and wholeness.

A comment on the poem by A. Alvarez, "Despite Everything, 'Daddy' Is a Love Poem" (*The Art of Sylvia Plath*, ed. Charles Newman [Bloomington: Indiana UP, 1971] 66), is another way to open up discussion of the poem. Ask students to discuss how that might be, or what it suggests (such as, the intensity comes from the depth of the speaker's longing for her father; or how thin the line between love and hatred can be).

A further quotation from the Alvarez essay provides another opening: "When she first read me the poem a few days after she wrote it, she called it a piece of 'light verse'" (66). Students can be asked if they think she was being serious or ironic, and, if she was serious, what she might have meant. They may recall the effect of hearing the light rhythms and sounds when the poem was read aloud. Some students seize the "light verse" suggestion with an almost obvious sense of relief. If this is true, suggest they analyze their reaction. Are they seeking to avoid the unpleasant effects that result from regarding the poem as serious?

PAIR IT WITH Charles Bukowski, "my old man" (p. 488).

Sylvia Plath

Metaphors   (p. 707)

WORKS WELL FOR   Figurative language; form; tone.

ENTRY POINTS   The logical way to begin discussion of a riddle poem is to ask students to give the answer and explain what the clues mean. Some students may recognize it immediately; but be aware that many others will be puzzled by it (perhaps all poetry seems a riddle to them, and these images and figures can seem particularly confusing).

Once the puzzle has been solved, ask students to explain the metaphors in each line — how they "work" as figures (what is compared to, or equated with, what; why the comparison or equation is effective and meaningful).

Also direct attention to the poem's form. It is an example of syllabic verse (same number of syllables in each line, without a regular pattern of stresses). See if anyone points out the witty appropriateness of having nine lines of nine syllables each in a poem about pregnancy.

PAIR IT WITH   Jean Toomer, "Face" (p. 741).

Sir Walter Ralegh

The Nymph's Reply to the Shepherd   (p. 707)

WORKS WELL FOR   Sound; imagery; *carpe diem.*

ENTRY POINTS   While this poem can be read on its own, it works best if discussed together with Christopher Marlowe's "The Passionate Shepherd to His Love." Using the same quatrain stanzas and *aabb* rhyme scheme and echoing some of Marlowe's diction, Ralegh provides a realistic counterpart to Marlowe's highly idyllic pastoral scene.

Have both poems read aloud. Ask someone to describe what is appealing in Marlowe's poem, in content and style (see p. 140); get others to help characterize the poem effectively. Then ask students to describe Ralegh's poem and to compare it — in content and style — to Marlowe's.

One characteristic that should emerge from the discussion is an early appearance in England of the *carpe diem* theme. If students have read Marvell's "To His Coy Mistress," they might notice similarity between its opening and Ralegh's opening (probably not enough to indicate that Marvell was echoing Ralegh). And comparing Ralegh's poem to Robert Herrick's famous "To the Virgins" will bring out a good deal of common imagery, in addition to shared theme.

PAIR IT WITH   Christopher Marlowe, "The Passionate Shepherd to His Love" (p. 687); also Robert Herrick, "To the Virgins, to Make Much of Time" (p. 669), and Andrew Marvell, "To His Coy Mistress" (p. 688).

Dudley Randall
Ballad of Birmingham   (p. 708)

WORKS WELL FOR   Ballad; irony.

ENTRY POINTS   This is a poem that after a first reading reads differently. Ask students to discuss the differences between the first and subsequent readings.

List various examples and types of irony in the poem and discuss their impact in the poem and on the reader.

Compare the poem to a traditional ballad (for example, "Sir Patrick Spens") and discuss the stanza structure, the meter, the rhyme and rhyme scheme in the poem. Is the poem in every way typical of the ballad form? Discuss the ballad-like use of dialogue in the poem. What impact does it have? What would be lost in the poem were it approached without the dialogue?

Discuss the speaker's relationship to the subject, the mother and the child. What is the speaker feeling? Discuss the speaker's tone and attitude. What other tones might have been created for this poem? Discuss why this tone is effective. Discuss what other tonal approaches might also be effective.

Discuss what makes this poem not only one that preserves this terrible piece of history but also one that is relevant today. Include in the conversation the students' ideas about what makes a poem one of lasting impact and importance.

PAIR IT WITH   "Sir Patrick Spens" (p. 598).

Ishmael Reed
Poetry Makes Rhythm in Philosophy   (p. 709)

WORKS WELL FOR   Rhythm; diction; figurative language.

ENTRY POINTS   Some students may initially have difficulty following what this poem is getting at. It could be a good example for discussing what can be enjoyed and appreciated, what a reader can feel in and through it, even if one doesn't comprehend everything in it.

Ask students to consider what the poem is saying about what is privileged in society and in the academic world, and what is more valued in general. Have the students list examples from their own experience of this valuing, devaluing, and privileging, and discuss what they record. Discuss whether the students think the title is setting up an argument about poetry's value versus that of philosophy. Talk about hierarchy of values. Discuss why the intellectual world has historically elevated philosophy above poetry, words above music.

Ask them to talk about the speaker, the speaker's attitude, feelings, ideas, and realizations, and about what in the speaker's tone makes it harmonize with the poem itself.

Focus on the lines "'Rhythm makes everything move'" (l. 8) and "nature can't / do without rhythm but rhythm can / get along without nature" (ll. 18–20). Talk about how these ideas about rhythm apply to other parts of life. Perhaps have the students make a list of aspects of their lives where rhythm plays an integral part. Talk about how the conversation in the poem about rhythm fits the rhythm of the poem and how the rhythms in the poem are their own argument for being.

Ask students to discuss what is implied by lines 29–31, "All *harrumphs!* must be / checked in at / the door," and what the speaker means when he says, "'Progress,' you know" (l. 37). What views or attitudes toward progress are implied by what he says and by his tone?

Discuss the timing of Bird vanishing right after the notion of progress is raised and right before the steel band enters the room.

PAIR IT WITH Lawson Fusao Inada, "Plucking Out a Rhythm" (p. 673).

Adrienne Rich

Diving into the Wreck (p. 710)

WORKS WELL FOR Diction; figurative language; symbols; myth.

ENTRY POINTS Some students will find this poem confusing and difficult — and, granted, it is a complex and challenging work. You might begin by focusing on the allusion to Cousteau, who traveled widely as adventurer and explorer. You might suggest (as Rachel Blau DuPlessis has) that this is a journey poem, with a hero (a woman), a quest (to find and critique old myths), and a buried treasure (the buried knowledge of the "wreck" that relations between the sexes has become and a self-knowledge that can come only through diving and exploring with objectivity and openness).

Discuss the "wreck" as a figure. What figure is it? If it is a figure, talk about what it might lead one to consider as its meaning or meanings. Talk about "diving into the wreck" as a metaphorical or symbolic action. (Many critics interpret the poem as diving into the wreck of obsolete myths, the patriarchal myths that govern relations between men and women. The speaker is searching for the reality, the truths, behind the myth, on the assumption that one needs to know the old stories, the old traditions, before one can set out to change them. This poem, however, does not take the last step, of proposing change, though the androgyny of lines 72–77 points in the direction of a new myth that could replace the old.)

In light of such an interpretation, you might ask students to consider the following images, figures, or symbols and talk about what they might represent and/or what their role is in the poem:

1. The book of myths
2. The camera
3. The grave and awkward mask
4. The ladder
5. The sea
6. The damage that was done
7. The mermaid and the merman
8. The water-eaten log
9. The fouled compass

Talk about the possible meanings and implications of the lines "The words are purposes. / The words are maps" (ll. 53–54), "the thing I came for: / the wreck and not the story of the wreck / the thing itself and not the myth" (ll. 61–63), and "a book of myths / in which / our names do not appear" (ll. 92–94).

PAIR IT WITH   Joy Harjo, "She Had Some Horses" (p. 537).

Alberto Ríos

Nani   (p. 713)

WORKS WELL FOR   Words; images; speaker.

ENTRY POINTS   Ríos has said that this poem is about "talking but it's not about words," yet "words" is used eight times in it. Ask students to discuss what he means by his statement and how the poem embodies this idea. Then ask them to focus on each time "words" appears and discuss what this poem says and means about words, used literally or figuratively, especially in lines 32–33, "what were the words / I could have been, was."

Ask students to describe and discuss the relationship between Nani (the diminutive for Nana, grandmother) and her grandson. Discuss what brings these two generations together in light of the speaker's being a second-generation Hispanic American and his grandmother being the first to immigrate to the United States.

Ríos grew up on the border between Mexico and the United States. He has said that in one sense he was raised in both countries. Consider how this crossing and blending of borders reveals itself in the poem.

There are moments of magical realism in the poem. Ask someone to point them out and ask the class to discuss what they create in the poem and how they may affect a reader.

The poem is rich with sensory images. Have the class make a list of images and the senses to which they appeal, and discuss their effectiveness: What makes this range of sensate material especially appropriate for this poem?

Ask the class to discuss the poignancy of the speaker's saying, "I wonder just how much of me / will die with her, what were the words / I could have been, was" (ll. 31–33).

PAIR IT WITH   Helena María Viramontes, "The Moths" (p. 391).

Luis Rodriguez

Running to America   (p. 714)

WORKS WELL FOR   Form (lines, lists); tone.

ENTRY POINTS   Much of the power in this poem comes from its clarity and directness. Ask the class to discuss why that is so. Discuss the levels of meaning suggested by the title.

Much of the speaker's feeling is embodied and evoked by the ways the lines are written: their lengths, where they break, their relentlessness of construction and rhythm, timing. Talk about what these effects cause in terms of the feelings and mood of the speaker.

Discuss the possible connotations of the first line — "They are night shadows." What makes it effective as the first line of the poem?

While the poem is indeed written in a style that is clear and direct, the images in the poem are complex and worthy of exploration: for their implications and meanings, for their role in the poem, for their appropriateness to the subject, and for the way particular images evoke a larger picture. Ask the class to discuss what makes the images of the poem particularly powerful.

Discuss why in line 21 the speaker says about the men, "You see something like this in prisons."

In the last stanza, the speaker says that after the people have crossed the border into the United States they will "Then run to America." Discuss what Rodriguez means by this.

PAIR IT WITH   Vijay Seshadri, "The Refugee" (p. 720).

Wendy Rose

Loo-Wit   (p. 715)

WORKS WELL FOR   Figurative language; lines; sound.

ENTRY POINTS   Consider the effects of personification in the poem (especially the personifying of Mt. St. Helens). Ask students to discuss what makes this usage appropriate and meaningful in light of Native American culture.

The speaker has the voice of a traditional storyteller. Characterize this voice and discuss what makes it both effective and appropriate.

Ask students to discuss various interpretations of having the volcano be an old woman. Discuss the possible implications and associations one might derive from the images in the last stanza: the boot scraping, the floor creaking, and the blanket being pulled from her thin shoulder. Discuss the possibilities for meaning in the volcano image, in the volcano's violent eruption, and in the speaker saying at the beginning that "this old woman / no longer cares / what others think" (ll. 2–4).

PAIR IT WITH   Diane Glancy, "Aunt Parnetta's Electric Blisters" (p. 248).

Benjamin Alire Sáenz

Elegy Written on a Blue Gravestone (To You, the Archaeologist)   (p. 716)

WORKS WELL FOR   Images; figurative language; tone.

ENTRY POINTS   You might start discussion of this poem with the image of the gravestone. Ask students to talk about what one associates with gravestones and what the gravestone might represent or connote in the poem. Then focus on the speaker and discuss the tone of the poem and what attitudes can be discerned from it. Talk about what lies behind the speaker's distress.

This is a poem of address. Talk about why it is addressed to an archaeologist — is it a literal archaeologist, a metaphorical one, or both? (Note lines 21–22: "the blatant irony: to end your days doing what you / hated. Fated to become an archaeologist.") If the term is metaphorical, discuss what it means and to whom the poem might be addressed. Discuss the effect of the strategy of using address as an approach to what the poet is saying.

Review the definition of *elegy* (in the Glossary, p. 1506) and then consider why this poem is an elegy and what it elegizes.

Discuss whether the poem is sentimental in its intensity and focus. Is there any redemption or resolution in the poem? How appropriate and effective is it that there either is or isn't?

PAIR IT WITH   Thomas Gray, "Elegy Written in a Country Churchyard" (p. 660).

Sonia Sanchez

An Anthem   (p. 717)

WORKS WELL FOR   Form (lines, stanzas, lists); voice; tone.

ENTRY POINTS   Ask students to identify what the poem is speaking out against, what it is speaking for, and what makes it a poem in behalf of peace. Ask what they think the opening line, "Our vision is our voice," might mean. Consider what makes this poem "an anthem."

Discuss how to characterize the speaker, the speaker's voice, tone, and attitudes. Talk about whether the speaker and Sonia Sanchez are one and the same and about the arguments for either side. Discuss for whom and to whom the speaker speaks.

Talk about the white space in the poem. It is a kind of "negative space," a space where something dynamic is happening. Ask students to discuss the role of the spaces in the poem and what part they play. What goes on in those spaces?

The poem opens with a capital letter. After that, even with new sentences, there are no capitals. Ask students to reflect on the effect of this.

Talk about the speaker asking for courage. What does that suggest? What are the reasons the speaker would feel the necessity to ask for courage?

PAIR IT WITH   Jayne Cortez, "Into This Time" (p. 626).

Cheryl Savageau

Bones – A City Poem   (p. 719)

WORKS WELL FOR   Form (parallelism, lists); images; rhythm; juxtaposition.

ENTRY POINTS   You might begin by asking about the title. Why is it called "Bones"? Why is it then followed by the words "A City Poem" when the poem itself focuses on the natural world? (Remind the class, if necessary, about juxtaposition or contrast — in this case implied juxtaposition.)

Ask students to describe or characterize the speaker, supporting what they say with evidence from the poem. Whom is the speaker addressing? Discuss the irony used by the speaker and what effect the speaker is hoping to have on the one addressed.

What is the effect of using the litany, the repetition? What is the effect of the vividly concrete images? What makes the voice of the poem haunting? What along with these parts of the natural world does the speaker want the one addressed to remember, to never forget, to carry within always?

Discuss what is suggested by the last two lines — "forget that you are walking / on the bones of your grandmothers."

PAIR IT WITH Jonathan Swift, "A Description of the Morning" (p. 737).

Vijay Seshadri

The Refugee (p. 720)

WORKS WELL FOR Form (sonnet); figurative language.

ENTRY POINTS This poem lends itself to a discussion of juxtaposition. As a way into the poem, ask students to note the juxtapositions in the poem: those of setting, image, age, and situation. Discuss what these juxtapositions create in the poem and in the reader's mind as well. What are the resulting effects, and how are these crucial to the meanings in the poem?

Discuss who the refugee is. Along with thinking of him in the particular, discuss whether he also can be seen as representative, metaphorical, and archetypal.

Ask students to consider the effect and appropriateness (or irony) of writing the poem as a sonnet. (The poem could provide a good opportunity for reviewing sonnets and discussing what is unusual about this one — the use of slant rhymes, the lack of meter; what's the point of using some features of a sonnet but not its traditional iambic pentameter? You might compare the handling of form here with Gary Miranda's "Love Poem — p. 693.) Discuss the effect of the white space left between the octave and sestet. If the white space is considered a part of the poem (should it be?), ask students about what they think is happening in that space. What does the ellipsis at the end of the octave suggest?

The poem has several provocative lines. Ask the students which they were particularly struck by and discuss what they found to be meaningful in the lines individually and in the context of the poem. They may single out other lines, but these may be particularly stimulating for discussion: "He feels himself at his mind's borders" (l. 1); "He sees each rifle as we who see him, / in the crystal blizzard of a century's static" (ll. 9–10); "try to reach him with our two-bit magic" (l. 11); and "pinned like a flower on the genocidal past" (l. 14).

Discuss the speaker's complicity in the refugee's situation (consider such references as "our two-bit magic" in line 11 and "But he escapes us to roam in the garden" in line 12).

Talk about the conflict between innocence and violence in the poem. Note the images that reveal this conflict and discuss their effectiveness.

PAIR IT WITH   Ana Doina, "The Extinct Homeland — A Conversation with Czeslaw Milosz" (p. 636).

William Shakespeare

My mistress' eyes are nothing like the sun   (p. 720)

WORKS WELL FOR   Figurative language; tone (irony).

ENTRY POINTS   Students sometimes read this as the speaker affirming that he cares deeply about his lover even though she is not all that beautiful, or not beautiful according to prevailing standards of beauty. Such a reading seems to miss the point emphasized in the last two words: "false compare." This is a poem more about poetry than about a woman.

The poem pokes fun at the farfetched conceits used in conventional love poetry, influenced by the sonnets of Francesco Petrarca (1304–1374) and those who followed in the Petrarchan tradition. For Shakespeare's speaker to say his mistress's eyes are not like the sun does not deny their brightness: It only points out the exaggeration, and even falseness, of the conceit. (One way to bring this out is to have students turn Shakespeare's negatives into positives: "Her breasts are white as the snow.") The poem implies that a poet should avoid clichés and use more realistic standards in choosing figurative language.

PAIR IT WITH   Marianne Moore, "Poetry" (p. 694).

Percy Bysshe Shelley

Ozymandias   (p. 721)

WORKS WELL FOR   Form (sonnet); irony; speaker.

ENTRY POINTS   This is an accessible, provocative poem that students are drawn to and often like very much. You might have a student read it aloud and then ask the class to explain what it says (as a way to find out if they are picking up and are able to explain its poignant irony).

Ask students to comment on the layers through which the information is conveyed: The speaker of the poem hears from a traveler the words written on the statue (presumably composed by Ozymandias, but inscribed by someone after his death). Ask them to comment on how those layers contribute to the effect of the poem.

Ozymandias was the Greek name for the Egyptian king Rameses II of Egypt (1304–1237 B.C.E.). The first-century-B.C.E. Greek historian Diodorus Siculus, in his *Library of History*, quotes the inscription on the pedestal of his statue (at the Ramesseum, across the Nile from Luxor) as "King of Kings am I, Osymandias. If anyone would know how great I am and where I lie, let him surpass one of my works" (trans. C. H. Oldfather, Loeb Classical Library [London: Heinemann, 1961] 1.47).

PAIR IT WITH   Benjamin Alire Sáenz, "Elegy Written on a Blue Gravestone (To You, the Archaeologist)" (p. 716).

Percy Bysshe Shelly
Ode to the West Wind   (p. 721)

WORKS WELL FOR   Images; sounds; form (terza rima sonnets).

ENTRY POINTS   Shelley's great lyric poem develops a conventional image of the English Romantic poets, wind and seasonal change representing a movement toward creative inspiration and spiritual insight. In many languages (Hebrew, Greek, and Latin, for example), the words for wind, breath, spirit, and inspiration are the same or closely related. The west wind of Shelley's poem, therefore, is a "spirit" (from the Latin *spiritus*, also the root word of *inspiration*). In the autumn it sweeps everything to death or extinction; in spring it renews nature and brings everything back to life. This cycle forms the central image of the poem, extended to nature (sections 1–3); to himself, having lost the imaginativeness and creativity he had in earlier years (section 4); and to the divine (section 5), as he asks the west wind to fill him with the divine inspiration he needs to resurrect his poetic voice.

Read a section or two, or have a strong student reader do so, and ask students to listen to the poem's handling of sounds, especially its use of assonance and rhyme, as a way of reinforcing the content (especially in a poem about the wind).

Ask students to analyze the form (fourteen-line sections — sonnet form, built out of terza rima tercets and a couplet). Ask them to reflect on the value of using such traditional but reconfigured components in a poem on this subject.

PAIR IT WITH   John Keats, "To Autumn" (p. 677).

Kazuko Shiraishi
Dedicated to the Late John Coltrane   (p. 724)

WORKS WELL FOR   Images; form (lines, parallelism, repetition); sound; rhythm.

ENTRY POINTS   Ask the students to read the poem even if they are not familiar with the great saxophonist John Coltrane (1926–1967). Then give them whatever biographical information you wish as well as a musical context for reading the poem by playing, perhaps, cuts from Coltrane's famous 1959 album *Giant Steps* or his 1964 album *A Love Supreme*. After doing so, ask the students to read the poem again and then discuss the differences, if any, in their experience of the poem before and after they have the biographical and musical contexts.

This is a poem of address, obviously to John Coltrane. However, there are indications throughout the poem that the actual audience for the poem is not Coltrane or at least not Coltrane alone. Ask students to note places in the poem that give them the sense that the poem is for a wider audience. Discuss who that audience is and what the poet hopes the effect is on readers.

Talk about the vision of the poem. In the best sense, the poet is using Coltrane to lead the reader to realizations. Discuss what these may be and what in the poem supports any of the students' conclusions.

Discuss what it is that the speaker feels the "people" desperately need. How does the poem reveal these things?

Talk about the ways Coltrane is described in the poem. Have the students write down what they conclude about Coltrane from the description and then compare their ideas. Talk about the images used to describe Coltrane. What do they evoke? How might one say they fit his life or his playing? How might they fit jazz or the era in which Coltrane played?

Discuss the effects of juxtaposing Coltrane's jazz music and nature. Talk also about why the poet may have decided to juxtapose these.

Discuss the impact Coltrane had on the speaker, perhaps the poet. What in the poem reveals why the speaker/poet loves Coltrane? Coltrane was a deeply and complexly spiritual man. In what ways is that brought into the poem?

PAIR IT WITH   Al Young, "A Dance for Ma Rainey" (p. 759).

Charles Simic

Begotten of the Spleen (p. 728)

WORKS WELL FOR   Images; allusions; form (stanzas, lines); juxtaposition.

ENTRY POINTS   Most students (understandably) find this a difficult poem. You will probably find it necessary to go through it stanza by stanza with the class. The poem is constructed as a juxtaposition of the holocaust and Christianity. Ask students to trace such connections through the poem and to begin considering the result and effect and meaning of joining them. Allusions play a large role in the poem. Help students identify most or all of them and discuss how the associations carried by the allusions enrich the poem and amplify its impact.

Discuss the bitterly ironic tone of the poem, why it is effective, and what might make it appropriate. Discuss what makes the horrific imagery also very poignant. When asked if he is a surrealist, Simic has answered, "Yes, if you mean by that a realist." Discuss what the students think he means by this and how it applies to this poem.

If one effect of juxtaposition is to put unlike things together in order to create a new reality or a deeper insight into each of what is combined, discuss how that is achieved in this poem.

Ask students what they think the poem "adds up to," what its point is, and why.

Simic has a stunningly wry sense of humor, often a very dark sense of humor. Ask students whether they feel that is evident in this poem and, if so, whether it seems effective and appropriate.

PAIR IT WITH Bei Dao, "Night: Theme and Variations" (p. 774).

Gary Soto

The Elements of San Joaquin (p. 729)

WORKS WELL FOR Structure; images; figurative language; speaker.

ENTRY POINTS The poem vividly depicts experiences and reflections of a fieldworker in California, perhaps a migrant worker or a former migrant who has now settled in a home (that he weeds the yard in the evening might suggest it is his own place). Discuss the speaker's relation to the subject. How involved do the students think the speaker is? What part does he play in the whole of the poem? Talk about if they feel he has distanced himself from the scenes or seems to be a part of it all. What is the role of the speaker as the one who "tells the story" of this poem? Do the students think this is a valid and valuable role? Who is the *you* in the poem? Why is a *you* addressed directly?

Consider the structure of the poem, the way it is divided into different "elements." What does that structure create? How does it affect the reader? Talk about why the poet chose these particular elements.

Within the harshness of the poem there is rich sensuous experience and beauty and affirmation. Ask the students to pick out such images and to talk about why these are important even if they do not redeem the situation. Talk also about why these aspects are not sentimental and not a rationalization for having to live this life. Ask students to talk about what the vivid descriptions lead them to feel, connect with, imagine, and reflect on. Which descriptions in particular strike them and why?

Ask students to discuss what the speaker means in line 29 when he says, "And I take on another life." Discuss why the speaker suddenly says, at the end of the section titled "Fog," "One hundred years from now / There should be no reason to believe / I lived" (ll. 91–93). Discuss how this line strikes the students. Discuss what the speaker means in line 111, "We won't forget what you failed to see."

The poem is rich with assonance. Talk about why that particular element of sound is appropriate for this poem, what it suggests in terms of meaning, and how it enriches the poem.

The final stanza is complex but powerful. Ask the students to talk about its meaning, techniques, and impact.

PAIR IT WITH   Thomas Gray, "Elegy Written in a Country Churchyard" (p. 660).

Wole Soyinka

Flowers for My Land   (p. 732)

WORKS WELL FOR   Form (lines, stanzas); images; figurative language; tone.

ENTRY POINTS   You might begin by discussing how the poet weaves together issues, flowers, biblical allusions, decay, human anatomy, violence, domesticity, academic stance, the natural world, and music into a tapestry depicting his land and what is being done to it or made of it — physically, socially, and politically. Ask students to talk about the sum total of this integration of disparate elements in terms of what is created, the purpose of doing so, and the resulting impact. Ask them to consider the use of collage structure, what it implies in terms of what the speaker is experiencing, what makes it appropriate for the poem, what that structure embodies in terms of the situation portrayed.

Ask students to think about the poem's form, its use of stanzas and rhyme, and to talk about what form adds to the poem, why it is fitting, why its variations are appropriate, what the rhyme and the ways it is used imply.

Talk about if this poem is "culture specific." If students feel that it is, discuss what culture it particularly applies to. If students feel it goes beyond the context in which it was written, discuss what other cultures or cultural groups, in the most general sense, they feel it speaks to and speaks for.

Look closely at lines 76–80, "Come, let us / With that mangled kind / Make pact, no less / Against the lesser / Leagues of death, and mutilators of the mind." To whom does the speaker refer? Why would the speaker want to "make pact"? What might be that pact?

Discuss the call to action at the end of the poem — "Orphans of the world / Ignite! Draw / Your fuel of pain from earth's sated core." Talk about what the students think the speaker is calling for in particular and discuss whether the students think the poem is relevant still.

PAIR IT WITH   Sonia Sanchez, "An Anthem" (p. 717).

Edmund Spenser

One day I wrote her name upon the strand   (p. 735)

WORKS WELL FOR   Form (sonnet); figurative language; sound.

ENTRY POINTS   Spenser's sonnet is one of a number of early modern poems that claim to immortalize the poet's love in verse. It sets the speaker's lover, with her "virtues rare" (l. 11), apart from other women and, like John Donne's "A Valediction: Forbidding Mourning" (p. 638), declares that their love for each other is special and will last eternally.

Suggest that students pay close attention to the language and figures of speech: What's the effect of "strand" in line 1 instead of "sand"? What's the effect of switching from the neutral "waves . . . washèd it away" in line 2 to the metaphor in line 4 of "the tide . . . made my pains his prey"? Ask students to comment on the effect of repetitions ("vain" in line 5, "mortal" in line 6) and the word play/allusion in "die in dust" in line 10 (with the contrast between "dust" and, in line 12, "heavens").

Ask students to discuss the variations on writing, from scratching in the sand with a stick, to inscribing a name in the heavens, to the writing of the poem itself, and the significance of the act of writing as an effort to achieve permanence.

Ask students to discuss the meaning of the closing couplet, especially the closing phrase, "and later life renew."

PAIR IT WITH   Gary Miranda, "Love Poem" (p. 693).

Wallace Stevens

The Emperor of Ice-Cream   (p. 735)

WORKS WELL FOR   Imagery; tone; humor.

ENTRY POINTS   Many students will find the poem confusing and may need some help getting oriented. You might start by asking students to describe the scene. If no one jumps in, tell them the scene is a wake or funeral and see if that helps them begin figuring out details. The wake is for an old woman and takes place in her apartment or house. The mourners take a sheet, with fantail pigeons embroidered on it, from a dresser to cover her body (furniture made of deal — fir or pine boards — is inexpensive, but has a glossy finish to make it look more costly). The mourners seem to be neighbors or friends, from a run-down neighborhood. Women come in everyday clothes. Boys bring flowers wrapped in old newspapers, not florist tissue. The food is not brought in but prepared in her kitchen by a friend or neighbor. The ice-cream maker is a burly cigar-roller (unless one takes "curds" literally, as the coagulated part of milk from which cheese is made, in which case he would seem to be whipping up some sort of cheese spread). That he is making ice cream might be favored by the title and by alliteration: cream, cups, concupiscent, curds. (In a letter, Stevens wrote, "The words 'concupiscent curds' . . . are merely expressive. . . . They express the concupiscence of life, but, by contrast with the things in relation to them in the poem, they express or accentuate life's destitution, and it is this that gives them something more than a cheap lustre" (*Letters* [New York: Knopf, 1966] 500).

Then ask students about the emperor. If the cigar-roller is making ice cream, they may suggest that he is the emperor of ice cream. Once they know that the poem involves a wake, they may suggest (as many critics have) that the emperor is death. Or the cigar roller and death may merge and end up the same. And ask why emperor of *ice cream*. It's important that students think in 1920s terms about ice cream, not today's terms. Lacking the kind of refrigerated equipment we have now, ice cream in the 1920s was a rare treat, not an everyday occurrence. An obvious connection between ice cream and death is coldness; see if students come up with others. They may not be inclined to think of positive qualities like sweetness and smoothness as connections, but there is reason to believe that Stevens did: He wrote in a letter, "ice cream is an absolute good" (*Letters* 341).

Another difficult phrase appears in line 7. Of it, Stevens wrote in the same letter, "The true sense of Let be be finale of seem is let being become the conclusion or denouement of appearing to be. . . . The poem is obviously not about ice cream, but about being as distinguished from seeming to be" (*Letters* 341).

The tone of the poem, thus, seems celebratory: It celebrates the deceased, and it celebrates those who gather to honor her in style, despite their own poverty and the lackluster surroundings. They celebrate life, and they celebrate death as a part of life.

Ten years after its publication, in a 1933 letter, Stevens refers to this as his favorite among his poems because it "wears a deliberately commonplace costume, and yet seems to me to contain something of the essential gaudiness of poetry" (*Letters* 263). Invite students to discuss how the poem fits his description and how that can be helpful in understanding the poem.

PAIR IT WITH   Mark Doty, "Tiara" (p. 639).

Virgil Suárez

Las tendederas/Clotheslines   (p. 736)

WORKS WELL FOR   Images; form (stanzas, lines); tone.

ENTRY POINTS   This is a memory poem, telling a story about an event the speaker remembers vividly for several reasons. The narrative is straightforward; most students should be able to follow it. Ask them to talk about the differences between the speaker at the time of this experience and the speaker as he relates the story. What besides a difference in age distinguishes the two? Think about tone, attitudes, feelings, realizations, reactions.

The poem takes a turn near the end and leaps into the present. Talk about what the speaker says at the end of the poem, what it may mean, why he includes the reference to traveling the open roads of the United States, and why he says what he does, noting especially his saying, "I think / about how much debris time & distance / have kicked up into my eyes" (ll. 49–51).

Ask students to talk about what the structural elements add to the poem, what their effects are, why they are appropriate, how they affect individual readers. Pay particular attention to the use of three-line stanzas, the staggered construction of the stanzas, the multiple compound sentences, and the repeated use of "&" for "and."

Discuss the violence in the poem. What does it suggest or signify or represent? What lasting impact did it have on the speaker?

Ask students to give some examples of ironies in the poem. Discuss what they reveal about the father, the family, the family's situation, their experience in two cultures, the way the speaker looks at things.

Talk about what is implied by having the title in Spanish and English in light of the poem.

PAIR IT WITH   Julia Alvarez, "How I Learned to Sweep" (p. 560).

Jonathan Swift

A Description of the Morning   (p. 737)

WORKS WELL FOR   Heroic couplet; images.

ENTRY POINTS   Ask students what the title led them to anticipate before they went on to read the poem: See if they thought it would show idealized nature in a rural setting as a "ruddy sun" comes up. Swift's anti-pastoral poem depends on that expectation for its fullest effect. Instead of the country scene, Swift gives us a montage of realistic details characteristic of morning in the city. Ask students to go through the couplets, clarifying what each brings out and reveals about what city life is like. Ask them also to point out examples of humor when they occur.

This is a good poem for studying heroic couplets. Swift's couplets are tight, varied, and effective, though he was not as skillful at them as his contemporary and friend Alexander Pope, the acknowledged master of the form.

PAIR IT WITH   Dennis Brutus, "Nightsong: City" (p. 548).

Mary Tall Mountain

Matmiya   (p. 738)

WORKS WELL FOR   Images; figurative language.

ENTRY POINTS   Mary Tall Mountain said that she spoke always with her late grandmother. Ask students to talk about ways the poem reveals and embodies this. Discuss the possible meanings and effects of the speaker's weaving together her grandmother and the natural world.

The poem is visionary and metaphorical in the sense of transformation. Talk about the effects of visionary and metaphorical experience and how it manifests itself in this poem. Discuss the discrepancy between the visionary experience and what is usually considered reality.

Discuss the tone of the poem and what it reveals about the relationship of the speaker to her grandmother.

Discuss why the poem ends with the speaker simply saying, "Matmiya, / I see you sitting." What makes that so evocative? What does it evoke in the reader? What might this ending suggest in terms of impact and stance in the world both for the speaker and the reader?

PAIR IT WITH   Judith Ortiz Cofer, "Cold as Heaven" (p. 558).

Alfred, Lord Tennyson

Ulysses   (p. 739)

WORKS WELL FOR   Dramatic monologue; blank verse.

ENTRY POINTS   The note on page 739 clarifies the context of this dramatic monologue, as the now elderly Ulysses addresses his men and challenges them to join him in undertaking a new, presumably last, voyage beyond the Strait of Gibraltar and into the unknown Atlantic.

One way into the poem is the character of Ulysses, as it develops through what he says. Ask students to summarize his character (a charismatic leader, someone who is bored sitting at home, a figure who wants adventure and challenge, and so on). His character comes out partly through contrast with his son, Telemachus — ask students to follow that lead. If Ulysses goes on this new adventure, he will leave behind his faithful wife Penelope, who waited twenty years for him to return. What do students think about that? How does it contribute to his character?

Another approach is to think of it as a poem about how an older person looks at life. This senior citizen, at least, doesn't want to sit around getting older and waiting for death to arrive. Ask students to find indications in the poem of how to deal with old age.

The poem can also be approached as a speech, considered for its rhetorical effectiveness. Ask students to outline it as a speech and evaluate its effectiveness as a persuasive speech. What techniques does he use to set up his case and convince his men to accompany him?

PAIR IT WITH   Derek Walcott, "Sea Grapes" (p. 745).

Dylan Thomas

Do not go gentle into that good night   (p. 741)

WORKS WELL FOR   Structure (villanelle); sounds; tone.

ENTRY POINTS   The speaker is addressing his father, who is dying. Ask the class to talk about the speaker: how he feels, his tone, his attitudes toward his father and toward what is happening, and his attitudes toward himself. Describe and discuss the relationship between the father and the speaker. Talk about what the speaker wants from the father, especially why he would want him not to "go gentle into that good night." Ask students to evaluate the speaker's reaction: Is it typical? Is it similar to how they think they would react in a similar situation?

Talk about the different types of men alluded to in each stanza. Discuss why the poet chooses these and what their role is in the poem, what they may represent. Why does the poet use these in relation to his father?

The poem is a villanelle. Refer students to the definition on page 1520 and ask them to discuss ways this form adds to the meaning and the effect of the poem. Talk about what happens to the impact or tone or meaning of the repeated lines when they appear in a new context.

Discuss the use of paradox in the poem. For example, talk about the speaker saying in the last stanza, "Curse, bless, me now," or about such uncommon modifiers as "blinding sight" (l. 13), "sad height" (l. 16), and "fierce tears" (l. 17) and their effect in the poem.

PAIR IT WITH   John Yau, "Chinese Villanelle" (p. 757).

Jean Toomer

Face   (p. 741)

WORKS WELL FOR   Form; images; figurative language.

ENTRY POINTS   Ask students to talk about the effect of the speaker discussing only the subject's face and about the effect of the title being simply "Face."

This poem is especially useful for discussing figures, particularly the transformational quality of metaphor. Discuss the usage, effectiveness, result, and impact of metaphors (and a simile) in the poem.

Talk about the tone of the poem and what it suggests about the speaker as well as the speaker's relationship to the subject. Describe the distance between the speaker and the subject, speculating on the difference between what seems to be the subject's impact on the speaker and the way the speaker in the poem describes the subject.

Discuss the possible meanings and effects of undermining the beautifully lyrical image of the next-to-last line — "purple in the evening sun" — with the harsh last line — "nearly ripe for worms."

PAIR IT WITH   Alberto Ríos, "Nani" (p. 713).

Quincy Troupe

Snake-Back Solo 2   (p. 742)

WORKS WELL FOR   Rhythm; sound.

ENTRY POINTS   The poem is from Quincy Troupe's collection *Avalanche*. With that title in mind as a metaphor for Troupe's use of diction and syntax in the poem, ask students to discuss its appropriateness as a description of this poem's effect on the reader.

Read the poem, focusing on its rhythms. Discuss whether one can understand the poem primarily through its rhythms and rhythmic structure. Discuss whether one could say that rhythm itself is a primary subject of this poem. Why would that be so? What makes the idea of rhythm itself so important in the poem?

Troupe has said that he wants to work with "heightened everyday speech." Talk about this in light of the poem. He has also said he wants to use language in such a way that the primary effect is evocative. Discuss this position in relation to the poem.

Characterize the speaker of the poem. Describe the tone and what it reveals about the speaker's attitudes and stance toward the world.

This is an excellent poem to use for a discussion of various sound elements. Ask students to pick out examples of sound elements and discuss what role they play in the poem and how they affect the way one experiences the poem.

One might say that the poem is impressionistic in its use of language. Ask the students to pick out passages that they do not understand on a literal level and discuss the "impressionistic meaning" of the passages.

PAIR IT WITH   Ishmael Reed, "Poetry Makes Rhythm in Philosophy" (p. 709); Kazuko Shiraishi, "Dedicated to the Late John Coltrane" (p. 724).

Gerald Vizenor

Shaman Breaks   (p. 744)

WORKS WELL FOR   Form; juxtaposition.

ENTRY POINTS   Some students may have difficulty catching what the poem is about. If so, you might ask them to read Vizenor's biographical sketch on page 1464 and then to focus on the first word of each section: "colonists," "tourists," and "soldiers." That ought to get them to pick up a contrast between Native Americans and outsiders who are encroaching on them and destroying (breaking) the physical manifestations of their culture ("the old stone man," "the old stone woman"). The poem affirms, nonetheless, the persistence of the spirit and values of native culture.

You may need to explain what a shaman is (a priest or medicine man, in certain religions that are based on a belief in good and evil spirits, who can influence these spirits). After doing so, discuss the poem in light of the title. What does it mean that a shaman "breaks"? (That the shaman breaks down, loses influence?) In what ways does the shaman break? Who and what breaks the shaman? Consider the different meanings of the word *breaks* and discuss all that apply to this poem. (Are the old stone man and woman figures — perhaps divine images — carved in stone and now breaking apart? Do they represent the inner strength of the people? Are they figures in myths that are no longer believed in as before?) Discuss whether the image of the shaman can be read as representing things other than itself and, if it does, what it might represent.

Discuss the possible purposes for the poem's being composed in three sections. What role do the stanzas play within each section? Talk about how the short lines affect the reader. What do they evoke? Why are they appropriate for this particular speaker? Notice also the line breaks. What do they add to the poem's impact and the speaker's tone?

List juxtapositions in the poem. What do they represent, and what is the resulting effect of placing them in juxtaposition?

Discuss the final image and what it may suggest and mean — "wild stories / break from the stones." Notice the reappearance of the word *break*.

PAIR IT WITH   Ray A. Young Bear, "From the Spotted Night" (p. 760).

Derek Walcott

Sea Grapes   (p. 745)

WORKS WELL FOR   Form (stanzas, lines); allusions; myth.

ENTRY POINTS   Walcott has spent much of his life composing work that creates a history of the Caribbean. It combines historical events, myth, personal history, critique, and an evocation of place and people. Discuss how this poem fits into that project. Focus on the speaker and discuss the speaker's attitudes and stance toward what has happened in the Caribbean.

The poem lends itself to a discussion of allusion. The notes on page 745 identify the details associated with the story of Odysseus. Ask students to talk about why the poet drew on other cultures from the past and what the effect of doing so is in the poem. How might it relate to the history project described in the previous paragraph? Discuss the last line: "The classics can console. But not enough."

The poem is structured in three-line stanzas with a single line at its end. Discuss what the consistency of stanza structure implies, the effect of the three-line stanza, and the impact of the single line at the end.

Talk about the title, the image of sea grapes. Why would the poet choose this image as a title? What effect does the title have as one reads the poem? In the third stanza, "sour grapes" appears. This is a rather common cliché. Ask students whether they think it is to be read as a cliché. Why would such an erudite poet use a cliché?

Discuss the speaker's assertion in lines 10–12 that "The ancient war / between obsession and responsibility / will never finish."

PAIR IT WITH   Alfred, Lord Tennyson, "Ulysses" (p. 739).

James Welch

Christmas Comes to Moccasin Flat   (p. 746)

WORKS WELL FOR   Diction; images; juxtaposition.

ENTRY POINTS   A way to initiate discussion of the poem is to ask students to describe what Christmas is like in Moccasin Flat and then to ask why Christmas matters there anyhow. The poem focuses on cultural conflicts — ask students to list and talk about examples revealed directly and indirectly in the poem. Discuss the poem in the context of the associations connected to Christmas. Note the juxtapositions and discuss the bitter ironies that result from these combinations.

Discuss the speaker. What do you think the speaker's role is in the poem? What is the speaker's relationship to the situation? What is the speaker's attitude toward the situation?

Discuss the tone and meaning when the speaker says the chiefs feel "an urge to laugh pounding their ribs" (l. 11). Discuss what is meant or implied by Medicine Woman predicting five o'clock by spitting at her television.

Talk about the poignancy of the presence of the children in the poem and the kind of story they beg to hear.

Discuss whether television in the poem is a metonymy. If it is, what is it a figure for?

PAIR IT WITH   Jim Barnes, "Return to La Plata, Missouri" (p. 577).

Roberta Hill Whiteman

The White Land   (p. 747)

WORKS WELL FOR   Images; sounds; tone; myth.

ENTRY POINTS   You might help orient students to this poem by suggesting that it seems to deal with place, and myths, and how place relates to identity. The "white land" is not identified — perhaps it suggests an arctic landscape (as suggested by the "polar" in line 15) or perhaps any snow-covered landscape. Line 19 mentions a plane that is carrying the speaker away, presumably from the white land back toward the "wooded horizon" (l. 20). Perhaps "over the white land" in line 2 indicates their arrival (could it be returning to the home territory of the *you*, which thus might try to keep the *you* there — line 22?)

Ask students to discuss who the *you* is. What are the possibilities, and what in the poem supports any conclusions?

Talk about why in line 10 the speaker says "time has no time" and "Fate is a warlord." What might these mean in the context of the poem, and what do the students think of these ideas?

Talk about why the bears leaving no footprints would rouse their joy (ll. 15–16). Are these literal bears? What indicates they aren't? If not, what are they?

Discuss the speaker's subtlety of tone. How would you describe the tone? What does the tone reveal about the speaker? What does it say about the speaker's attitudes and decision about a stance toward this situation?

Notice the sudden shift in tone, focus, attention, texture, and imagery in the next-to-last line and discuss the possible meanings and implications of this change: "The dishwater's luminous; a truck / grinds down the street."

PAIR IT WITH   Louise Glück, "Parable of Flight" (p. 659).

Walt Whitman

From Song of Myself   (p. 748)

WORKS WELL FOR   Rhythm; form (free verse); imagery; use of lists; use of symbols.

ENTRY POINTS   This poem was first published in 1855 as an untitled section of *Leaves of Grass*. It is important for its expression of American culture and politics shortly before the Civil War and for its experimentation with free verse. Whitman revised and expanded the poem constantly until the end of his life. We have used, as most texts do, the sixth edition (1891–92); it is longer, more carefully crafted, and more conventionally punctuated.

Section 1 introduces the persona and begins to set out the scope and method of the poem; section 7 is an example of Whitman's use of historical panoramic miniatures; section 21 develops Whitman's theme of sex and nature; section 24 extends the handling of the persona; section 47 recapitulates major themes of the poem; and section 52, the final section, deals with the absorption of the persona into the converted reader.

Read some of the poem aloud or have a good student reader do so. Ask students to listen to the rhythms. As one way to get students to reflect on those rhythms and where they came from, have them read Yusef Komunyakaa's comparisons of Whitman and Langston Hughes on page 1276, especially his comment on the influence of arias from Italian opera. Other suggestions of influence include the rhythms of ocean waves and the rhythms of the King James Bible.

Ask students to discuss what Whitman means by the self (incorporating both the sense of individualism that developed in the eighteenth and nineteenth centuries, and the individual as part of a collective whole — America). Whitman's poem could be discussed in conjunction with the half dozen poems dealing with self at the end of Chapter 14.

Note also Komunyakaa's sentence saying that Whitman's vision (and Hughes's) was "driven by an acute sense of beauty and tragedy in America's history." Ask students to discuss the vision of America that emerges from Whitman's poem.

PAIR IT WITH   Langston Hughes, "Freedom's Plow" (p. 1258).

Richard Wilbur

Love Calls Us to the Things of This World   (p. 752)

WORKS WELL FOR   Form; images; figurative language; juxtaposition.

ENTRY POINTS   The poem opens with the speaker awaking so suddenly that his soul hangs outside his body for a moment and experiences the air filled with angels. Ask students to discuss the effect of this juxtaposition of the sacred and the profane, the spiritual and the earthly, and the possible meanings it suggests. Juxtaposition, as it connects or relates dissimilar things, is used to create something original from the combination or to give us a fresh perspective. Discuss ways this poem does either.

Ask students to clarify what the soul — still outside the speaker's body — shrinks from and why, and why the soul says what it does in lines 18–20. Then, as sun rises further, the soul reenters the body and speaks again, but now "In a changed voice" (l. 25). In what way or ways does it change? What does the changed voice say, and why? How does the title relate to what is happening? What does it mean that "love calls us to the things of this world"? Where does love appear in the poem?

There are several unusual and perhaps easily overlooked modifiers in the poem. Discuss how the following alter one's usual perceptions and what effect their use creates in the poem: "*halcyon* feeling" (l. 9); "*impersonal* breathing" (l. 10); "*terrible* speed of their omnipresence" (l. 12); "*rapt* a quiet" (l. 14); "*punctual* rape of every blessèd day" (l. 17); "*clear* dances" (l. 20); "*bitter* love" (l. 23).

Wilbur is a master of formal techniques. Point out examples of such formal elements in the poem and comment on his ways of using them.

PAIR IT WITH   William Carlos Williams, "Spring and All" (p. 753)

William Carlos Williams

Spring and All   (p. 753)

WORKS WELL FOR   Images; form.

ENTRY POINTS   The poem describes the beauty of spring (and all that goes with it), which he notices, ironically, along the road to a hospital for contagious people. (You might want to point out that Williams was a physician who wrote poetry between appointments and in the evenings.) Ask students to notice and discuss the juxtaposition of the natural setting with the hospital setting, particularly in the details used in describing things in nature, and to talk about what such juxtapositions suggest and mean.

The descriptions of the natural world in this poem are certainly vivid, but they also seem to suggest further meaning. Talk about what the students think may be the further meanings and implications drawn from these descriptions and how they are related to the hospital and its entrance.

Williams often approached things much like an objectivist, submerging the subjective aspects of experience and offering the reader only the "objective." Talk about the ways this approach can be seen in this poem. Talk about what makes the descriptions in the poem effective, arresting, memorable.

Notice how Williams focuses every line and attends to every line break. Talk about how that affects one's reading and what such effects create in the poem.

PAIR IT WITH   Percy Bysshe Shelley, "Ode to the West Wind" (p. 721).

Nellie Wong

Grandmother's Song   (p. 754)

WORKS WELL FOR   Form (pantoum); images.

ENTRY POINTS   You might begin by asking students to pick out examples of loss or separation in the poem. To what extent do they think loss and separation are subjects of the songs the grandmother sings? Discuss the blending of celebration and mourning in the poem. What is being suggested by having the poem be about a grandmother's song rather than a mother's song? (Is her longing for the old traditions stronger than it would be in the next generation?)

This poem is a pantoum, a poem consisting of a variable number of four-line stanzas rhyming *abab*, with the second and fourth lines of one stanza used as the first and third lines of the next stanza. The first and third lines of the first stanza are repeated in reverse order as the second and fourth lines of the final stanza, so that the poem ends with the same lines with which it started.

After explaining the form to the class, ask them to discuss what makes this form especially appropriate for the subject of this poem. The pantoum comes full circle, ending with the same line that began it. What effect does that have in this poem, and what makes this usage particularly poignant here? Ask students to note the rhyme words and discuss what they suggest either directly or ironically or both.

Which lines shift in meaning or implication when they are repeated in a new context? Ask the students to describe the differences between the initial use and the repeated use of the lines.

PAIR IT WITH   Gish Jen, "Who's Irish?" (p. 272).

William Wordsworth

The world is too much with us   (p. 755)

WORKS WELL FOR   Form (sonnet); figurative language; allusion.

ENTRY POINTS   This sonnet, embodying the Romantic love of nature and despair over feeling separated from nature and its inspirational effects, connects with many students as an environmental poem (we too are out of touch with nature, we too have given too much away and lost touch with nature and its positive influences in the process). Ask students to describe what the poem is saying to check if they are catching such implications (some may stumble over "world," equating it initially with nature, until it's suggested to them that they think of it as "worldliness," as in "getting and spending" in line 2). Having students discuss it together with Gerard Manley Hopkins's "God's Grandeur" (p. 524) could help clarify its themes.

Part of the loss is the decline of spirituality ("out of tune" in line 8). Thus the speaker suggests that the pagan world had a deeper sense of spirituality than his (Christian) world. Ask students to work through the implications of the sestet: Why is the speaker forlorn? Why would a glimpse of Proteus or Triton make him less forlorn? What does seeing them have to do with the problem stated in the octave?

It's a good poem for examining and assessing figures of speech.

PAIR IT WITH   Duane Niatum, "First Spring" (p. 696).

Sir Thomas Wyatt

They flee from me   (p. 756)

WORKS WELL FOR   Form; irony; puns.

ENTRY POINTS   Wyatt's lovely poem about his wandering lover appeals to students once they become comfortable with the twists that create its best effects. Ask the class to work out the meaning of the poem and to pick out things they like (perhaps the sensuous description in lines 11–13 and the enchanting line 14, "Dear heart, how like you this?").

They'll need to work through the deliberate ambiguity of the first stanza, all of which seems to describe only wild animals — perhaps deer — except for the word *naked* and the question of why animals would be roaming about in his chamber. Then comes the contrast between his past successes — no longer dealing with animals — and one memory in particular.

It was not a dream, he says in the final stanza — but can we be sure? And does it matter? What is clear is that the woman he loves has moved on, though the reason is cloaked in irony. Have students work through the last six lines carefully. The *Oxford English Dictionary* defines *newfangledness* as "(objection-able) modernness or novelty." What does the speaker mean by that, and by his freedom to move on, bestowed by her "goodness" (l. 18)? Be sure they explore the pun in line 20, and the way line 21 gains its power and effective-ness by using implication rather than an explicit explanation.

PAIR IT WITH   Kamala Das, "In Love" (p. 632).

John Yau

Chinese Villanelle (p. 757)

WORKS WELL FOR Form (villanelle); figurative language.

ENTRY POINTS This is a poem of address. Talk about who is being addressed. Discuss the speaker's relationship with and attitudes toward the one addressed. (It is a poem of loss. It could be a lover; it could be a culture.)

Review the requirements for a villanelle (see the Glossary, p. 1520) and ask the class to discuss how this poem fulfills and varies from them. For example, are there any implications in the poet's abandoning the usual rhyme scheme and meter for a villanelle? How does his varying the wording of the lines affect the way one reads the poem? Talk about how the repeated lines vary subtly each time they appear in a new context. Discuss how that adds to the possible levels of meaning in the poem. Talk about why the poet calls the poem a *Chinese* villanelle.

The poem uses several different figures. Ask the students to note them and to discuss their role in the poem and their effect on the reader.

Discuss the way the speaker mixes emotional expression with natural images, sometimes directly, sometimes simply by placing them alongside one another. What is the resulting effect of this, and what might it suggest about the speaker, the one addressed, their relationship, and the speaker's relationship to the world as a whole?

PAIR IT WITH Dylan Thomas, "Do not go gentle into that good night" (p. 741).

William Butler Yeats

The Lake Isle of Innisfree (p. 757)

WORKS WELL FOR Images; sound; rhythm.

ENTRY POINTS This beautiful poem is early and accessible Yeats, the sort of poem students love. They can understand it and relate to it. Innisfree is a small island in a lake, Lough Gill, in County Sligo, in the heart of what is now called Yeats country in western Ireland. You might show students a map to give them a sense of location — though of course the important location is in Yeats's imagination, rather than in physical region. Yeats says his father once read him a passage from Henry David Thoreau's *Walden*, which planted in his mind the dream of one day living in a cottage on the "little island called Innisfree."

This is one of the poems in which Yeats began to find his own voice or, as he put it, "with anything in its rhythm of my own music." Ask students to discuss its rhythms. If they don't comment on the diction and syntax of the opening line, ask them about it (do any hear in it an echoing of the King James Bible, for example?). Yeats comments that "a couple of years later I would not have written that first line with its conventional archaism," having decided that he should use "nothing but the common syntax."

Ask students to pick out images, phrases, and sounds they like in the poem and explain what makes them striking and effective.

PAIR IT WITH   Maxine Kumin, "The Sound of Night" (p. 466).

William Butler Yeats

The Second Coming   (p. 758)

WORKS WELL FOR   Myth; imagery; allusion.

ENTRY POINTS   This is later and more inaccessible Yeats, especially for beginning students of poetry. For such students you'll probably need to walk through the poem and help them see its meaning, especially the way it fits into Yeats's personal mythology. The note on page 758 gives a succinct summary of the poem's movement, but students may need to be shown where and how those points appear in the poem, and particularly how they relate to — are embodied in — the poem's powerful imagery.

PAIR IT WITH   Linda Hogan, "The History of Red" (p. 670).

Al Young

A Dance for Ma Rainey   (p. 759)

WORKS WELL FOR   Rhythm; sound; tone.

ENTRY POINTS   The speaker addresses Gertrude "Ma" Rainey (1886–1939), a well-known singer who has been given the title "Mother of the Blues." You could have a student do some research on Ma Rainey and give a report; or a student could do a short research paper on Ma Rainey and how she is depicted in this poem. Ask students to describe what the speaker's feelings and attitudes are toward her, with specific support from the poem. Discuss the speaker's tone and how it reflects his feelings. Discuss why this poem is called a dance.

Although it's a poem of address, it reaches beyond Ma Rainey to address factors in the African American experience that led them to sing the blues. Talk about what the poet through the speaker hopes to lead the reader to realize and reflect on. Ask the class to discuss the following lines — why the speaker says them, what layers of meaning and implication they have in the context of the poem, and what impact they have on the students as they read them:

> "I'm going to hover in the corners / of the world" (ll. 7–8)

> "throbbing with that sick pain / I know / & hide so well" (ll. 26–28)

> "that pain . . . first felt by some stolen delta nigger / swamped under with redblooded american agony" (ll. 29–35)

> "our beautiful brave black people / who no longer need to jazz / or sing to themselves in murderous vibrations / or play the veins of their strong tender arms / with needles / to prove we're still here" (ll. 42–47)

Talk about the importance of the rhythms of the lines and the sounds produced by assonance and consonance to the impact of the poem.

PAIR IT WITH   Langston Hughes, "The Weary Blues" (p. 1266).

Ray A. Young Bear

From the Spotted Night   (p. 760)

WORKS WELL FOR   Images; myth.

ENTRY POINTS   You might ask students to look for and talk about ways the speaker combines images from two cultures and two worldviews in the poem and why the speaker does so.

The poem is about the destruction, and the continuing destruction, of native culture. The narrator holds fast to the spirit and vision of native culture, such as the stars being spots in the night. He holds fast to a native vision still extant all around him. The shirt is native and its persistent embodiment of native culture has gone from being an emblem of resistance to a weapon, meaning it will remain and be worn and will now be seen as a statement against the destructive culture.

The poem opens in a blizzard. Ask students to discuss why that setting is appropriate for the poem, what tone it sets, how it affects the reading of the whole poem, and if it can be seen as a symbol or synecdoche. Who is the mystical whistler? Why a whistler? Why mystical?

Discuss what the speaker's saying "In the abrupt spring floods / swimmers retrieved our belief" (ll. 7–8) may mean.

Talk about the moments of reverence in the poem, including their ironies, and discuss what that tone in itself says and suggests.

Discuss what the speaker means by believing that "someone wears / the shirt and rearranges / the heavy furniture" (ll. 24–26).

Discuss whether the speaker's saying "nothing / is actually changed" (ll. 27–28) is paradoxical or ironic.

PAIR IT WITH   Gerald Vizenor, "Shaman Breaks" (p. 744).

READING POEMS IN TRANSLATION

Jorge Luis Borges

El otro tigre   (p. 764)

The Other Tiger   (p. 765)

WORKS WELL FOR   Images; symbol.

ENTRY POINTS   See the discussion of the poem's meaning on pages 763–64.

The epigraph is a phrase from *Sigurd the Volsung* (1876), a retelling of the Icelandic *Volsunga Saga* by Victorian author and craftsman William Morris (1834–1896). The phrase is from Book 2, a section in which Regin tells Sigurd about his kindred and the gold that was accursed from ancient days. The phrase appears in the following passage:

> And to me, the least and the youngest, what gift for the slaying of ease?
> Save the grief that remembers the past, and the fear that the future sees;
> And the hammer and fashioning-iron, and the living coal of fire;
> And the craft that createth a semblance, and fails of the heart's desire;
> And the toil that each dawning quickens and the task that is never done;
> And the heart that longeth ever, nor will look to the deed that is won.
> (ll. 439–44)

Poetry, like the craft of working in iron, can create only a semblance, not reality, not the essential tiger.

Our intent in this section is to bring out some important points about translation, mainly that no translation can do justice to the original. Every translation is an interpretation, just as every reading of a poem is an interpretation. A translation cannot be an objective, exact reproduction of the poem, equal to the original. Putting the poem into different words makes it a different poem.

You might ask students to find and read a translation of "El otro tigre" on the Web and compare it to the authorized translation by Alastair Reid included in the book. You also might suggest that they search for the original Spanish version of the poem on the Web using a search engine such as Yahoo! or Google and then use the search engine's "Translate this page" function to translate the poem into English. The resulting translation, which just turns the Spanish words into the nearest equivalent words in English, exemplifies an attempt to convey the meaning but with no effort made to convey a sense of the poetic qualities of the original. Students who know Spanish can compare the translations to the original and decide which translation they think does the best job of conveying the meaning, style, and tone of the original. For students who do not know Spanish, the point is not which translation they prefer: An inaccurate translation of a poem might be more readable and enjoyable than a more accurate one. One important thing is that they see that the translations differ from each other: Ask them to focus on various elements — images, rhythm, diction, syntax, line length, line breaks, tone, and internal structure, for example — and discuss the similarities and differences in the ways the translators worked with them. A second is that they understand that translators use different criteria for deciding how to approach the task of translating (to remain as close as possible to the wording of the original, for example, or to produce a poem that reads well as English poetry, even if it is not as close to the words and meaning of the original).

Jorge Luis Borges

Mi último tigre   (p. 768)

My Last Tiger   (p. 769)

WORKS WELL FOR   Symbol; archetype.

ENTRY POINTS   This piece is included in Spanish and English to provide another opportunity for students to compare a translation with the original and to compare different translations with each other. Here too you might suggest that students find and read other translations of "My Last Tiger" on the Web and compare them with each other and with Kenneth Krabbenhoft's translation in the book (and, of course, ask students who read Spanish to compare the translations with the original).

This piece, like the next one, is also included to provide a larger context for the first poem, to show that both a translator and a reader need to see a poem in context with other, related works by the author in order to do justice to the poem. "Mi último tigre" provides students a biographical explanation of how tigers became an important personal and archetypal symbol in Borges's life and thought and art. And it illustrates nicely Borges's philosophical idealism, his assertion that a physical animal is no more real than the image of a tiger, whether a visual or a verbal image.

PAIR IT WITH   Jorge Luis Borges, "El otro tigre"/"The Other Tiger" (pp. 764, 765) and "The Gold of the Tigers" (p. 770).

Jorge Luis Borges

The Gold of the Tigers   (p. 770)

WORKS WELL FOR   Images; symbol; archetype.

ENTRY POINTS   This poem, like the previous piece, is included to provide a larger context for "The Other Tiger," illustrating how Borges develops tigers, through imagery and archetype, in another poem. It is also interesting to compare this poem with "My Last Tiger," to note how he handles similar material in biographical prose and an imaginative poem.

PAIR IT WITH   Jorge Luis Borges, "My Last Tiger" (p. 769).

POEMS IN TRANSLATION

Anna Akhmatova

The Song of the Last Meeting   (p. 770)

WORKS WELL FOR   Figurative language; archetypes.

ENTRY POINTS   Akhmatova suffered terribly in Soviet prisons. Ask students to discuss the poem in light of that information. What difference does it make to know that when reading the poem? What in the poem reveals what the speaker used to survive and to maintain her spirit?

We aren't told the occasion of the poem — why she's putting a glove on the wrong hand, what the steps lead to, whose house it is, why it is dark, why candles are burning with an "indifferent-yellow flame." Ask students how we as readers should deal with that. Could the vagueness indicate that those details are insignificant? Should we concentrate not on what is said but on what isn't said?

In that case, students should consider similarities, or connections, between the speaker and the personified autumn (used as an archetype?). They should consider why the speaker is ready to die or accept death. In that light, they might speculate on what the "last meeting" might be (meeting with whom? Why the "last" meeting?) and on how "song" relates to the poem (is the poem the song of the last meeting, or is the poem describing or commenting on the song of the last meeting?).

Ask the class to think about what makes such a depressing poem life-affirming, perhaps even inspiring.

Talk about the possible meanings for the structure of the poem — four stanzas of four lines. What possible ironies might there be in the structure?

PAIR IT WITH Emily Dickinson, "Because I could not stop for Death" (p. 635).

Yehuda Amichai

Wildpeace (p. 771)

WORKS WELL FOR Form; figurative language; allusions.

ENTRY POINTS Ask students to discuss what the title means. What kind of peace does the speaker want? In what ways is this unusual, perhaps even subversive, to the common notions of what peace is? If this is a subversive notion, what then makes it positive rather than destructive? What kind of peace does the speaker seem not to want? What might be some possible reasons for not wanting that kind of peace?

Ask the class to describe the nuances and variations in the speaker's tone. When does the speaker alter the intensity of tone? Why? What makes that effective and appropriate for what the speaker wants?

Ask students to discuss why knowing "how to kill" makes the speaker "an adult" (ll. 6–7) and how they react to that idea.

Ask students to identify ironies in the poem and to comment on their effect. Ask if anyone recognizes any allusions in the poem. (For example, compare line 3 with the image of perfect peace in Isa. 11:6 — "The wolf also shall dwell with the lamb." And compare line 11 with the instructions in Joel 3:10 for preparing for war: "Beat your plowshares into swords.") If students don't recognize any allusions, identify them and ask the students to discuss what the allusions add to the poem, carrying something of their context and history with them.

Discuss what it may mean when the speaker offers the rather surreal image in lines 8–9, "And my son plays with a toy gun that knows / how to open and close its eyes and say Mama."

There is no regularity to the length of the lines. The poem's structure seems to have evolved from the poet attending to other elements. Discuss what the elements may have been that led to the lines being of these varying lengths.

Talk about the effect of having the long first stanza followed by a pause in the white space followed by a shift in tone and focus in the short, four-line stanza at the end.

PAIR IT WITH Wislawa Szymborska, "The End of the Beginning" (p. 784).

Reza Baraheni

Autumn in Tehran   (p. 772)

WORKS WELL FOR   Form; images; symbol.

ENTRY POINTS   The author describes the poem as a nonpolitical political poem. It tells of the death of many people who died in the horrendous Evin prison (see the note on page 773), but, Baraheni says, "it avoids being political and polemical by making a rather minute study of death and decay in metaphors and allusions, and finally it invokes the archaic symbols of poetry, the Shaman and Ozan, to lament and glorify the death of so many people, so many 'worlds.' . . . But the poem, as a poem, stands away from being political. It is an internal dialogue of the figures and the objects, and the spaces and line-breaks and in-line breaks, that shape the form of the poem."

The poem is an open-air marketplace for the reader's senses. Have the class notice the rich sensory content of the poem, perhaps listing all the images in connection to the various senses, and then discuss the overall effects of these images. In what ways does the poem restore the reader to the rich mystery of the senses?

Have the students discover the various shifts in the poem: shifts in perspective, tone, focus, feeling, idea, attention, and mood. They might discuss what these shifts reveal about the actual complexity of the most common of human experiences.

The poem's ending is open. It lends itself to a variety of implications. Have the students discuss this ambiguity and its appropriateness for the poem itself and as an ending.

PAIR IT WITH   Anna Akhmatova, "The Song of the Last Meeting" (p. 770).

Julia de Burgos

Returning   (p. 773)

WORKS WELL FOR   Form (lines, parallelism); figurative language.

ENTRY POINTS   This poem is what is often referred to as a "personal lyric," one in which the *I* of the poem is not only a singular person speaking about a singularly emotional experience, but also stands for the part of the self that is profoundly affected by experience. It's as if the *I* is a location, a place where the inner life of thought, imagination, memory, and feeling fuse in an overwhelming way. Discuss ways this poem seems to embody this idea of "personal lyric."

Ask students to discuss the various meanings of *returning* and the ways the title affects one's reading of the poem, or how it relates to the poem.

A personal lyric often centers on the speaker. Focus on the speaker and discuss what the speaker is going through and what can be inferred about what the speaker has gone through. Talk about the speaker's tone, intensity of tone, degrees of feeling embodied in the tone. What does the tone reveal about the speaker's attitudes?

A personal lyric is most effective when the reader can identify with the *I* of the poem. Ask students if they found themselves able to identify with the speaker and why or why not.

The speaker is addressing her- or himself. Inquire about the effect of that and about the shift to the word *soul* at the end of the poem. Talk about why the poem begins with "Indefinitely," and whether the word is meant to be connected to the title — returning indefinitely. Talk about the final image: "shadowing my own shadow." What may it imply?

PAIR IT WITH   Richard Wilbur, "Love Calls Us to the Things of This World" (p. 752).

Bei Dao

Night: Theme and Variations   (p. 774)

WORKS WELL FOR   Images; juxtaposition; tone.

ENTRY POINTS   Ask the class to talk about the ways the poet works with the ideas of collapse, destruction, and disappearance. What is the relationship of these to "night"? Discuss what layers of meaning there are in the poem in terms of what the poem implies is collapsing, being destroyed, or disappearing.

One could easily miss the juxtapositions in the poem. There are combinations and collisions of time, generations, values, tradition, culture, and such concepts as stillness/movement, creation/destruction, beauty/ugliness, secular/spiritual, the natural/the human-made, tender/harsh, dark/light, present/past. Ask students to discuss the role of these juxtapositions in the poem.

Talk about the ominous feel in the ending. What effect does it have on a second reading? In what ways does it affect the whole poem? Discuss what it may mean to call "night" a theme and what it means that there are variations on this theme. How does the title affect the way one reads the poem?

Discuss the inner structure of the poem in terms of the images, the ways the images when connected create "a whole greater than the sum of the parts," and the tonal variations. Focus on the speaker and talk about what the speaker's attitudes are toward this situation.

Talk about the effect of the use of list structure in the poem.

PAIR IT WITH   Charles Simic, "Begotten of the Spleen" (p. 728).

Faiz Ahmed Faiz

A Prison Daybreak   (p. 775)

WORKS WELL FOR   Images; figurative language.

ENTRY POINTS   Ask students to talk about the title, with its play on words; how the title sets up the poem; and how, when reading the poem, the reader is led to reflect all the more on the title.

Discuss personification in the poem. Ask about the effect with this subject of personifying the moon, eyes, whirlpools, night, day, breezes, poison, a lock, and a window. In light of the situation the speaker portrays, what ironies might there be in the use of personification?

Talk about what the speaker does to survive. What in the poem directly and indirectly reveals his way of surviving?

Talk about the speaker in terms of sensory experience. Notice how much of the speaker's experience comes through the senses. What does this create? How does it affect the speaker's imagination and his feelings and those of the reader? Talk about the mixture of beautifully luminous images with the horrific conditions of the prisoners. What are the effects of this mix?

Ask the class to discuss the ending in terms of hope and despair. Why would the speaker say they wait for a "rebel prince of legends" (l. 37)?

This poem lends itself to a discussion of ambiguity. Some might say that the poem is structured around ambiguity. Explore the poem for different ambiguous moments, phrases, words, and images. Discuss what is ambiguous about each and why they are appropriate for the poem.

PAIR IT WITH   Nazim Hikmet, "Letters from a Man in Solitary" (p. 776).

Nazim Hikmet

Letters from a Man in Solitary   (p. 776)

WORKS WELL FOR   Images; speaker; tone.

ENTRY POINTS   Ask the class to talk about this as a poem of address. Describe the relationship between the speaker and his wife. What are the ironies? What does that dynamic create in the poem, and how does it affect the reader?

Focus on the speaker and discuss what the speaker is experiencing. Talk about how the poem creates the experience of being in solitary. Noting the tone, talk about what the speaker's attitudes are and what the class thinks of those attitudes. Hikmet suffered as a political prisoner. Consider this in light of the poem, and discuss what difference knowing this makes.

Perhaps the most startling things in this poem are its celebration of natural beauty, the prisoner's enormous capacity to love, and his joy. Discuss why these are convincing, never sentimental, and not a rationalization to survive his conditions.

Talk about the structural elements in the poem. In what ways do they evoke the situation, express what the speaker is feeling, and create a tension between the "structure" of his condition and the poet's structuring of the poem? Attend to the use of sections, varying line lengths, intensity of line rhythms and tones, emphasized line breaks, indentation, lists within the poem, and changes of tone in the speaker's voice.

Talk about what makes this poem both heartrending and inspiring.

Compare this poem to "A Prison Daybreak." What do they have in common? In what ways do they differ?

PAIR IT WITH   Faiz Ahmed Faiz, "A Prison Daybreak" (p. 775).

Miroslav Holub

Elementary School Field Trip to the Dinosaur Exhibit   (p. 779)

WORKS WELL FOR   Allusions; images.

ENTRY POINTS   Ask students to describe what thoughts and feelings they associate with the words "field trip" (a chance to get out of school, to do something different, maybe exciting?). Then ask them to say what comes to mind from the words "dinosaur exhibit." (See if they *visualize* dinosaurs in an exhibit they have seen in a museum — if so, ask them to compare that to the experience in the poem, of a little boy who can't visualize what a dinosaur looks like, who needs to find a different way to gain some conception of what a dinosaur is like, as described in the third section of the poem.)

Discuss what the students make of the opening two lines. How do they affect the whole poem?

But that is just the start. The poem goes on to raise larger, epistemological questions, especially in stanza 4. Work through the stanza carefully. (Why "insanely" blank? Does "like Händel's Concerto Grosso" go with the line before it, or the line after, or neither? What does "a step aside" mean? Why would his mother say such a thing to him?) Ask students to discuss the meaning of lines 17–19, "but the hand already knows / that nothing is in the mind / that hasn't been in the senses."

Ask students to discuss the allusions in the poem, what they add, how they fit in (St. Georges; Rambos; Händel's Concerto Grosso). Push them especially to talk about the biblical allusion in line 26: Why would a dinosaur, Triceratops, be considered "Abel's younger brother"? (Abel, of course, is the younger of Adam's two sons in Gen. 4:1–15 and was killed by his older brother, Cain.)

Talk about what the last two lines may imply: "the last dinosaur / meeting the last man."

PAIR IT WITH   Anita Endrezze, "The Girl Who Loved the Sky" (p. 476).

Taslima Nasrin

Things Cheaply Had   (p. 780)

WORKS WELL FOR   Images; tone (irony, hyperbole).

ENTRY POINTS   Ask the class to explain what the poem is about, to discuss what are the "things" that are cheaply had. Discuss possible meanings of the first line: "In the market nothing can be had as cheap as women." The speaker has a voice that is somewhat reportorial and unemotional. What does that add to the poem's meaning and ambiguity? Talk about how this stance affects the reader. Ask if there are ways that the poet conveys emotions, even though the speaker is not intensely emotional.

Talk about the shift from the longer first section to the shorter second section. Consider if anything takes place in the white space. Discuss the meaning and effect of the change from focusing on the women to the cur and then to the image of the lock over the women's mouths.

Discuss the meaning and effectiveness of the image of the lock and why it is a golden lock.

Attend to and discuss the effect of the external structure of the poem, including the deeply indented lines and its use of a type of litany format by repeating "If they."

Ask students to note the ironies in the poem and comment on their impact and role. What do they reveal?

PAIR IT WITH   Marge Piercy, "Barbie Doll" (p. 494).

Pablo Neruda

The Dead Woman   (p. 781)

WORKS WELL FOR   Speaker; form; rhythm.

ENTRY POINTS   This is a poem of address. Ask students to consider who the *you* is. Could the *you* be a literal woman — the speaker's beloved, his "love" (l. 22) — and the poem an unusual love poem? If they think so, ask them to explain and support their answer from the text. Could the *you* be something other than, or in addition to, a woman? If students think it might be, ask them to explain what in the poem leads them to think so.

Pablo Neruda was a member of the Chilean government. In what ways could that biographical information affect one's reading of the poem? Talk about whether this is something one should know when reading the poem. Is this information necessary to make the poem complete or does it limit the poem? Could the poem be a political poem? (Could the *you* perhaps be the country he loves?) If students think it might be political, ask them to clarify what they mean, to find evidence in the poem for what they say, and to talk about what makes using a love poem effective as an approach to the political issues.

Focus on the speaker and his tone. What are his attitudes toward the one he loves and toward all that he cares about? What in the poem would support any conclusions?

Read again each stanza and discuss the speaker's tone and what he is feeling in each. In what ways does his tone and in what ways do his feelings change in themselves and in intensity in each stanza? Talk about why he changes throughout the poem. Discuss the effect of the blunt title and how it affects one's reading of the whole poem.

Talk about what the speaker may mean at the poem's end when he says that he "shall go on living . . . because you know that I am not just one man / but all men."

Poets have often taken on the role of the voice of those who are voiceless. Discuss in what ways this poem embodies that calling.

PAIR IT WITH   Langston Hughes, "Freedom's Plow" (p. 1258).

Octavio Paz

The Street   (p. 782)

WORKS WELL FOR   Images; symbol; paradox.

ENTRY POINTS   Ask students to describe what is going on in the poem. If they are hesitant at first, ask if it might deal in some way with identity. (For the person behind the speaker to duplicate the speaker's every move suggests that it is the speaker, or some aspect of the speaker.) Talk about what it may mean that, at the end of the poem, the speaker is following someone and when that person turns, he sees nobody.

Focus on and describe the speaker. Talk about the tone of voice and what the speaker may be feeling and experiencing.

Ask the students if the street is a metaphor or a symbol or a metonymy. If so, ask them to explain which, and why, and then talk about what they think the figure creates in the poem.

Discuss the implications of line 8, "Everything dark and doorless," in terms of what meanings it could embody or suggest and which meanings fit the context of the poem.

Octavio Paz once said, "When you say life is marvelous, you are saying a banality. But to *make* life a marvel — that is the role of poetry." Discuss what he meant and whether that is the case for this poem.

PAIR IT WITH   Julia de Burgos, "Returning" (p. 773).

Dahlia Ravikovitch

Clockwork Doll   (p. 782)

WORKS WELL FOR   Form (sonnet); irony.

ENTRY POINTS   Discuss the image of the clockwork doll and the image of the proper doll, what each represents, and what lies behind the creation of each. Then talk about what the speaker means by saying in line 7, "But I was a doll of a different sort." Talk about the implications of the words *clockwork* and *proper* and *different sort* as they are used in this poem.

Consider the poem to be dealing with the ways a self and/or an identity can be created. Ask the class to discuss the differences between the ways each self or identity is created. Talk about what the poem implies about the consequences of becoming each particular self or identity.

Ask students to describe the speaker and to discuss what the speaker is feeling and what attitudes the speaker holds toward herself and the society she finds herself in.

Talk about what it might mean when the speaker says that "they left me alone with the dogs and cats" (l. 10).

The final tercet is vivid, rich with colors and sensate images. Discuss what might be being suggested by this sudden shift in tone and image and energy.

Ask students to discuss the form. See whether they identify it as a sonnet; ask them how that form seems fitting to the content. The poem uses slant rhyme or off rhyme. Ask students to talk about why that use is appropriate for what the poem is dealing with.

PAIR IT WITH   Marge Piercy, "Barbie Doll" (p. 494).

Masaoka Shiki

Six Haiku   (p. 783)

WORKS WELL FOR   Images; form.

ENTRY POINTS   You may need to review what haiku is: The definition given in the glossary (p. 1509) is "a lyric form, originating in Japan, of seventeen syllables in three lines, the first and third having five syllables and the second seven, presenting an image of a natural object or scene that expresses a distinct emotion or spiritual insight." Ask the class to discuss how any of these haiku fulfill the requirements. You might point out to the class, however, that just as some writers create variations on the sonnet (a sixteen-line sonnet or a sonnet without rhyme or without meter, for example), so some writers vary the form of the haiku, retaining its spirit but altering the number of syllables or lines to create a startling effect.

Ask the students which if any of the haiku lead them to have an "aha" experience and have them say what happened for them, how the haiku affected them. Notice how different senses are used in this series of haiku and discuss them in light of sensory experience and what the combinations create.

Discuss any of the haiku in terms of the shift or juxtaposition between the first two lines and the third line.

These haiku have some subtle implications. Some might argue they even have social and/or political implications. Ask the students if they see any such implications and ask them to explain what these are and why they think these are such. Then talk about whether any students think this is an inappropriate reading of haiku.

You might suggest that the students try writing a series of haiku, perhaps doing one a day as a kind of discipline or meditation. Ask them to discuss what they experienced.

PAIR IT WITH   William Carlos Williams, "The Red Wheelbarrow" (p. 468); Xu Gang, "Red Azalea on the Cliff" (p. 785).

Wislawa Szymborska

The End and the Beginning   (p. 784)

WORKS WELL FOR   Images; irony.

ENTRY POINTS   This is a war poem with a difference — it focuses on the clean-up job after conflict has ended. A good entry point is diction and tone in the first stanza: Ask students to discuss the words (such as the connotations of "tidy up") and ironies.

Ask students to discuss the juxtapositions, ironies, and surprising phrases (the biting ideas and ironies of stanza 5, for example). Discuss the role of the title in this poem. What does it apply to?

Ask the class to consider whether the tidying up is only physical. See if they pick up on lines 33–34: "From time to time someone still must / dig up a rusted argument." If not, point them to it and ask them to discuss its metaphors and meaning.

Talk about the last stanza. Ask students to think about what it says in terms of their own lives and how it applies to history generally.

Talk about the ways that the structural elements are meaningful in relation to what the poem deals with. Consider the stanza structure, the space between stanzas, the line length, line breaks, and what is focused on in each stanza.

PAIR IT WITH Julia Alvarez, "How I Learned to Sweep" (p. 560).

Xu Gang

Red Azalea on the Cliff (p. 785)

WORKS WELL FOR Apostrophe; paradox.

ENTRY POINTS The poem employs apostrophe, addressing the red azalea. Ask students to think about why the speaker might be talking to the azalea. Ask if the azalea might be a synecdoche, and if so, a part of what whole?

The poem in part is about beauty and nature. Talk about the speaker's views of beauty that appear throughout the poem. But clearly there's more to it than that. Discuss why the red azalea makes the speaker "shudder with fear" (l. 3) and why line 4 is juxtaposed with lines 1–2. What is conveyed in line 5, "Beauty, always looking on at disaster"? Ask students to pick out ironies and paradoxes in the poem, and to discuss their effect.

Discuss what the speaker may mean by saying at the end of the third stanza that "Then an azalea would surely bloom in his heart," and at the end of the poem when the speaker says, "Sometimes the past years look / Just like the azalea on the cliff."

Talk about the structure of the poem in terms of the effect of the stanzas, the varied line lengths, the inner imagistic structure, and the use of address. Perhaps compare the poem to the series of haiku on page 783. What are similarities and differences?

PAIR IT WITH Mary Oliver, "Goldenrod" (p. 699).

Reading Drama

In a typical class, you are likely to find students who are very familiar with drama and theater — possibly having performed in high school or college plays — and others who have never even attended a live performance. That diversity in background makes this unit challenging to teach. The approach in this chapter is very basic — explaining to students who need it what a page of drama looks like and what to expect and look for as they begin reading, while also giving more experienced students some fresh insights into the nature of drama. The emphasis in this unit is on reading plays as literature, not assessing performances as drama, but we hope instructors will encourage students to attend a play, especially if they haven't before, or perhaps will require the whole class to attend a campus performance and then spend a class period, or part of one, discussing it as a group.

A difficulty in teaching drama in a course like this one is the length of plays. It's difficult to have students read a full-length play, or even part of one, while also reading a chapter on elements (and spending class time on it). In an attempt to remedy this, we have included one-act plays in Chapters 17–20. Most of them are short enough to be read in addition to the pages that discuss the elements of drama. Most aspects of drama can be taught as effectively through a short play as through a full-length play. We believe, however, that including at least one full-length play in a course is important to give students experience with how the greater length allows for in-depth development.

We assume that most (or all) instructors using this book will want students to study Chapter 17, on character, conflict, and dramatic action, and Chapter 18, on setting and structure. Some instructors, however, may decide not to ask students to read Chapter 19, on theaters and their influence, or Chapter 20, on dramatic types (genres) and their effects. We think the latter chapters are valuable for learning how to get the most out of reading a play, but we also are aware of the time constraints that we all face. If you decide not to require Chapters 19 or 20, we suggest you consider at least listing them as suggested reading and explaining what students may find of value in them.

CHAPTER 17 Character, Conflict, and Dramatic Action

Alice Childress

Florence (p. 795)

STARTER Even though set is not covered until the next chapter, we find that a helpful way to start discussion of this play is — without using the term *set* — to ask a student to come up and draw a diagram of the stage layout, sketching as much as she or he can remember and then having the rest of the class chip in with additional details or refinements.

ENTRY POINTS The prompts following the play and the discussion of the play in the rest of the chapter cover its characters, plot, conflicts, dialogue, and dramatic action pretty comprehensively. You might ask students if they have questions about the play's content or techniques or about specific details, but it's a pretty straightforward play that they should be able to follow and understand.

You might follow up on "Approaching the Reading" question 5 (p. 806) and ask students if the play is still relevant and worth reading even though it was written more than fifty years ago. See if they agree with what we said in that paragraph about the value of reading it for the way it brings to life conditions people faced in earlier eras and for the universal issues it explores.

A further way to approach it is as a play dealing with borders. Ask students to make a list of different types of borders that appear and are confronted in the play (for example, the low railing dividing the waiting room as a physical border, the social/cultural borders between North and South, the metaphorical borders separating economic classes, the metaphorical barriers that prevent people from entering or succeeding in various careers, and so on).

PAIR IT WITH   Alice Walker, "Everyday Use" (p. 101).

Caleen Sinnette Jennings
Classyass   (p. 812)

STARTER   This is a short play, taking around ten minutes to perform. Ask a group of students to perform it for the whole class.

ENTRY POINTS   Students like this play because of its brevity, rapid pace, smart-assed dialogue, and satisfying retribution on a guy who had it coming — and because it deals with college students, perhaps types they can identify readily from their own experience.

The "Approaching the Reading" questions (p. 818) focus on the characters, conflicts, and use of dialogue in the play. Ask students to describe the two main characters and to point out the conflicts in the play. Ask them to focus on the opening speech and describe how it sets the stage and tone for the rest of the play.

Much of the play's effect is created by its satire on stereotypes and stereotyping. Ask students to give examples and discuss the point the play makes about them. Consider the names and how they relate to this theme.

Compare the final speech in the play with the opening speech. Has Amadeus learned a lesson? What evidence of that is there? Ask students to comment on the effectiveness of the final lines of the play.

PAIR IT WITH   John Updike, "A & P" (p. 386).

CHAPTER 18 Setting and Structure

Susan Glaspell

Trifles (p. 822)

STARTER   Ask students to draw a sketch or diagram of the set for *Trifles*, using stage directions throughout the play for guidance.

ENTRY POINTS   This is a very teachable play, one that students enjoy discussing. In the chapter we discuss the play's setting and structure, but not its characters, conflicts, and themes, wanting to leave those for class discussion. We will follow up here on some of the "Approaching the Reading" questions on page 833.

You might start with plot, asking someone to summarize the plot to make sure students clearly understand the action, and then direct attention to some particular features, such as the use of gaps (have students point out examples of gaps and how they tried filling them on first reading). Discuss the opening stage directions: The men come in first, the women behind them, and the women stand together apart from the men, signaling visually one of the key contrasts and conflicts of the play. Other features include the use of detective story conventions ("has anything been moved?"). Notice also the tight construction of the plot, which deals with a slightly more than twenty-four hour period but is presented in actual time (the stage is never empty — the time covered and the performance time are the same).

This is a good story for exploring conflicts and contrasts. Ask students to identify conflicts (Mr. Wright vs. Mrs. Wright, Mr. Wright and the canary, the men vs. the women, the inner conflict in Mrs. Hale because she neglected Mrs. Wright, and the inner conflict in Mrs. Hale and Mrs. Peters over whether to tell the men about the dead bird). Do the same for parallels and contrasts in the structure: the parallels between Mrs. Wright and the canary ("she was kind of like a bird herself — real sweet and pretty" — p. 830; both liked to sing; both lived in cages; both are broken by Mr. Wright; and more), between the bird and Mrs. Peters's kitten (when it was killed by a boy with a hatchet, she "would have . . . hurt him" if she hadn't been held back — p. 831); between the quietness of Mrs. Peters's house after her baby died and the quietness there must have been in the Wrights' house after the canary died; between the choking of the bird and the choking of Mr. Wright; and so on. Notice how lines near the end begin to take on double significance.

Ask students to describe the main characters: Mr. and Mrs. Wright (whom they should be able to describe even though neither appears in the play), Mrs. Hale, and Mrs. Peters. Ask how much we learn about the latter characters by paying attention to stage directions.

Have the class discuss the relevance and significance of the title. Someone should notice the irony involved with it — use that to inquire about other uses of irony. Discuss the significance and appropriateness of the last line.

This could be a good play for discussing borders, the things that separate people in it. Ask if Mrs. Hale and Mrs. Peters did the right thing in covering for Mrs. Wright (by taking out the uneven stitching in the quilt, by hiding the canary even after the County Attorney told them, "I would like to see what you take" — p. 826). Mrs. Peters says on page 827, "The law is the law." Later, Mrs. Hale accuses herself for not visiting Mrs. Wright: "That was a crime! That was a crime! Who's going to punish that?" (p. 831). The two women become in effect prosecutor, judge, and jury, convicting Mr. Wright of crimes against Mrs. Wright and freeing her on the grounds of implied self-defense (of her personhood, not her life) — note that when Glaspell rewrote the play as fiction in 1917 she entitled the story "A Jury of Her Peers." Ask students why Mrs. Hale and Mrs. Peters end up feeling as they do about Mrs. Wright (the key lines seem to be, "I might have known she needed help! I know how things can be — for women. . . . We all go through the same things — it's all just a different kind of the same thing" — p. 831).

PAIR IT WITH   Bessie Head, "The Collector of Treasures" (p. 421); Zora Neale Hurston, "Sweat" (p. 263).

David Ives

Sure Thing   (p. 839)

STARTER   Arrange for two students to act out part of the play.

ENTRY POINTS   A good way to initiate discussion is to have two people act out a page or two of the play, or the whole play, so students can see and hear conversation stop as the bell rings and start over. Ask the class to talk about the effect of watching as opposed to reading and then about what the play is getting at by the stopping and backing up and repeating. It also provides an opportunity to discuss how the characters should be interpreted — do the student actors bring out the characters well? Could the characters be interpreted differently? Should the characters be portrayed as changing and developing? In what sense or direction do they develop?

The "Approaching the Reading" questions (p. 848) suggest several ways to approach the play and initiate discussion of its setting, structure, and handling of characterization. All of them offer good entry points for the play.

The chapter's introduction to the play says that in it "we watch two characters as they attempt to connect with one another. But there's a twist: If the character does not connect or slips up, she or he backtracks and tries again" (p. 838). Suggest that the class discuss this description of the play. Is it adequate and accurate? If so, what's the point of having characters backtrack and try again? (Could the characters be trying out different faces, creating different images of themselves, attempting to mesh with the image the other person is creating? Could the play be suggesting that that's what *all* personal encounters — not just boy-meets-girl ones — usually involve?) If not, can they suggest a better way to explain what the play is about?

Ask students to discuss the title. The words are used several times in the play. Does their meaning change or develop? Is the title ironic? Is the use of "sure thing" in the play ironic? Or sometimes ironic and sometimes not?

PAIR IT WITH   Dagoberto Gilb, "Love in L.A." (p. 55).

Theaters and Their Influence

CHAPTER 19

Luis Valdez

Los Vendidos   (p. 864)

STARTER   Ask students to bring to class a list of features in the play that make it work, that they think are particularly effective.

ENTRY POINTS   Students usually find this play funny and fun to read. Like most works with surprise endings, it should be read twice, since details and actions take on new meaning in light of the ending. Use the lists students compiled for their Starter assignment to talk about what makes the play work — to point out and discuss what is clever or interesting or humorous about it (for example, the parallels between a used car lot and a used Mexican lot, including the very audaciousness of the idea of a used Mexican lot; the parody of the language and type of advertising in used car lots; the mixture of English and Spanish, with Spanish used often for witty effects; the satisfaction that the secretary who denies her heritage by anglicizing the pronunciation of her name gets what she has coming to her by being taken in by a clever Hispanic).

In the introduction to the published version of *Mambo Mouth* (New York: Bantam, 1993), John Leguizamo writes, "Some reviewers and members of the press insinuated that I was perpetuating stereotypes rather than lambasting them. . . . But if my years of performing comedy have taught me anything, it's that you've got to be strong to make fun of yourself. In creating *Mambo Mouth*, I felt that mocking the Latin community was one of the most radical ways to empower it." Have students point out stereotypes in the play (that Mexicans are lazy and dirty, that they fight a lot and get arrested). Ask them to what extent Leguizamo's comments apply also to *Los Vendidos*.

Ask students to point out uses of satire in the play and to evaluate their effectiveness. The aim of his "actos," Valdez said (see "Approaching the Reading" question 2 on p. 873), is to "inspire the audience to social action. Illuminate specific points about social problems. Satirize the opposition. Show or hint at a solution. Express what people are feeling." Invite students to discuss the extent to which *Los Vendidos* achieves those aims.

Ask students to discuss the relevance and effectiveness of the title, perhaps using a word play to mean both "those who are sold" (the used Mexicans who seem to be for sale on the lot) and "the sellouts" (as Honest Sancho appears to be and Miss Jimenez certainly is). Ask students to watch for ways the play involves borders, literal and metaphorical (the literal borders of the car lot; metaphorical borders between Anglo and Hispanic cultures, between languages, between social classes, between political outlooks).

PAIR IT WITH   Dagoberto Gilb, "Love in L.A." (p. 55).

John Leguizamo

From Mambo Mouth: A Savage Comedy   (p. 874)

STARTER   Show the class the Pepe section performed by John Leguizamo in the film version released in 1992 by Uni/Polydor and available in VHS.

ENTRY POINTS   Ask students to discuss the difference between reading Pepe's monologue and watching Leguizamo (an excellent actor and comedian) perform it.

Remind students that the monologue by Pepe, funny and effective as it is by itself, is one section of a one-actor play. Part of the comedy and enjoyment of *Mambo Mouth* derives from watching the same actor take on the different roles and the cumulative effect as one character follows another.

Ask students what Leguizamo is satirizing in the Pepe monologue and what serious point he is making. In the introduction to the published version of the play (New York: Bantam, 1993), Leguizamo writes, "Some reviewers and members of the press insinuated that I was perpetuating stereotypes rather than lambasting them. . . . But if my years of performing comedy have taught me anything, it's that you've got to be strong to make fun of yourself. In creating *Mambo Mouth*, I felt that mocking the Latin community was one of the most radical ways to empower it. I love the world I come from, and only because I do can I poke fun at it." Ask students to discuss how the play could be a way of empowering the Latino community.

Ask the class to comment on the title. What is implied by "mouth" and calling it a "mambo mouth"? What is suggested by the subtitle "A Savage Comedy"?

The published version of the play includes this dedication: "This book is for all the Latino people who have had a hard time holding on to a dream and just made do." Ask students how this might apply to the part of *Mambo Mouth* they read and watched.

PAIR IT WITH   Martín Espada, "The Saint Vincent de Paul Food Pantry Stomp" (p. 649).

CHAPTER 20 Dramatic Types and Their Effects

Milcha Sanchez-Scott

The Cuban Swimmer (p. 890)

STARTER Ask students to come to class with ideas on how this play could be staged — what sets and props might be used for a play whose setting is on and in the ocean.

ENTRY POINTS Some students will find parts of this play (especially the ending) hard to understand. It might do well to start by asking the class to go through the play by scenes and summarize what goes on in each, focusing on the conflicts. They might also divide the characters into groups: (1) Margarita, who is involved in a conflict with nature (the ocean), with other swimmers (presumably they are professionals, she an amateur), and with her father; (2) her father, who is trying to get her to fulfill his ambitions — thus, he is involved in generational conflict and a struggle with issues of identity, in part growing out of being an immigrant; (3) the rest of the family, in conflict with the father and each other; and (4) the sports reporters. Students might notice that one group is in the water (Margarita with the other, unseen swimmers); two groups are on the boat; and one group is in the helicopter.

The first "Approaching the Reading" question (p. 902) asks students to pick out examples in scenes 1–4 of various types of comedy, such as witty dialogue, satiric comedy, and parody. Ask students to point out parts they think are especially funny and to explain what humor contributes to the play and its overall effect.

The tone changes in scene 5. That is partly a result of the action, as Margarita begins to cramp and panic and wants to quit, and partly a result of the father's reaction. His character is developed most fully in the play — ask students to talk about what he is like, in scenes 1–4 and in scene 5, where he loses all perspective in his desire for Margarita to win the race (and for himself as coach to be victorious).

Students will want to talk about the final scene even without urging. See how they approach it and what questions they raise. Get them to discuss tone and how they think the scene should be staged and played — that is, is it serious? Satiric? Comic? It definitely involves magical realism, discussed on page 47. If students have read examples of magical realism, such as Gabriel García Márquez's "A Very Old Man with Enormous Wings" (p. 415), Helena María Viramontes's "The Moths" (p. 391), or Agha Shahid Ali's "I Dream It Is Afternoon When I Return to Delhi" (p. 597), ask them to point out features of the genre in this scene. If they aren't familiar with magical realism, you may need to point such features out. Mixed with the magical realism is religious imagery. Prayers and other religious language are present throughout the play. In scene 5, the stage directions call for Margarita to stretch out her arms "as if on a cross" (p. 900). The final speech of the play is full of religious imagery, including allusions to Christ: "This is indeed a miracle! It's a resurrection! Margarita Suárez . . . is now walking on the waters" (p. 902). Is Margarita to be taken as a type of Christ? If so, is the tone serious or ironic? The decision on that makes a huge difference in the theme of the play, what it all adds up to (see "Approaching the Reading" question 4 — p. 902). What it adds up to might deal with the issue of identity, especially of the father and daughter: Each seeks an individual identity but is defined until Margarita's death (or "death") only in relation to the other, all of this being complicated by the confusion created by being "outsiders" in a new culture (consider the title: the *Cuban* swimmer, not American or Cuban American).

To some extent this is a play about language. There is the mixture of Spanish and English throughout the play. Ask students about the effect of that mixture: Is it confusing? Realistic? There is the parody of sports reporters and the clichés they use. There is the religious language. There is the language of gesture and symbol. You might ask students to discuss what the play is saying about language and communication through its handling of language and miscommunication or lack of communication.

PAIR IT WITH   Gish Jen, "Who's Irish?" (p. 272).

David Henry Hwang

As the Crow Flies   (p. 903)

STARTER   Ask students to pick out two or three examples of humor in the play, ones they think would get the biggest laughs in a theater.

ENTRY POINTS   Typical of Hwang's work, the play depicts the confrontation of Eastern and Western cultures, complicated by Chinese myths or, in this case, folk beliefs. Ask students to summarize what happens in the play, calling attention to its humor (perhaps ask them to report what they wrote down for their Starter assignment) as well as to the conflicts, cultural and personal.

Magical realism appears most frequently in works of Spanish or Hispanic writers, as in the Milcha Sanchez-Scott play *The Cuban Swimmer*, discussed earlier, but it is not restricted to them. Ask students if characteristics of magical realism, or a quality similar to it, appear in this play. See if that proves helpful in understanding the last part of the play. Or would it be more helpful to read it just as symbolic?

In a monologue, Mrs. Chan says, "We are born traveling. We travel — all our lives. I am not looking for a home. I know there is none" (p. 908). Invite students to discuss the significance of these lines, in various directions: as they help to understand her character and situation; as they bring out archetypal implications and a wider significance for readers and viewers. Follow the references to "home" in the last few pages of the play. Consider how they relate back to these lines and how they shape the meaning and significance of the ending.

Ask students to discuss how the title relates to the play, particularly the references to crows in the final two pages.

Ask students to discuss Hannah and her second role as Sandra. What's the point in the final lines of the play?

PAIR IT WITH   Agha Shahid Ali, "I Dream It Is Afternoon When I Return to Delhi" (p. 597).

Writing about Drama

CHAPTER **21**

Some students will feel relief in being able to write about drama instead of writing about poetry — drama has plot and character, with which they feel more confident and comfortable than with poetic techniques and approaches, partly because they know them through fiction. Encourage students to review the material on writing about stories in Chapter 8, much of which applies to drama as well, and to review the suggestions in Chapter 8 about writing short papers generally, much of which this chapter builds on but doesn't repeat.

One-act plays work well in providing topics for short papers, just as they are convenient for class discussion. Full-length plays also can be used for short papers, of course, usually by focusing the paper on a single scene, passage, technique, or theme. If you assign papers on full-length plays, you might work with the class on the techniques needed for focusing on an aspect of the play, examining it in depth, and drawing connections between it and the play as a whole. Keep in mind that full-length plays can often provide good topics for research papers.

A Collection of Plays

Henrik Ibsen

A Doll House   (p. 926)

WORKS WELL FOR   Problem play (see pp. 887–88); character; symbols.

ENTRY POINTS   Some students may have difficulty following the details of the plot, especially regarding Nora's financial transactions and legal difficulties, in the context of the laws and approaches of the time. Invite questions about the storyline or ask students to summarize what goes on in the story. Compiling a list of conflicts can help clarify the plot and the issues it deals with — conflicts between people, conflicts between people and society, and internal conflicts (all apply especially to Nora: her conflicts with Torvald, Krogstad, and society generally, and within herself). You might note also the careful compression of plot: The events occur over a three-day period, Christmas Eve, Christmas Day, and the day following; the various strands woven over many years come together in that season (ironically) and form a turning point in all their lives.

A good place to enter the play is with its title image. Ask students to describe what they think of when they hear the term *doll house* and then to explain how that relates to the play. For a child, a doll house is not so much a place to play with dolls as the place where the dolls live — so it's the home of dolls, not of real people or adults. It's an unreal place, a place that exists in the imagination. The doll house image treats both Nora and Torvald as dolls — both are playing games in an unreal world. The doll house lends its image to Nora's life and her world, shaping her relationship first to her father and then to her husband; it defines her understanding (and that of society in her day) of the role a woman is supposed to fill, as helpless, obedient, using feminine wiles to gain her ends; and it defines her storybook sense of what a husband should be — strong, courageous, protective. All of this coincides perfectly with

Torvald's view of things: The doll house fits his impressions of himself and his ideas of the role a wife should fill.

Ask students to put the doll house into larger context (outside it is a bigger world, a "real" adult, male world of economic pressures and legal rules, a ruthless world with little space for unrealistic idealism) and to explain how Nora has been forced out of the smaller world into the larger one. That is, through the necessity of raising money for the trip to save her husband's life, she has come into contact with that larger world. The play shows those two worlds crashing into each other: The collision is inevitable once she gets outside the doll house. And after she leaves the safe, self-indulgent nest of Torvald's care, she eventually will have to judge it from outside and will find it lacking, particularly because the reality does not fit the image, as she can't help but learn.

Students will want to talk about the characters, and they should. Ibsen sought to create psychological realism in his characterizations — suggest that students keep that standard in view as they discuss the characters: Does he achieve such realism? (See the discussion of nineteenth-century realism on pp. 856–58.) Are the characters believable? Ask students to describe Nora and Torvald (for Torvald, what he seems through Nora's eyes, and how other people view him), drawing on what they say and do and what is said about them, but also drawing on foils set up in the play: How does Mrs. Lind accentuate qualities of Nora? How does Dr. Rank bring out aspects of Nora and Torvald? What does the relationship of Mrs. Lind and Krogstad show about the relationship of Nora and Torvald? Dr. Rank is particularly interesting: Ask why he is in the play. Does he have any role other than bringing out aspects of Nora and Torvald, as, for example, Nora's innocence in not knowing about sexually transmitted diseases, and her wanting Rank to love her but not tell her he loves her? She is playing a game with him, and reality must not impose.

And students will want to talk about the climax of the play, when Nora decides to leave Torvald. Be sure students understand the impact of this action — in literary and social terms — in the late nineteenth century. Audiences were conditioned to expect happy endings — for a play like this, they would anticipate a tearful reconciliation between a contrite husband and an understanding wife. Their literary sensibilities were unsettled and their social values were shocked to have the play end instead with the door slamming as Nora abandons her husband and children. As critic John Gassner put it, "An anarchist's pistol shot could not have reverberated more frighteningly in the Victorian world than the closing of that door."

Ask students to discuss what happens to the relationship between Nora and Torvald after he reads and reacts to Krogstad's letter, and why Nora decides she must leave, rather than try to repair the relationship. Does her action seem consistent with her earlier character and adequately motivated? Are there foreshadowings of it? Is it the culmination of feelings or ideas she had suppressed through the years? Is it believable that she could leave her children behind? (That seems foreshadowed early in the play.)

Ibsen once said, "A dramatist's business is not to answer questions, but merely to ask them." You might ask students to consider to what extent that seems to apply to *A Doll House*. If it does, what questions was Ibsen asking in it? Are those questions still applicable today? Do the questions stay the same, or do they change as time passes and readers change?

Finally, you might ask students if the play seems relevant and worth reading today in light of the huge social changes that have occurred since the play was written.

PAIR IT WITH Nahid Rachlin, "Departures" (p. 371).

Arthur Miller

Death of a Salesman (p. 980)

WORKS WELL FOR Modern tragedy; characters; symbols.

ENTRY POINTS Many students will have difficulty following the action as they read this play, particularly with the shifts in time, the shifts on the stage (signaled in the opening stage directions; the handling of set is discussed on pp. 859–60), and the shifts in Willy's mental state. For those who are not experienced readers of plays, it would be helpful to show them how to pick up the cues that signal such changes. And it probably would be a good idea to have the class summarize what goes on in the portion of the play assigned for that day.

You might alert students to look for gaps in the play and point out to them that Miller creates gaps to heighten emphasis and increase dramatic tension. As active readers (or viewers), they need to be raising questions about what is left out at a given point, anticipating how the gaps might be filled, and watching for the answers the plays supplies. (Why was Biff out of touch with his mother for three months? What happened to Biff that caused him to change? What is the barrier between Biff and Willy that has changed their relationship so significantly?)

One way into the play is to ask students to pick out its key conflicts, such as Willy vs. Biff, Willy vs. Linda, Willy vs. Charlie, Willy's internal conflicts, Willy vs. Howard Wagner, employees vs. employers, the lower middle classes vs. society.

Another approach is to focus on characters. Ask students to describe Willy, Linda, Biff, Happy, Charlie, and Bernard, through what they say and do and what is said about them, but also through the pairings and contrasts (Willy-Ben, Biff-Happy, Biff-Bernard, Willy-Charlie, Willy-Howard). Willy is the most important character to explore in depth: Is he a good husband? Is he a good father? (The answers are likely to be mixed: yes, but . . .) Did he instill good values in his sons? Is he a good salesman? Is he (and was he) a successful salesman? Does he understand himself well? Does he understand the way to succeed? Why won't he work for Charlie? Why does he commit suicide?

A central theme in the play is identity: Linda, Charley, and Bernard seem to know themselves well and be comfortable with who they are. But Willy, Biff, and Happy don't. Ask students to discuss this, especially for Willy, particularly for how his identity relates to his career. Does being a salesman (what he sells is never indicated) give him a sense of purpose and self-worth the way another career might have? How do the references to building fit in? What do the references to planting, gardens, and seeds contribute? (Do they function as symbols?)

The play is skillfully constructed, including the contrasting pairs discussed in the previous paragraph. The time covered in the present is about twenty-four hours, with flashbacks filling in events from earlier years. The day covered in the present is one in which several events coincide, especially Biff coming home for a visit and Willy being unable to drive to New England and then being fired. The play uses foreshadowing effectively: Ask students to give examples (such as Willy's reaction to Linda's darning stockings — p. 1016; Willy saying, "I got nothing to give him" — p. 1027; Willy earlier smashing into a bridge railing — p. 1008).

Invite students to discuss the play in the broader context of the American dream. Have someone clarify what that means and then ask how the play relates to it. What larger social issues does the play raise? Is it a play that continues to be relevant and meaningful in the twenty-first century, or is it of interest mostly as a historical document?

You might also initiate a discussion of the nature of modern tragedy: Ask students to discuss how *Death of a Salesman* is similar to and different from earlier tragedies, such as *Oedipus Rex* and *Othello*. Chapter 20 lays the groundwork for such a discussion. (See pp. 884–85 for *Death of a Salesman*.) Go on to the broader question of why people read and watch tragedies: Why not stick to stories with happy endings? What is the appeal or value of watching stories about tragic events?

PAIR IT WITH   Jhumpa Lahiri, "Interpreter of Maladies" (p. 285).

William Shakespeare

Othello the Moor of Venice   (p. 1054)

WORKS WELL FOR   Tragedy; plot; character.

ENTRY POINTS   The skill with which the plot is constructed can perhaps be best illustrated by an outline, which might also help students see the play as a whole and grasp relationships between its parts:

I. THE BACKGROUND
   a. *Injuries* — Rodrigo was passed over by Desdemona, and Iago by Othello; they tell Brabantio about his daughter's marriage.

    b. *Accusations* — We meet Othello after hearing negative things about him, as Brabantio accuses him of using enchantments over Desdemona.

    c. *Defense* — The Duke analyzes thoughtfully reports about the attack upon Cyprus and the accusations against Othello, who defends himself eloquently and is cleared.

  II. THE TRAP IS SET: The characters arrive at Cyprus, the enemy fleet is destroyed in a storm, a holiday is declared to celebrate, Iago gets Cassio drunk, and Cassio is dismissed by Othello.

 III. THE TRAP IS BAITED: Desdemona promises to help Cassio get reinstated at the same time that Iago plants suspicions in Othello's mind and warns him to watch his wife and Cassio closely. Othello does not analyze things thoughtfully, as the Duke did in Act I, but allows the seed of jealousy to grow and demands that Iago give him proof of Desdemona's unfaithfulness — visual evidence ("oracular proof"). Note: the play includes a great deal of "sight" imagery.

 IV. THE TRAP CLOSES: Iago fills Othello's mind with images of Desdemona being unfaithful — thus Othello sees in his mind's eye the "oracular proof" he sought; he sees what he thinks is further visual evidence as Cassio seems to laugh about being with Desdemona and then as Cassio has Desdemona's handkerchief. Othello says she must die.

  V. THE TRAP KILLS: Iago goads Rodrigo to kill Cassio, but Cassio escapes and Iago kills Rodrigo to silence him; Othello remonstrates with Desdemona, does not listen to her, and smothers her; when Othello learns the truth about Desdemona, he kills himself.

    Othello is at the center of the play and discussion might start with his character. Ask students to list his character traits, both strengths and weaknesses (he is an admired soldier and military officer, a man of nobility, a man of great integrity and humanity). But he is in many respects an outsider in the city of Venice. Have students add to their list various ways in which Othello is an outsider and how that contributes to his character: For example, he is a black man in a white society (which undermines his confidence that Desdemona can continue to love him); he is a soldier in a civilian setting (he knows how to deal with the clear-cut rules and expectations of the military and its culture of trusting one's comrades, but is unsure of himself in Venice's civilian society, thus providing Iago — whom he trusts as a fellow soldier — the opportunity to manipulate his mind); he is an alien, perhaps a hired soldier, living in Italy; he is outside of Desdemona's social group by age as well as race and nationality (because he is much older, he can be made to believe she won't continue to care for him). (Othello is not an outsider in religion. Presumably he was born Muslim, but he is now a baptized Christian, according to Iago in 2.3.302–3.)

Students should also discuss Iago's character. Again, a list of traits would help (negatives surely will predominate, but make sure they notice the positives, too — he must be a man of charm and even charisma because everyone trusts him — trust is part of his name, "honest Iago"). In scene 1 of act 2, as the company waits for Othello's ship to arrive, Iago is witty, outgoing, and ingratiating. But he is also filled with hate, envy, and vindictiveness. Students should look for motivations for what he does to Othello — some can be found: Othello did not give him the promotion he thinks he deserved, and he suspects Othello may have slept with his wife (1.3.368–71). But for the most part motivation is lacking: He is a descendent of the Vice, the evil tempter in medieval morality plays. Iago becomes a devil figure: Othello wants to check if Iago's feet are cloven, like the devil's (5.2.286), and he refers to Iago as a "demi-devil" in 5.2.301. Iago seems to push Othello as far as possible almost for sport.

One can also ask if things got out of hand — that Iago intends only to poison Othello's life by making him jealous (3.3.214); but when Othello is unable to live with suspicions and jealousy (3.3.179–80), events force Iago further and further to results he perhaps did not originally anticipate. Note also Iago's mode of operation: He plants ideas using suggestiveness but never makes positive statements on which he might be challenged later; he is opportunistic, using what comes to him (the handkerchief, for example, and what characters do or say); he has a slow, apparently thoughtful, hesitant way of talking that makes him seem to say less than he knows (3.3.120); he uses reverse psychology (by saying in 3.3.475 "but let her live," Iago plants the idea that Othello should kill Desdemona).

The skillfulness of the plot is evident in the use of foils and other character pairings. Othello and Iago contrast in many ways. Emilia is a foil for Desdemona, evident especially in 4.3.59–79, where Emilia admits that she might cheat on her husband for the right price, while Desdemona says she would not do so for the whole world (see also 4.2.161–64). Desdemona in her goodness and love contrasts with Iago in his evil and hatred. Scenes are connected carefully through foreshadowing and repetitions.

Students may raise questions regarding the believability of the play. So much depends on coincidences. And it seems incredible that when Emilia sees how upset Desdemona is about the loss of the handkerchief, she does not tell Desdemona where it is. Without question the plot strains credulity. But you should point out to students these problems arise mostly as we read the play and can stop to think about what's happening. On the stage, the plot moves along so rapidly, with such tightness and unity, that the problems don't have a chance to occur. The same is true of the handling of time in the play. The events on Cyprus occur in the space of about twenty-four hours, and the marriage of Desdemona and Othello occurred only shortly before they left Venice to sail to Cyprus. Yet Iago convinces Othello that Desdemona has been unfaithful to him often ("she with Cassio hath the act of shame / A thousand times committed," 5.2.212–13), though there was no time for all of that to occur. Shakespeare skillfully creates a sense of double time, in which events must move rapidly, for Iago's scheme would be exposed in the course of time. On the other hand, events seem to move slowly, allowing the possibility for many events to occur.

Othello fits the pattern of medieval tragedy in that he starts in prosperity and then falls into adversity. Ask students about their impression of him at the end of the play. Does he regain a sense of heroic dignity and respect, or does he die defeated and despised?

(The staging of Elizabethan plays is discussed on pp. 853–56, using *Othello* as the main example. Elizabethan tragedy is discussed on pp. 882–83, with *Othello* discussed briefly to illustrate.)

PAIR IT WITH   Arthur Miller, *Death of a Salesman* (p. 980).

Sophocles

Oedipus Rex   (p. 1145)

WORKS WELL FOR   Tragedy; plot; character; dramatic irony.

ENTRY POINTS   Spend some time going over the masterful handling of plot in *Oedipus Rex*, noting such features as the *in medias res* opening, the way exposition is introduced, the steady development of the action, the way attention is deflected from Oedipus (including the use of Teiresias and then Kreon as red herrings), the way the various threads begin to converge with a powerful sense of inevitability, the way Iokaste's death and Oedipus's blinding are contrived to occur offstage, as was conventional for violence in Greek drama.

Ask students to discuss characters, particularly that of Oedipus. What are his strengths and weaknesses? Point students to the definitions of *hamartia* and *tragic flaw* in the Glossary (pp. 1509 and 1519): Ask them to discuss which is the better term to apply to this play. Oedipus's combination of a quick temper and intense anger is often cited as a tragic flaw; to us the error in judgment he makes in trying to escape his fate is more central to the play than his anger (see our discussion of this point on p. 881).

The use of foils (Glossary, p. 1509) is important for characterization. Ask students to pick out and discuss uses of characters as foils to Oedipus, especially Teiresias (the bearer of divine wisdom, which contrasts to Oedipus's reliance on human knowledge) and Kreon (a steadier, more rational person than Oedipus, one who does not overreact in anger as Oedipus does).

Ask students to discuss the use and importance of irony in the play (such as the fact that the murderer Oedipus is seeking is himself, that the blind Teiresias can see the truth more clearly than Oedipus with his good eyes) and dramatic irony (that the reader or audience becomes aware of the truth before Oedipus and Iokaste do and thus watches them moving steadily toward disaster).

Bring up the role of the chorus, which speaks for the community and provides the voice of reason, order, and balance in the play. (Greek theater, including such conventions as the chorus, are discussed on pp. 851–53.)

Suggest that students watch for imagery of light and darkness, and of eyes and sight.

Have students talk about why Oedipus blinds himself instead of committing suicide, as Iokaste does.

A key question students should deal with is how Oedipus is to be viewed at the end: as a broken, defeated, pitiable man, or one who retains, or regains, strength and dignity by accepting responsibility for his actions and inflicting just punishment on himself for them.

ENTRY POINTS   Raymond Carver, "Cathedral" (p. 217).

August Wilson

Fences   (p. 1186)

WORKS WELL FOR   Character; symbols; the blues.

ENTRY POINTS   A good way into this play is to focus on borders: Ask students to pick out as many examples as they can of physical walls and borders (for example, prison walls, the outfield fence in baseball, and of course the fence Troy is working on throughout the play, with its question of whether Rose wants the fence to keep people out or to keep people in) and of figurative walls and borders, especially the various kinds of barriers between characters, interfering with relationships. Have students talk about whether fences should be considered as a symbol, and if so, what they might symbolize.

Discussion of characters is important for the play, especially the character of Troy. Ask students to come up with a list of character traits for him. More importantly, they should examine what is behind his attitudes and actions: the way his father treated him, for one thing, and his bitterness at the discrimination that prevented him from becoming a major league ball player. Have them try to understand his disappointments and frustrations in life — the dreams that were deferred indefinitely. Ask them to talk about Troy's relationship with Alberta: Why is he unfaithful to Rose?

Then discuss Rose: ask students to list her character traits, including her patience with and support of Troy and her generosity in being willing to become mother to his illegitimate child. How has her life been? What dreams did she have? Has she achieved them? Look closely at her speech replying to Troy's complaint that he has been standing in the same place for eighteen years (pp. 1224–25).

Ask students to discuss Cory's character. We don't see as much of him as of Troy and Rose, but we see enough to know about his dreams and his struggles and to imagine Troy's effect on Cory's life and personality. That effect becomes clear in the final scene: Ask students go through it carefully and discuss what it brings out about for both Cory and Rose.

Students will probably want help in understanding the ending, with Gabriel attempting to blow his horn, able to open the gates of heaven even though he cannot make a sound.

The blues form an important motif in the play, especially in the final scene. Ask someone to describe the blues and to begin a discussion of their relevance to the play and their effect in it.

Ask students to discuss the connection between the play's epigraph (p. 1186) and the play itself.

(The staging and set design for *Fences* are discussed on pp. 860–62.)

PAIR IT WITH   James Baldwin, "Sonny's Blues" (p. 138); Langston Hughes, "The Weary Blues" (p. 1266).

Langston Hughes: Dreams Deferred

The three chapters in Part 5 offer an opportunity to pursue an author in depth, either as a part of class discussion or as the subject matter for student papers, particularly research papers. In many textbooks, multiple works by a single author are included in the genre sections of the book — several short stories, for instance, or a number of poems. That seems appropriate especially for authors who work mostly in one genre. But many authors work in more than one genre. For these writers, we believe that reading from several genres is invaluable in gaining a comprehensive understanding of the author's work, comparing how the author handles similar themes in various genres, and examining how the author's techniques carry over or differ from one genre to another.

Although Langston Hughes offers many subjects and themes for consideration, in our choice of works to include we have focused on dreams, partly because of the importance of that theme in his work and also because it connects meaningfully with so many other authors and works in this book: the dreams of the Garcia family in Julia Alvarez's "Daughter of Invention" (p. 10), of the unnamed, invisible narrator in Ralph Ellison's "Battle Royal" (p. 237), of Dikeledi Mokopi in Bessie Head's "The Collector of Butterflies" (p. 421), of the Mexicans crossing the border in Luis Rodriguez's "Running to America" (p. 714), of the aging Odysseus about to cross the Mediterranean in Alfred, Lord Tennyson's "Ulysses" (p. 739), of Willy in Arthur Miller's *Death of a Salesman* (p. 980), or of Troy in August Miller's *Fences* (p. 1186). Topics for discussion or writing can stay within this chapter, exploring the development of themes and techniques in Hughes's works, or move between this chapter and other parts of the book, comparing Hughes's themes and techniques with those of other writers.

In addition to dreams, several pieces in the chapter deal with music, especially jazz and the blues. Music too is important to Hughes, in theme and technique, as it is to numerous other authors included in this book. Discussions or papers could examine the importance of music to Hughes himself or could develop comparisons between Hughes and, for example, James Baldwin, Amiri Baraka, Sterling A. Brown, Jayne Cortez, Christopher Gilbert, Lawson Fusao Inada, Ishmael Reed, and Kazuko Shiraishi.

Judith Ortiz Cofer: Thinking Back Through Her Mothers

As we explained for Chapter 22, the three chapters in Part 5 offer an opportunity to pursue an author in depth, either as a part of class discussion or as the subject matter for student papers, particularly research papers. In many textbooks, multiple works by a single author are included in the genre sections of the book, for instance, as several short stories or a number of poems. That seems appropriate especially for authors who work mostly in one genre. But many authors work in more than one genre. For these writers, we believe that reading from several genres is invaluable in gaining a comprehensive understanding of the author's work, comparing how the author handles similar themes in various genres, and examining how the author's techniques carry over or differ from one genre to another.

In selecting works for this chapter, we focused on the importance of mother and motherland in Judith Ortiz Cofer's life and work. Mothers (and grandmothers) are influential in several of the works in the chapter, as a motif that can be traced through her own work or related to mothers or grandmothers as influential figures in works by many other authors in this book — Julia Alvarez, James Baldwin, Eavan Boland, Alice Childress, Toi Derricotte, Cornelius Eady, Gish Jen, Jamaica Kincaid, Joyce Carol Oates, Tillie Olsen, Katherine Anne Porter, Alberto Ríos, Amy Tan, Helena María Viramontes, Alice Walker, and Nellie Wong among them.

We also selected works that relate to Ortiz Cofer's sense of being situated between two homes — the island and the mainland — and two languages — the Spanish of her birthplace and the English of her education and later life. That sense of bifurcation appears in her creative work and in her autobiographical writings. It can be used as a topic for discussion or papers within her own work, noticing how it is developed in different ways in various genres, or in comparison with other writers whose works depict characters experiencing a similar sense of belonging to two cultures, such as those by Julia Alvarez, Lan Samantha Chang, Sandra Cisneros, Toi Derricote, Ana Doina, David Henry Hwang, Nikki Giovanni, Gish Jen, Li-Young Lee, John Leguizamo, Alberto Ríos, Milcha Sanchez-Scott, Leslie Marmon Silko, Gary Soto, and Luis Valdez.

Sherman Alexie: Listening for Stories

As we explained for Chapters 22 and 23, the three chapters in Part 5 offer an opportunity to pursue an author in depth, either as a part of class discussion or as the subject matter for student papers, particularly research papers. In many textbooks, multiple works by a single author are included in the genre sections of the book, for instance, as several short stories or a number of poems. That seems appropriate especially for authors who work mostly in one genre. But many authors work in more than one genre. For these writers, we believe that reading from several genres is invaluable in gaining a comprehensive understanding of the author's work, comparing how the author handles similar themes in various genres, and examining how the author's techniques carry over or differ from one genre to another.

The works in this chapter focus especially on the place of stories in Alexie's life and in his culture. Many of the works are themselves stories, which are important for Alexie to tell, and both his stories and poems deal with stories and storytellers (notably Thomas Builds-the-Fire). In addition to exploring this theme within Alexie's works, it can be connected to related themes in such works as Charles Bukowski's "my old man" (p. 488), Judith Ortiz Cofer's "Not for Sale" (p. 134) and "Silent Dancing" (p. 1295), and Toni Morrison's "Recitatif" (p. 300). Alexie's works (including his essay "Superman and Me" on p. 4) also deal with fathers, offering many comparisons with other works, and their references to sports provide a motif some students may find interesting to pursue. They could consider relating Alexie's works to one or more of the following: Patricia Goedicke's "My Brother's Anger" (p. 559), A. E. Housman's "To an Athlete Dying Young" (p. 672), Arthur Miller's *Death of a Salesman* (p. 980), Gustavo Pérez Firmat's "José Canseco Breaks Our Hearts Again" (p. 701), Milcha Sanchez-Scott's *The Cuban Swimmer* (p. 890), Virgil Suárez's "A Perfect Hotspot" (p. 381), and August Wilson's *Fences* (p. 1186).

LITERARY RESEARCH

Reading Critical Essays

We have included this chapter because we think that before students begin reading critical essays for a research paper, they need some help in learning how to read critical studies. The critical essay is a genre different from others students encounter in a literature course. It will be helpful for them to have you discuss the nature of scholarly essays and spend some time going through a critical essay with them — perhaps Susan Farrell's essay in this chapter, one of the critical studies included in Chapters 22–24, or another essay of your choice.

Such discussion should focus on helping students understand how to identify the thesis of an article, the arguments used to support it, and methods employed by the critic. But the most important part of this chapter may be the last two paragraphs on using critical thinking to evaluate what they've read. Most students need help in understanding what to do with the critical essays they read, how to apply critical thinking: Their impulse is to treat a critical essay as authoritative and accept it as their own interpretation. The best way to counter this is to underline the importance of comparison as the basis of critical thinking about a critical essay. Reiterate that students should read interpretations by several critics, not stop with one or two, and compare them with each other and with their own reading of the work to determine both strengths and weaknesses in what they say.

CHAPTER 26 Writing a Literary Research Paper

We regard the research process and research papers as important parts of a Writing and Literature or Introduction to Literature course, and important ways to teach critical thinking. Primary research is particularly valuable, of course: It teaches students to challenge a text, to determine what aspects need to be clarified or answered, and to explore necessary research methods to go about finding the needed information. Reading and evaluating critical studies helps students to think comparatively, critiquing and refining their own ideas as they learn how other readers have approached the same texts and the same issues.

It's important to remember that research papers do not have to be long papers. The research process and incorporation of outside materials can be applied in a two- to three-page paper as well as in a ten- to twelve-page paper. Some teachers require research (primary or secondary) for all papers, instead of only in a long paper near the end of the course. This allows for learning through repetition, going through the process several times instead of just once. And it teaches students to think in research terms each time they approach a paper.

This chapter is too long to give to students as a single assignment. It can be broken into a number of segments that can be assigned at different points, or as a series of steps in the research process. Here is one way of dividing up the chapter:

Step 1 (pp. 1376–80): The nature of a literary research paper (it's not a report) and the types of research and sources (primary, secondary, and tertiary)

Step 2 (pp. 1380–84): Searching for sources (books, articles, electronic sources)

Step 3 (pp. 1385–86): Evaluating sources

Step 4 (pp. 1387–91): Taking notes and incorporating sources in a paper

Step 5 (pp. 1392–93): Avoiding plagiarism

Step 6 (pp. 1393–1405): Documenting sources; parenthetical citations and Works Cited page

Step 7 (pp. 1405–13): Sample student research paper

In addition to Kristina Martinez's paper on pages 1408–13, two other essays that might provide useful models for a short paper involving research or a longer paper are Philip C. Kolin and Maureen Curley's *Explicator* article "Hughes's *Soul Gone Home*" (p. 1273) and Susan Farrell's "Fight vs. Flight: A Re-evaluation of Dee in Alice Walker's 'Everyday Use'" (p. 1366).

Stories, Poems, and Plays Grouped by Topic

AGING

Stories

Gabriel García Márquez, *A Very Old Man with Enormous Wings*, 415
Gish Jen, *Who's Irish?*, 272
Naguib Mahfouz, *Half a Day*, 435
Katherine Anne Porter, *The Jilting of Granny Weatherall*, 364
Helena María Viramontes, *The Moths*, 391

Poems

Rita Dove, *The Satisfaction Coal Company*, 641
T. S. Eliot, *The Love Song of J. Alfred Prufrock*, 645
Robert Herrick, *To the Virgins, to Make Much of Time*, 669
Timothy Liu, *Thoreau*, 682
Clarence Major, *Young Woman*, 687
Andrew Marvell, *To His Coy Mistress*, 688
Janice Mirikitani, *For a Daughter Who Leaves*, 693
Judith Ortiz Cofer, *Cold as Heaven*, 558
Alberto Riós, *Nani*, 713
Mary Tall Mountain, *Matmiya*, 738
Alfred, Lord Tennyson, *Ulysses*, 739
Nellie Wong, *Grandmother's Song*, 754

Plays

David Henry Hwang, *As the Crow Flies*, 903
Arthur Miller, *Death of a Salesman*, 980
August Wilson, *Fences*, 1186

Poems

W. H. Auden, *Musée des Beaux Arts*, 600
Eavan Boland, *The Pomegranate*, 613
e. e. cummings, *in Just-*, 629
Alfred, Lord Tennyson, *Ulysses*, 739
Derek Walcott, *Sea Grapes*, 745

Plays

Sophocles, *Oedipus Rex*, 1145

COMING OF AGE (GROWING UP)

Stories

Sherman Alexie, *This Is What It Means to Say Phoenix, Arizona*, 1329
Toni Cade Bambara, *The Lesson*, 183
Lan Samantha Chang, *The Eve of the Spirit Festival*, 228
Ralph Ellison, *Battle Royal*, 237
Nathaniel Hawthorne, *Young Goodman Brown*, 252
Langston Hughes, *One Friday Morning*, 1249
Jamaica Kincaid, *Girl*, 283
Toni Morrison, *Recitatif*, 300
Joyce Carol Oates, *Where Are You Going, Where Have You Been?*, 75
Judith Ortiz Cofer, *Abuela Invents the Zero*, 1292
Judith Ortiz Cofer, *Not for Sale*, 134
Virgil Suárez, *A Perfect Hotspot*, 381
Amy Tan, *Two Kinds*, 189
John Updike, *A & P*, 386
Helena María Viramontes, *The Moths*, 391
Alice Walker, *The Flowers*, 20
Richard Wright, *The Man Who Was Almost a Man*, 395

Poems

Julie Alvarez, *How I Learned to Sweep*, 560
Elizabeth Bishop, *In the Waiting Room*, 506
Eavan Boland, *The Pomegranate*, 613
Sandra M. Castillo, *Exile*, 618
Rosemary Catacalos, *David Talamántez on the Last Day of Second Grade*, 620
Countee Cullen, *Incident*, 519
Anita Endrezze, *The Girl Who Loved the Sky*, 476
Richard Garcia, *Why I Left the Church*, 653
Nikki Giovanni, *Nikka-Rosa*, 534

Plays

Memoirs

DEATH

Stories

Poems

Plays

DREAMS/SURREALISM

Stories

Poems

Louise Erdrich, *The Red Convertible*, 67
Dagoberto Gilb, *Love in L.A.*, 55
Diane Glancy, *Aunt Parnetta's Electric Blisters*, 248
Zora Neale Hurston, *Sweat*, 263
Tillie Olsen, *I Stand Here Ironing*, 353
Judith Ortiz Cofer, *Not for Sale*, 134
Katherine Anne Porter, *The Jilting of Granny Weatherall*, 364
Virgil Suárez, *The Perfect Hotspot*, 381
John Updike, *A & P*, 386
Alice Walker, *Everyday Use*, 101
Richard Wright, *The Man Who Was Almost a Man*, 395

Poems

Sherman Alexie, *The Business of Fancydancing*, 1323
Agha Shahid Ali, *I Dream It Is Afternoon When I Return to Delhi*, 597
Jimmy Santiago Baca, *Family Ties*, 601
Amiri Baraka, *AM/TRAK*, 602
William Blake, *The Chimney Sweeper*, 610
Sterling A. Brown, *Riverbank Blues*, 616
Rita Dove, *The Satisfaction Coal Company*, 641
Martín Espada, *The Saint Vincent de Paul Food Pantry Stomp*, 649
Nikki Giovanni, *Nikka-Rosa*, 534
Robert Hayden, *Those Winter Sundays*, 462
Gerard Manley Hopkins, *God's Grandeur*, 524
Philip Levine, *What Work Is*, 681
Robert Lowell, *Skunk Hour*, 683
Orlando Ricardo Menes, *Letter to Mirta Yáñez*, 690
David Mura, *Grandfather-in-Law*, 535
Edwin Arlington Robinson, *Richard Cory*, 552
Benjamin Alire Sáenz, *Elegy Written on a Blue Gravestone (To You, the Archaeologist)*, 716
Gary Soto, *The Elements of San Joaquin*, 792

Plays

Alice Childress, *Florence*, 795
Henrik Ibsen, *A Doll House*, 926
Arthur Miller, *Death of a Salesman*, 980
Luis Valdez, *Los Vendidos*, 864
August Wilson, *Fences*, 1186

EXILE

Stories

Julia Alvarez, *Daughter of Invention*, 10
Lan Samantha Chang, *The Eve of the Spirit Festival*, 228
Judith Ortiz Cofer, *Not for Sale*, 134
Amy Tan, *Two Kinds*, 189

Poems

Ana Doina, *The Extinct Homeland — A Conversation with Czeslaw Milosz*, 637
Naomi Shihab Nye, *The Small Vases from Hebron*, 697
Dwight Okita, *In Response to Executive Order 9066*, 698
Ricardo Pau-Llosa, *Years of Exile*, 700
Luis Rodriguez, *Running to America*, 714
Vijay Seshadri, *The Refugee*, 720
Derek Walcott, *Sea Grapes*, 745
Nellie Wong, *Grandmother's Song*, 754

Plays

John Leguizamo, From *Mambo Mouth: A Savage Comedy*, 874
Milcha Sanchez-Scott, *The Cuban Swimmer*, 890
Luis Valdez, *Los Vendidos*, 864

Memoirs

Judith Ortiz Cofer, *Silent Dancing*, 1295

FAMILY

Stories

Sherman Alexie, *This Is What It Means to Say Phoenix, Arizona*, 1329
Julia Alvarez, *Daughter of Invention*, 10
James Baldwin, *Sonny's Blues*, 138
Lan Samantha Chang, *The Eve of the Spirit Festival*, 228
Sandra Cisneros, *The House on Mango Street*, 91
Louise Erdrich, *The Red Convertible*, 67
Diane Glancy, *Aunt Parnetta's Electric Blisters*, 248
Bessie Head, *The Collector of Treasures*, 421
Gish Jen, *Who's Irish?*, 272
James Joyce, *Eveline*, 280
Jhumpa Lahiri, *Interpreter of Maladies*, 285
Mishima Yukio, *Swaddling Clothes*, 438

Poems

Plays

HEALTH/MEDICINE

Stories

Kate Chopin, *The Story of an Hour*, 167
Diane Glancy, *Aunt Parnetta's Electric Blisters*, 248
Jhumpa Lahiri, *Interpreter of Maladies*, 285

Poems

Elizabeth Bishop, *In the Waiting Room*, 506
Louise Erdrich, *A Love Medicine*, 478
Michael S. Harper, *Nightmare Begins Responsibility*, 664
Linda Hogan, *The History of Red*, 670

HOME/GOING HOME

Stories

Julia Alvarez, *Daughter of Invention*, 10
James Baldwin, *Sonny's Blues*, 138
Sandra Cisneros, *The House on Mango Street*, 91
James Joyce, *Eveline*, 280
Bharati Mukherjee, *Orbiting*, 315
Katherine Anne Porter, *The Jilting of Granny Weatherall*, 364
Alice Walker, *Everyday Use*, 101

Poems

Jim Barnes, *Return to La Plata, Missouri*, 577
Lorna Dee Cervantes, *Freeway 280*, 575
Ana Doina, *The Extinct Homeland — A Conversation with Czeslaw Milosz*, 637
Rita Dove, *The Satisfaction Coal Company*, 641
Cornelius Eady, *My Mother, If She Had Won Free Dance Lessons*, 642
Nikki Giovanni, *Nikka-Rosa*, 534
Judith Ortiz Cofer, *The Birthplace*, 1289
Derek Walcott, *Sea Grapes*, 745

Plays

Langston Hughes, *Soul Gone Home*, 1270
Arthur Miller, *Death of a Salesman*, 980
August Wilson, *Fences*, 1186

IDENTITY

Stories

Poems

LOVE

Stories

Poems

Plays

ORIGINS

Poems

PARENT/CHILD

Stories

Poems

Plays

Essays

Screenplays

PROGRESS/CHANGE

Stories

Poems

RACE

Stories

Poems

Plays

TRADITION/S

Stories

Poems

VIOLENCE

Stories

Poems

WAR

Stories

Poems

WOMEN'S ISSUES

Stories

Poems

WORDS

Poems

Essays

WORK

Stories

Poems

Plays